Enfants Terribles

Susan Weiner

ENFANTS TERRIBL

Youth and Femininity
in the Mass Media
in France, 1945–1968

The Johns Hopkins University Press   Baltimore and London

9 8 7 6 5 4 3 2 1

The Johns Hopkins University Press
2715 North Charles Street
Baltimore, Maryland 21218-4363
www.press.jhu.edu

Library of Congress Cataloging-in-Publication Data
Weiner, Susan, 1946–
    Enfants terribles : youth and femininity in the mass media
in France, 1945–1968 / Susan Weiner.
        p.   cm.
Includes bibliographical references and index.
    ISBN 0-8018-6539-5 (alk. paper)
    1. Mass media and youth—France.   2. Women in mass media.
3. Teenage girls—France.   I. Title.
    P94.5.Y722 F838   2001
    302.23′082′094409045—dc21
00-009533

A catalog record for this book is available from the British
Library.

Title page illustration is from the first issue of French
Mademoiselle (1962).

A shorter version of chapter 1 appeared in *Contemporary
European History* 8 no. 3 (November 1999): 395–410 under
the title "Two Modernites: from *Elle* to *Mademoiselle.*
Women's Magazines in Postwar France"; and an earlier
version of chapter 2 appeared in *French Literature Studies*
20 (1993): 93–102 under the title "Le Repos de la critique:
Women Writers of the Fifties."

Contents

Acknowledgments

A Fulbright Advanced Student Award for Dissertation Research got this project off the ground in the 1990–91 academic year. Grants from the Société des Professeurs Français et Francophones en Amérique and the University of Toledo allowed me to spend the summer of 1994 doing new research. With a Morse Fellowship in the Humanities from Yale University I was able to devote 1997–98 to research and writing. The Frederick W. Hilles Publications Fund administered by the Whitney Humanities Center at Yale contributed significantly toward assembling the illustrations.

Letters of support from Christopher Miller, Denis Hollier, Alice Kaplan, and Linda Orr were instrumental in my obtaining these grants.

Alice Kaplan taught me how to do detective work in the archives, the questions to ask as well as how to write about what I found. Her excitement for an unconventional dissertation topic and her willingness to guide me through it as a writer and a scholar were unflagging and inspiring. In a most exhilarating teacher-student friendship, Linda Orr taught me how to unravel literary texts with the possibility that I might not like what I saw. Toril Moi shared her knowledge about politics and esthetics in the post–World War II period. Jean-Jacques Thomas gave me the idea of looking at women's magazines. Janice Radway shared her insight about how to study popular culture.

Conversations with Anne-Marie de Vilaine, Christiane Rochefort, Christine de Rivoyre, Françoise D'Eaubonne, Christian Bourgois, and Pierre Assouline gave me a sense of the position of the young woman writer and the world of publishing in 1950s France. The Julliard, Gallimard, and Grasset publishing houses generously opened their archives to me.

Karin Badt, John Evelev, Nicholas Hewitt, Trent Hill, Denis Hollier, Emmanuelle Saada, Yael Schlick, Silvia Tandeciarcz, Caroline Weber, and Glenn Willmott read parts of the manuscript at various stages and gave me invaluable feedback. Ross Chambers got me interested in the *jeune fille* as a historical type. The Whitney Humanities Center at Yale and Michael Kelly at the University of Southampton (UK) invited me to present work in progress, expanded versions of which appear as chapters 4 and 5.

It is in conversations in the most informal of settings that friends Maria Bezaitis, Benoît de l'Estoile, Yvès Pagès, Yannick Saint-Raymond, Maurie Samuels, Debarati Sanyal, Vanessa Schwartz, Anne Simonin have helped me to best formulate my ideas.

Margaret Thorpe provided air-conditioned splendor, tranquility, and fine foods over the course of a summer of final revisions.

In the process that transforms a manuscript into a book, Lynn Higgins was the best of guides. Her enthusiasm and suggestions as a scholar of the period and an astute and sensitive literary critic were essential. She has helped me move toward personal and intellectual clarity as a writer.

Kennie Lyman joined forces with me in the final stages, her editorial skills honing every page at micro and macro levels. Maura Burnett and Sam Schmidt at the Johns Hopkins University Press have been a pleasure to work with, warm and professional in our every exchange.

Enfants Terribles

Introduction

Juliette Gréco, the black-clad muse of pseudo-existential angst in Saint-Germain-des-Prés, kohl-rimmed eyes framed by loose lank hair; Françoise Sagan, short curls and expressionless gaze, alternately the "bad girl" next door and a fast-driving Riviera jet-setter; Brigitte Bardot, voluptuous yet childlike, her gingham fashion imitated by mothers as well as daughters, her on-screen gyrations flanked by African drummers a target of the censors; Jean Seberg, the androgyne who had more appeal in France than at home in the U.S.; Françoise Hardy and Sylvie Vartan, the intellectual bohemian and the Americanophile kitten, rivals in song and style alike: in France, after the Liberation and prior to May 1968, an unprecedented number of young women found fame and often notoriety in the public eye. Some were writers, others actresses or singers, and all in a way were characters whose private lives and psychology were as open to conjecture as those of fictional characters. In the public imagination, these precocious public personae took their places alongside an array of characters from novels and films who in some way resembled them, with the combined effect of redefining what it meant to be young and female in France.[1]

An important forerunner of the type was the *garçonne* of the 1920s, a bourgeois androgyne of independent mind and character. Slim, short-haired, and childless, "loose in her morals and free in her clothes,"[2] the garçonne spoke to national anxieties about the disruptive effects of the recent war. Conservative cultural observers expressed the fear that this strange new female character appearing in the popular fiction of the time was a new social type as well, one whose androgynous public appearance was the most visible sign of the end of a familiar world of codes and prescriptions for young women's behavior.

This vanishing world was expressed in a single term and concept: the *jeune fille*. The jeune fille, distinct from the prepubescent *fillette* or *petite fille,* began to emerge as a specific category of identity in France as in the larger western culture in the eighteenth century, testimony to the growing interest in human physiological and hormonal development as well as to the newly acceptable temporal lapse between the onset of menstruation and marriage. In the nineteenth century, the term "jeune fille" entered common usage as a means to refer to the young unmarried woman of the upper classes.[3] The jeune fille was nubile yet intact, an intactness that familial and social forces worked to maintain at any price.

Anthropologists have taken every possible methodological approach —psychoanalytic, functional, structural, and ecological—to understand the persistence of the cultural imperative of female purity, but as Sherry Ortner argues, each of these approaches is most convincingly framed in terms of the historical and economic phenomenon of the emergence of the state and with it the patriarchal family.[4] It is a history that can only be alluded to in the present context, but what is particularly striking for our purposes is the change in the status of virginity from the epitome of individual asceticism and piety for all in the Middle Ages and Renaissance, to an ideal for girls alone by the late seventeenth and early eighteenth centuries.[5] The cultural underpinnings to female intactness remained largely spiritual in the privileged classes, where young women could set their sights on marriage or salvation, the latter, as Fénélon wrote in his *Avis à une dame de qualité sur l'education de Mademoiselle sa fille* (1687), a valuable and respectable opportunity for self-determination.[6]

Chastity as the only freedom imaginable for girls seems less constrictive in light of the new secular mood that emerged over the course of the eighteenth century, making spiritual justifications for virginity unnecessary and placing the female life trajectory squarely within earthly patriarchal control. With the epistemological shift toward science, biology became the means to most authoritatively represent the differences between the sexes. Rousseau's highly influential *Discours sur l'origine et les fondements de l'inégalité parmi les hommes* and *Emile* played a major role in redefining female specificity in terms of the reproductive capacity, the maternal function, and an accompanying natural modesty.[7] These natural tendencies were firmly fixed as moral qualities in society, where, as Rousseau wrote at the beginning of Book 5 of *Emile,* "[t]he male is male only at certain moments. The female is female her whole life . . . Everything constantly recalls her sex to her."[8] Under the influence of Rousseau's pedagogical discourse, early nineteenth-century French culture in its tendency to normalize the family made it a moral imperative to raise a properly modest jeune fille, whose outward signs of intactness were most important of all.

Girls of the nineteenth-century bourgeoisie were supposed to know very little about the anatomical particularity that their delicacy and reserve should translate. They received only fragmentary knowledge from their mothers about menstruation, enough to obliquely understand that their social value as "demoiselles" lay in its immanence: that of the "virtuality of maternity," the logical conclusion to the marriage always present on their horizons.[9] But the jeune fille was told nothing about the act by which this virtuality could and would be realized. Her limited but crucial public appearances defined her as ripe yet intact in mind as well as body, a dutiful daughter who would make a desirable wife, the unquestioned trajectory in Catholic families for whom virginity mattered above all else.[10] Piety was part of the profile, but less as a function of a girl's inner life than as a quality that she could display. Conduct books and novels — most of them written by men — as well as popular women's magazines, imagined and reinforced the social type of the nubile and sexually ignorant girl prized by all social classes. Diaries from this period reveal the extent to which girls themselves internalized the image of angelic femininity, resulting in a uniformity and conformity never before seen.[11]

Well after World War I, nineteenth-century images and models of an idealized girlhood continued to dominate. The *garçonne* of the 1920s proved to be a sign of freedoms that were not to come for young women for several decades. As late as 1937, conduct books could still evoke "trois routes pour jeunes filles": marriage and maternity, convent life, or spinsterhood. Those in the last category, whose French translation, "vieille fille," underscores its own social status as a contradiction in terms, should make the best of things by passing the time doing good works as schoolteachers or aunts.[12] Despite the fact that she would ultimately take none of these paths, Simone de Beauvoir was, nevertheless, groomed to do so, an upbringing she evoked vividly in the autobiography of her childhood and adolescent years, *Mémoires d'une jeune fille rangée.* Beauvoir as the "dutiful daughter" of the title was a practicing Catholic, one among several social roles that defined her as good: a good daughter, a good student, a good friend, and—implicitly—a virgin. But from the title on, Beauvoir's retrospective gaze on a French Catholic girlhood tempered its bittersweet nostalgia with irony: along with girlhood, this particular jeune fille left the Catholic faith behind for her own moral code.

By neither marrying nor keeping to the sorry social type of the vieille fille, by making intellectual life and not the Church her passion, Beauvoir was a Catholic girl who veered off the map into uncharted territory. For while a certain level of general culture was de rigueur for the jeune fille of the interwar years en route to marriage, spirituality could still be evoked as the loftiest of her qualities. The image of the spiritual virgin has a practically medieval resonance in a biography of a girl nonetheless entitled *Une jeune fille d'aujourd'hui* (1934). The description of the priorities of the aptly named Magdeleine, who died from an unnamed illness in 1920 at the age of twenty, could not be any clearer:

> Son intelligence est prompte, intuitive; son jugement sans défaut, sa volonté ferme. Elle a des connaissances très étendues, un goût littéraire sûr, une sensibilité artistique affinée. Elle est spirituelle, enjouée, d'une amabilité exquise et d'une distinction rare . . .
>
> Par dessus tout, au dessus d'elle-même, elle a placé Dieu. Cette vision l'enivre de sa beauté, l'attire irrésistiblement . . . [C]et amour réfléchi, cette aspiration continue, l'arrachent à la terre, la dressent tout entière vers l'éternité; elle y monte comme à une fête.[13]

> [Her intelligence is quick, intuitive; her judgment flawless, her volition firm. She has wide knowledge, confident literary tastes, a fine artistic sensibility. She is witty and gay, possesses an exquisite good nature and rare taste.
>
> Above all, above herself, she has placed God. This vision intoxicates her with its beauty, attracts her irresistibly. This thoughtful love, this continuous aspiration, pulls her away from earthly matters, raises her entire being toward eternity; she ascends as if she were on her way to a celebration.]

Magdeleine headed for sainthood with an anticipation likened to preparations for a high school dance; World War I only intensified her desire to do good, and found her volunteering at schools and hospitals.

But there are always exceptions to cultural ideals. As the 1842 diary of a girl identified as "Z.B." recounts of her friend Claire, "elle est dangereuse, sa conversation est d'une précocité effrayante pour de jeunes têtes bien candides et de jeunes imaginations bien pures qu'elle effarouche et dont elle soulève le voile d'innocence"[14] [she is dangerous, her conversation is frighteningly precocious for young and candid minds and pure imaginations whom she terrifies and whose veil of innocence she raises]. Like Z.B.'s description of her dangerous friend Claire, occasional tales of girls who were no longer "vraies jeunes filles," whether in mind or in body haunt cultural and literary histories. There is, for example, the sixteen-year-old Fleur-de-Marie in Eugène Sue's best-selling *roman-feuilleton, Mystères de Paris,* whose aristocratic birth is eventually revealed while her life of prostitution remains one of innuendo.[15] Or, in a text that continues to test cultural limits, there is the eponymous protagonist of the Marquis de Sade's *Juliette ou la prospérité du vice* (1797), libidinous counterpart to her sister Justine, the pious suffering virgin of *Les Infortunes de la vertu.*[16] As the titles indicate, Justine wallows in self-pity and the "misfortune of virtue" while Juliette prospers from vice: she does not suffer nor seem to submit. But while Sade may have tested the cultural limits of representation, he did not imagine an alternative sociosexual order. There is no "outside" to patriarchy: complicity is the only strategy available in order for Juliette to avoid her sister's passive status as victim.[17] The power Juliette seems to have is rather a survival tactic, that of a self-inscription in phallic desire, the very condition of the apprenticeship of femininity as a sociosexual role. As Luce Irigaray describes the process by which the girl gains access to discourse and the singular logic of the Symbolic, she must pretend to have phallic power: "faire «comme si» elle l'avait, «semblant» de l'être"[18] [acting "as if" she had it, "seeming" to be it]—nevertheless remaining subjected to it in the end.

It takes more than historical interpretation to understand Juliette's masquerade. Patriarchy is not only France of the late eighteenth century, but a psychosexual order predicated on male desire in its multiple manifestations. One must be aware of the dual nature of patriarchy as both historical and psychosexual in order to understand the complicity of Justine and the submissiveness of Juliette. The motivation for good behavior as well as bad is in part latent, inaccessible to immediate comprehension and unreadable in terms of what Joan Copjec calls "the positivity of the social."[19] In *Read My Desire: Lacan Against the Historicists,* Copjec argues that cultural studies must go beyond historicism, must seek out psychic and linguistic structures not readily apparent but at work nevertheless, in order not to construct a reality that is "Real-tight." This is the approach the present study takes to the historical phenomenon of the redefinition of the teenage girl in post–World War II France.

As Lacan theorized the relationship between the Symbolic and the Real, between the describable surface of appearances, language, and the social on the one hand and the latent generative principle by virtue of which the Symbolic never stops realizing itself on the other, their non-coincidence is the very condition of desire.[20] In feminist theorist Luce Irigaray's psychoanalytic understanding of the apprenticeship of femininity, the girl comes to inscribe herself in phallic desire and the Symbolic, which cannot and do not allow for the expression of her original desire—her own libido, her earliest relationship to her mother. As Irigaray writes of that moment, "elle fonctionne comme un trou . . . dans l'élaboration des processus imaginaires et symboliques. Mais cette faille, ce défaut, ce «trou», la femme dispose justement de trop peu d'images, de figurations, de représentations, pour pouvoir s'y re-présenter"[21] [it functions as a hole . . . in the elaboration of imaginary and symbolic processes. But this gap, this defect, this "hole," woman has too few images, figurations, representations, to be able to re-present herself in it]. Desire is usually well within patriarchal definitions in novels and films about teenage girls, but as we shall see, there are occasional moments of elusiveness.

When the desires of the adolescent female are figured as enigmatic, unreadable, or inarticulable, it is the juxtaposition with adult women and teenage boys that facilitates this presentation. Mothers and young men were categories of identity whose roles in the ideological imagination of postwar France were clear. Women were seen as the foundation of reconstruction and agents of cultural stability, boys as ciphers for recent history, current events, and the future direction of the nation. While we do see occasional parallel attempts to categorize and interrogate young women as a group, with few exceptions postwar culture imagined youthful femininity as untouched by the experiences of wartime or the politics of the world around them. "Girl," "teenage girl," "female adolescent," "young woman," this book uses the terms interchangeably, just as journalists, novelists, publishers, literary critics, filmmakers, and advertisers did in the postwar years. The actual parameters of age are necessarily and intentionally vague: any female who wanted to could take part in the qualities of a sexualized girlishness, outside of history and current events.

This separate status was mystifying to many readers, especially in juxtaposition to young men who were automatically aligned with the traumas of the Occupation, the ongoing Algerian war, and the tensions between an age-old sociopolitical *immobilisme* and the lure of the American way of life. When youthful malaise was so defined, angry young women became hard to find. This was the substance of novelist and journalist Geneviève Dormann's 1961 rhetorical query:

> Pourquoi, demandent certains, lorsque le mot jeunesse est prononcé, cite-t-on plus facilement des exemples de garçons que de filles? Pourquoi les «crises», les problèmes, les révoltes, les livres et les «bêtises» en général semblent-ils être plus l'apanage des adolescents que des adolescentes? Bref, où sont les filles et que font-elles?[22]

> [Why, certain people ask, when the word "youth" is pronounced, do we cite examples of boys more easily than examples of girls? Why do the "crises," the problems, the revolts, the books and the "follies" in general seem to be the exclusive right of adolescent boys rather than girls? In short, where are the girls and what are they doing?]

Dormann initially answered her own question by situating adolescent girls within a misogynistic and monolithic view of femininity. She did not see them as equal agitators in generational conflict and authentic political revolt, but rather as passive sufferers in the transgenerational feminine condition: a tendency toward lamentation and a fixation on the vicissitudes of the menstrual cycle.

For Dormann, girls were rightfully absent from images of youthful turmoil. Her point was intended to be practical and constructive: teenage girls should cease their excessive self-preoccupation and start to look at the world around them, as boys allegedly did. But she concluded the article with the following caveat: "le désespoir féminin est doux et latent" [mild and latent]. Where Dormann stopped, this book begins: rather than an equivalent female counterpart to the politicized "angry young man," the feminine experience of "crises, problems, and revolts" is the terrain of the self-obsessed, body-obsessed "bad girl," a term whose primary sense was, and always has been, sexual.[23]

Nadine Dubreuilh in Beauvoir's *Les Mandarins* (1954) offers an apt illustration of the bad girl and her "mild and latent" despair. Most dramatic in its status as a non-issue is Nadine's sexuality: she is not a virgin, a matter of fact and not concern, even for her parents. The problem rather is the association of her precocious sexual activity with a loss of psychological intactness, an evacuation of the idealism and optimism associated with youth. Unlike Magdeleine in *Une jeune fille d'aujourd'hui*, for whom wartime represented an opportunity to do good works, the Occupation has traumatized Nadine. Her lover, a Jewish Resistance fighter, was killed shortly before the Liberation. In the aftermath she is sullen, angry, and uncommunicative and passes the time in loveless affairs with older men.

While we find individual cases of bad girls in eighteenth- and nineteenth-century French literature, in the post–World War II period they became a recognizable cultural type. Nadine has strayed far from "trois routes pour jeunes filles": she seems to be heading neither for motherhood, sainthood, nor the good works of a maiden aunt. She is only one of many examples of the post–World War II period's redefinition of the teenage girl. Unlike the nineteenth-century model of the dutiful daughter, unlike the garçonne of the interwar years, whose rebelliousness was incarnated in her androgynous appearance, the postwar teenage girl's most distinctive characteristic was promiscuous and precocious sexuality, assumed, whether defiantly or matter-of-factly, as a right. Nadine does end up getting married: Beauvoir may have escaped categorization as a good girl or a bad girl in her own life, but in *Les Mandarins* she does not imagine an ending to female adolescence outside the conventions of patriarchy.

The bad girl's virtuous counterpart, the jeune fille, never fully disappeared in the postwar years: indeed, the French Communist Party and such Catholic groups as *Pour un foyer chrétien* continued to publish books and brochures destined for her, either for her "protection" or to help her in her role as a future mother, with the moral reconstruction of the nation clearly in mind.[24] Nevertheless, as early as 1952, the jeune fille was on her way to becoming what the Catholic man of letters François Mauriac called an endangered species:

> Qu'est-devenue cette jeune fille de notre adolescence, celle qui s'avançait sous les tilleuls, dans une musique de Schumann? N'est-ce pas une espèce en partie disparue? Mais quand, par hasard, nous rencontrons l'une d'elles, qu'elle nous paraît précieuse! Que son charme demeure puissant![25]

> [What has become of this girl of our adolescence, the one who moved slowly under the linden trees, while Schumann played? Is she not a partially extinct species? But when, by chance, we meet one of them, how precious she seems! How powerful her charm remains!]

Mauriac was reacting to what was seen at the time as the growing similarity between the lives of young men and women in the public sphere, specifically the increased female presence in the educational and professional trajectories traditionally reserved for males. Mauriac cautioned girls to slow down in their race for equal opportunities: "il y a quelque chose d'infiniment plus beau que de dépasser les hommes dans tous les domaines"[26] [there is something infinitely lovelier than exceeding men in every domain], he wrote: only women had the possibility of bringing children into the world, of raising them and initiating them to the life of the soul. Mauriac's nostalgia for *jeunes filles* who remained focused on their future reproductive and maternal roles went right back to Rousseau.

Though real, the social changes Mauriac referred to were not as far-reaching in the 1950s as he would have his reader believe. There was indeed a dramatic rise in the number of female university students: between the prewar period and 1945, their overall numbers doubled, with the most marked increases in law (from roughly 10 percent of law students in 1935 to 25 percent in the mid-fifties). Although the number of university students tripled in France between 1945 and 1967, with young women eventually counting for 44 percent, students themselves were only a small percentage of the entire population of French youth. If we look at the statistics for the population in France between the ages of fifteen and twenty-nine in June of 1953, for example, 1,366,000 were students; 1,724,000 worked in agricultural jobs; 1,884,000 worked in factories; the rest were artisans or in small businesses (366,000) or office workers (784,000).[27] In 1955, students counted for 11 percent of nineteen-year-olds and 9 percent of twenty-year-olds. The real numbers associated with the increased presence of female students were thus quite small.[28]

Social restrictions also underlie the impressive statistics on young working women. Most who worked did so out of economic necessity, leaving their positions on family farms, often unsalaried, for the same sort of urban employment girls had taken in the prewar period: dead-end factory jobs for wages two-thirds lower than men, sales clerking, domestic work.[29] The phenomenon of the growing visibility of young women in the *professions libérales*—medicine, law, management, engineering, and so on—was a bourgeois luxury. Most tellingly, this professional class, while on the rise, was only a fraction of the entire French work force: in 1954, for example, it accounted for 1.2 percent of working women and 2.9 percent of working men.[30] Social change in the first decade of what Jean Fourastié termed the postwar "trente glorieuses" was gradual: in terms of increasing gender parity in the public sphere, the "révolution invisible" he described was the privilege of the middle classes.[31] Most French people in the 1950s would probably not have a female university student or a young career-oriented professional woman in the family. It was rather in the realm of representation, where a major shift occurred in both the content and the form of images of youthful femininity, that the existence of Mauriac's jeune fille was most endangered in France.

Writers and artists have always been in the business of imagining gender, but after the Liberation, it was the phenomenally expanding mass media, rather than literature or art, that increasingly came to dominate French cultural conceptions of female adolescence. In its accessible — indeed, unavoidable — forms of communication, which reached a public of all ages, regions, levels of education, and social class, the mass media — the popular press, advertising, movies, the radio, and finally television — were in an unparalleled position from which both to present and to create a new image of the teenage girl: a position of power that was itself a truly new and significant sign of postwar cultural change. Central to this book's study of paradigms and shifts in the representation of female adolescence is the role of the mass media, which implicitly and explicitly set teenage girls apart from two ideologically overdetermined categories: mothers — not just homemakers anymore, but citizens and often working women — and adolescent boys. The result was that girls were both implicated in and excluded from various discourses of the reconstruction and reconfiguration of postwar French life.

This is a cultural history in which governmental policy played a minor role at best. In contrast to the explicitly formulated *politique de la jeunesse* of the two preceding regimes, the Popular Front and the collaborationist government at Vichy, Fourth Republic policy on youth was one of benign neglect. While the influential left-wing coalition of the Popular Front (1936–37) had actively encouraged access to cultural activities and the outdoors for working-class youth, Pétain, on the opposite end of the ideological spectrum, had also placed young people at the center of the Vichy vision of a society founded on a morally solid family. Since the association with fascism was so recent after the Liberation, Charles de Gaulle rejected any specific constitutional provisions for an autonomous Ministry of Youth such as had existed in Vichy, preferring instead to emphasize a class-based "éducation populaire" through the Ministry of Education. Even after De Gaulle resigned in 1946, austerity measures during the difficult reconstruction years meant cutbacks in government programs for young people. As for youth movements, the political, religious, and "neutral" groups that came out of the Resistance failed to establish themselves in postwar society. The only ones that continued to function did so as satellites of the Communist Party, and in the atmosphere of paranoia that accompanied the onset of the Cold War, their status was marginal. Prime Minister Pierre Mendès-France was the first postwar leader who specifically addressed the concerns of youth in the middle of the decade, but he was voted out of office before his policies could come into effect.

In an unrivaled position to create and disseminate images of youth, the postwar mass media figured youth as an easy cipher for collective sociopolitical tendencies, as a sign of the times, be it the recent past, current events, or future trends: victims of wartime and nuclear paranoia, mindless and apolitical consumers, experts in the latest technology. Underlying these formulations of youth was a consistent alignment with masculinity — and an almost as consistent elite status. Educated, middle-class teenage boys as the mass media imagined them became the synecdochal means by which the larger public came into contact with national and global politics and socioeconomic mutations, which would otherwise have been less sensational. At first this was largely the work of the press. After wartime paper rationing came to an end, a massive array of new publications appeared on the newsstands. Dailies and weeklies, magazines and journals, ranging from the popular to the intellectual, from Right to Left, furnished an ample and varied source of news and entertainment for a public who could not afford the price of new books. In feature articles and special issues of magazines, psychological "experts" and journalists alike made pronouncements about the beliefs and habits of "youth" as a distinct group, erasing the factors of both gender and social class. Facilely diagnosed in terms of the Occupation, the Cold War, and the new materialism, the "news" of youth eventually extended to the domain of the audiovisual as films, radio, television, and popular music put them literally in the spotlight.

The media generated a series of handy labels for each of these images: In the immediate postwar years, there were the "existentialists," the bohemian youth who frequented Parisian Left Bank nightclubs and were titillatingly linked to Sartre, a factor in the philosopher's own media visibility. In the early 1950s, the "J-3s" came to public attention. Originally a wartime ration category, the term was appropriated to refer to young people whose behavior, world view, or imagination exhibited a dark side that was attributed to the Occupation, no matter how far-fetched the connection may have been. At the end of the decade, other labels included "tricheurs," taken from the title of a 1958 Marcel Carné film in which the gang of protagonists must prove their nihilism to each other, and "Nouvelle Vague," from a 1957 survey of French youth by the news magazine *L'Express* whose banal findings were effaced by the catchiness of the expression. Finally in the early 1960s, the media referred to young people as "copains," the Americanized pop singers with whom fans easily identified and who became instant vehicles for an expanding market of young consumers.[32] Omnipresent in popular culture, invoked and analyzed in domains ranging from politics to psychology to the Protestant and Catholic churches, these labels provoked little serious scholarly attention at the time. Nor have images of postwar French youth generated interest among contemporary social theorists, who are less interested in questions of particular historical representations than in the invisibility of social class in the creation of youth as an ostensibly generic category.[33] In the British and American contexts, on the other hand, sociologists and cultural critics as early as the 1950s turned their attention to specific sectors of their postwar youth, focusing on juvenile delinquency and the working classes, which they continue to study today.

In one of the seminal works on the subject, *Subculture: The Meaning of Style,* Dick Hebdige discusses the series of youth cultures in postwar Britain through the 1970s: teddy boys, mods, hipsters, skinheads, and punks, "highly structured, visible, tightly bonded" groups, whose generational consciousness is rooted in working-class experience and expressed through a shared style of dress, dance, and music. Hebdige reads the chronology of subcultural styles over the course of the postwar period as "a phantom history of race relations since the War": as responses—rejection or assimilation, in some cases conscious, in others not—to the succession of black immigrant communities in Britain from 1945 on.[34] Just as in the French context, the pivotal role belonged to the mass media. But British youth cultures, according to Hebdige, were real: the media appropriated and redefined working-class forms of resistance to dominant culture and gave them the appearance of cohesion, thus providing well-defined and sensationalized images of subordinate groups for mass consumption.

The French case does not fit as neatly into Hebdige's analysis of representations of youth culture. While some young people in France probably shared the world view, habits, and psyche that constituted each successive type, the reality of the existentialists, the J-3s, the tricheurs, the Nouvelle Vague, and the copains was primarily discursive, taking shape when the media named and defined them, in their function as news and entertainment. This is not to dismiss their importance. Media categorizations had social repercussions, entering the lives of real young people whose participation, rejection, or deformation of these models generated new behaviors along with new definitions of what it meant to "be young" in post–World War II France.

Teenage girls are present in all of these media images of youth, but not in the same causal relationship with politics and history as their male counterparts. Within the peer group or the family as imagined by films, popular novels, feature articles, and news stories, bad girls were, instead, positioned as *enfants terribles:* in the *Petit Robert* dictionary, "personnes qui se signalent par une certaine turbulence, dans un groupe" [individuals who make themselves known in a group by virtue of a noticeable turbulence]—that group being alternately the age category "youth" and the gendered category of femininity. The best-known literary example is a brother and sister pair: Paul and Elisabeth in Jean Cocteau's *Les Enfants terribles,* a 1929 novel he adapted to film with director Jean-Pierre Melville in 1948. In a shared bedroom, Paul and Elisabeth create a hermetic and all-consuming though nonsexual world which remains in place even after their invalid mother's death. The magical space is transposed to a ghostly *hôtel particulier* after Elisabeth marries a fantastically wealthy American and is instantly widowed. In their various inventions and machinations inside the bedroom and in the world outside—teasing good girls, stealing random useless objects—Elisabeth dominates her frail brother and jealously guards him from any other attachments, in particular from Agathe, another orphan, who bears an uncanny physical resemblance to Dargelos, a dangerous and seductive friend from Paul's boyhood school days (they are played by the same actress, Renée Cosima, in the film).

The dictionary-worthy "turbulence" belongs primarily to Elisabeth, and not just because she is two years Paul's senior. She is the conjurer of the exaggerated theatricality of their existence as they perform for adult caretakers and their enchanted friend Gérard. Elisabeth's power is highlighted by Cocteau in her capacity for masquerade: she moves from one role, one identity, into the next. When she nurses Paul back to health, "elle se butait, devenait son personnage" [she stumbled, became her character]; she moves out of girlhood like a snake shedding its skin: "elle qui, jadis, agissait avec des armes garçonnières, se replia vers les ressources d'une nature féminine toute neuve et prête à servir" [35] [she who in the past acted with the defenses of a tomboy withdrew toward the resources of a feminine nature, brand-new and ready to serve]. It is in adolescence that Elisabeth realizes her dangerous potential as an enfant terrible. She concocts a plot to keep Paul for herself and both of them from the banality of others by intercepting his love letter to Agathe and coaxing her rival into a marriage with Gérard. Her machinations ultimately uncovered to the horror of all, Elisabeth stands remorseless, "seule contre tous," first as witness to Paul's slow and miserable suicide by poison, then as a resourceful participant with a revolver. Here the *Petit Robert* definition of *enfant terrible* rejoins that of the *American Heritage* dictionary: "one whose startlingly unconventional behavior, work, or ideas are a source of embarrassment or dismay to others."

In Cocteau's myth-inspired fiction, Elisabeth's power emanates from her intactness, making the death of her husband before the consummation of their marriage a structural necessity. She is "la pythonisse, la vierge sacrée"—prophetess and holy virgin—foretelling perhaps the metamorphosis of her singularly destructive and self-destructive powers into a new image of the female adolescent in the 1950s, whose powers reside rather in the precocious and often heartless deployment of her sexuality. The startlingly unconventional behavior and ideas of Cocteau's Elisabeth and their capacity to dismay others became increasingly visible in French fiction and film after World War II. Settings were no longer timelessly mythical, but contemporary: department stores and cafés, the Côte d'Azur, the nightclubs of Saint-Germain-des-Prés, the university corridors of Bordeaux— but young women continued to stand "seule[s] contre tous," their behavior presented as startling, inexplicable, and titillatingly dangerous.

Simone de Beauvoir was largely alone in her intimation in *Les Mandarins* that the experiences of wartime could sufficiently explain the behavior of wayward teenage girls after the Liberation. Novels and films presented the unapologetic expression of their sexuality as inexplicable, and it came as a shock to French critics and their public. Writing about Brigitte Bardot, Simone de Beauvoir called the actress's widely disseminated image of frank sexuality "the Lolita syndrome." Even though Bardot was older than Nabokov's underage character, the screen roles of "B.B." (bébé) played up her youthfulness to a point of exaggeration, taking part in what Beauvoir theorized as the "new feminine mystique":

Aujourd'hui la femme adulte vit dans le même monde que l'homme, mais la femme-enfant se meut dans un univers auquel il n'a pas accès. La différence d'âge rétablit entre eux la distance nécessaire pour faire naître le désir. Du moins c'est ce qu'espèrent ceux qui ont créé une nouvelle Eve en combinant «le fruit vert» et «la femme fatale».[36]

[The adult woman today lives in the same world as does the man, but the nymphet moves about in a universe to which he does not have access. The age difference restores the distance necessary to arouse desire. At least that is what those who have created a new Eve by combining the "unripened fruit" and the "femme fatale" hope for.]

Bardot played orphans and schoolgirls, characters typically imagined to be innocent, but who, in the hands of her directors, became devastatingly sexual. Much of the appeal of the sexualized orphan or schoolgirl as Bardot played her lay in what seemed to be a blithe unawareness of her appeal to older men, an appeal that gave her the upper hand, but only temporarily. Marriage to a father figure is the usual ending for a Bardot film, recuperating her sexuality for family life. Nevertheless, as Beauvoir writes, the characters B.B. played would never become ideal wives and mothers. The unapologetic pleasure in her own body that she exhibited on screen elicited a reaction from the French public that was disproportionately hostile: caustic reviews; letters from indignant parents to newspaper editors, politicians, and priests; blame for episodes of juvenile delinquency.[37]

Such an extreme reaction is a telling symptom of the ambivalence with which images and narratives of the young woman in possession of inappropriate sexual powers were created and received in France of the 1950s and 1960s. Bardot may have been shocking and titillating, but she and characters like her were always ultimately recuperated. Their sexualized rebelliousness and complicated plots and acts of self-determination were abruptly put to an end through marriage, senseless death, terrifying solitude, or punishment for bad behavior. French culture was ready to be outraged by teenage girls but not ready for their freedom from familial and patriarchal definitions, a precarious position from which we are still emerging on both sides of the Atlantic. Texts that define and usually punish the bad girl help us to understand just how threatening this new social category was in a France both reluctant and eager to embrace change. In her imperfect freedom, the enfant terrible stands willfully outside of the family, outside of the normative couple, in narratives and images that suggest or force her eventual and ineluctable reintegration.

Just as Joan Copjec calls for a cultural studies that seeks out what is inarticulable in cultural statements, Luce Irigaray insists upon the need to interpret the exclusion of femininity from the positivity of the social and to recognize how, with respect to the logic of the Symbolic, "un excès, dérangeant, est possible du côté du féminin"[38] [a certain disruptive excess is possible on the feminine side]. In the case of the bad girl, or enfant terrible, this disruptive excess is located in enigmatic moments that texts themselves do not attempt to explain. Such moments only take shape when the Symbolic breaks down and ceases to communicate through reason, when a certain inarticulateness makes itself elliptically available for detection. Inarticulateness is not a condemnation to nonexistence but an indication of an aspect of female identity that escapes the Symbolic. One of the goals of this book is to detect and discuss the vague "something else" that emerges alongside complicity with patriarchy in popular texts from 1945 to 1968.

Images of specifically feminine and sexualized *enfants terribles* circulated in a sociocultural sphere where universalizing discourses about adolescence translated as male. While such discourses are, as sociologist Olivier Galland writes, a "crucible for the expression of ideologies,"[39] the specificity of images of the sexualized teenage girl lies instead in their relationship to the culture's unarticulated anxieties—about its own intactness, both physical and psychological. The raw and summarily repressed ideological divisions of the Occupation, the attempt to articulate a "third way" between the superpowers in the Cold War, the loss of a French Algeria, the threats and hopes of the rural exodus and Americanization, and the accompanying decline of the traditional French way of life: the social fragmentation that resulted has not been fully assimilated to this day. Before World War II, France had been a world where the characters that popular culture offered its audiences were, for the most part, jeunes filles who had internalized well the prescription to be good and remain pure until marriage; in the 1950s, France was a world that was beginning to come apart. Would the social fabric hold? Fiction and film in the postwar period testify to the social vertigo brought about by the dissolution of what was literally and figuratively familiar, the jeune fille and the social fabric that contained her. *Enfants Terribles* argues that the post–World War II period was a historical moment where we do find narratives and images of youthful femininity in crisis and revolt, where girls struggled in new ways with their place in the family as daughters and their destiny as wives. Theirs was a struggle to assert an interstitial identity: it almost always originated in sexual (mis)behavior. In many cases, however, the sexuality they used as a source of power and self-determination revealed itself as powerless. In the broad range of images and texts from these years studied in the following chapters, *enfants terribles* come up against a final lesson: again and again they learn that there is no viable position outside of the codes that determine the "good girl," that one cannot escape heterosexuality, the family, and marriage.

This book explores the period between the end of World War II and the political eruptions of May 1968. In a world whose moral coherence had been challenged and where basic material difficulties persisted, political and cultural attempts to restore order betrayed a nostalgia for the nineteenth century, and even the *Ancien Régime*. Tellingly, one of the two most popular films of 1954 was Sacha Guitry's *Si Versailles m'était conté*; the other, *Papa, Maman, la bonne et moi*, was a comedy about the housing shortage.[40] Adult women were as pivotal to the latter-day Restoration as they were to creating comfort in the face of material difficulty. The Fourth Republic called upon them in their joint capacity as citizen and mothers, zealously expanding the state-financed program of *allocations familiales* to make it financially wiser for women to stay home and have numerous children than to seek employment in the public sphere. More equivocally, *Elle* magazine offered readers the novel fantasy of women effortlessly balancing a career and motherhood.

In the context of newly modernized definitions of femininity, which remained fundamentally traditional and centered on the home, and of the singular alignment of (male) youth with history and politics, teenage girls in popular fiction, film, and advertisements acted against domestic destiny while ignoring the events in the world around them in plots that served their own ends. Unlike Cocteau's widowed virgin Elisabeth they used loveless sex as their primary playing card. But the machinations of female adolescents ultimately troubled their own lives along with the lives of others. In that it often came with punishment, theirs was an imperfect freedom, one that profoundly characterized images of female adolescence in the years prior to the demands and promises of what looked like unfettered liberation in the late 1960s.

Through an analysis of *Elle* magazine from 1945 through 1962, chapter 1 studies redefinitions of adult femininity in the postwar period and their implications for teenage girls. After the Liberation, *Elle* positioned itself as the voice of modernity for adult women, the fantasy of having it all and serving the nation. By the mid-1950s, *Elle* acknowledged that its version of feminine modernity was not the only one: the true novelty and excitement lay in what *Elle* itself dubbed "the reign of the *adolescente*," the domain of daughters rather than mothers. *Elle* never quite succeeded in reorienting its content to appeal to both these readerships, and the first issue of *Mademoiselle* in 1962 could legitimately hail teenage readers with the declaration that "their" magazine had finally arrived.[41] Yet the brand of femininity advocated in *Mademoiselle*'s pages often bore an uncanny resemblance to its mature counterpart in *Elle*.

Constructed as ahistorical and apolitical, the enfant terrible emerged as a specific category of identity in popular fiction by young women writers and the mass marketing of these writers. This is the subject of chapter 2. Book publishers promoted novels by Françoise Mallet-Joris, Michèle Perrein, Christiane Rochefort, and Françoise Sagan for their shock value as documentaries of what it meant to be young and female in the modern world. In turn, literary critics writing for newspapers assumed that the novels were autobiographical and presented them to the public as such. Young women writers and their equally young female protagonists were both hailed and reviled as good bourgeois daughters gone astray: representatives of a new, rebellious breed of femininity that was precociously and guiltlessly sexual, unsentimental, disinterested in world events, and disdainful of conventional social mores. The novelty of the type was not without its textual repercussions: writers often "punished" their shocking characters by implicating them in unhappy and sometimes violent endings, from suicides to car crashes to loveless marriages. The right-thinking may have been titillated and outraged by signs that the jeune fille was an endangered species, but the process of her extinction in popular culture did not exclude sobering punishments for bad behavior.

How were representations of female adolescence different when youth rather than femininity took center stage? This is the subject of chapters 3 and 4. The postwar ideology of femininity maintained adult women as a stabilizing force that teenage girls were seen to threaten. The meaning of youth as a generic category, however, underwent a chain of metamorphoses that paralleled the social, economic, and political metamorphoses of the nation itself: the aftermath of the Nazi Occupation and the beginnings of the uncomfortable imbalance of remembering and forgetting that Henry Rousso has termed "the Vichy syndrome"; the Cold War; urbanization and the decline of traditional small town family life; the growth of consumerism and "technological society," as Jacques Ellul called it; the expansion of the mass media; and the lure and anxieties of Americanization. While it is doubtful that these changes affected youth more than any other social group in France, it was primarily through representations of youth that attitudes about changes in the French way of life were expressed. Chapter 3 focuses on the representation of young men as traumatized victims of the Occupation and the Cold War, traumatized anew by *enfants terribles.* Chapter 4 turns to the relationship between discourses about youth and certain aspects of their real experiences, namely the simultaneously pivotal role of the radio in their new status as a consumer category and in the war in Algeria, and how increasingly blurred gender roles allowed female characters to evoke the ongoing war.

Chapter 5 examines the ostensibly objective tool that legitimated the images, theories, and diagnoses of youth advanced elsewhere: the sociological survey. In their pretension to being scientific and using empirical methods, surveys offer the most dramatic illustration of the over-historicized categorization of (male) adolescence from which girls are excluded. These surveys never even acknowledge, in their ambitious claim to definitively portray French youth, the gendered limits of their inquiry. My analysis ends with Jean-Luc Godard's film *Masculin/Féminin* (1966) and its iconoclastic statement that youth is indeed a gendered category. With Godard, youth no longer only meant male; for the first time, the questions of difference and representation were taken on, both seriously and comically. *Masculin/Féminin* appeared in a climate of international political agitation in which the voices of young people were increasingly heard, culminating in the student and worker uprisings of May 1968. With May '68, the image of the young activist—a media product as well, though linked to actual events—came to efface all the labels that had preceded it. Armed with utopian ideals, the *soixante-huitards* were, in a sense, the point of rupture in the chain of meanings assigned to youth. But by no means should this imply the radical separation of the soixante-huitards from this chain. The events of May must be understood in light of the categorizations that had been imposed upon youth from 1945 on. It is my hope that we will eventually cease to see May 1968 as the unique and unrehearsed moment in which young people emerged into the public eye in postwar France. This book represents one step towards that end.

Unless otherwise noted, all translations are mine.

 # From *Elle* to *Mademoiselle*

Today an international fashion magazine known for marketing French style to young women, *Elle* had a very different look in its early years. From 1945 through the late 1950s, *Elle* projected the image of a reader who was, at the time, uniquely modern. She was a mother, a citizen, and a working woman, whose wide-ranging expertise in "making do" during the Occupation carried over to her home in the postwar years. Only her talents in her salaried job could equal the skill, ease, good humor, and sense she demonstrated in the domestic sphere. That was the novelty of *Elle*: for the first time, a women's magazine displayed the fantasy of having both a fulfilling career and a traditional home life. To whom was such a fantasy proffered? Most probably, not only to mature women who had, or wished to have, their own homes and jobs, but also to adolescent girls. There were no general magazines which explicitly targeted the young female audience in 1950s France.[1] Political groups that came out of the Resistance, religious groups such as the Protestant *Jeunes Femmes Françaises,* and agricultural interest groups published their own magazines, pamphlets, and newsletters written by and for young women, but circulation was necessarily limited to their own members. The short-lived French *Mademoiselle,* (1962–64), unrelated to the American magazine in existence since 1935, was the first weekly for the general audience of teenage girls. It was followed in 1963 by *Salut les copains,* which targeted teenagers of both sexes. Before then, girls had to make do with the women's magazines on the market.

For the present study, *Elle* is of pivotal interest because of its transformation, over the course of the 1950s, from a magazine specifically targeting adult women readers to one that tried simultaneously to appeal to teenage girls, both as a media audience increasingly visible in French culture and as a consumer group in its own right. As the audience of teenage girls became more explicitly defined in other cultural channels, the monopoly held by the home-oriented *Elle* over the general women's magazine market was ripe for contest. *Elle* is an important point of access to understanding the story of this contest between two modernities: how the immediate postwar version of female modernity—maternal, nationalistic, and institutionally approved—was usurped by the renegade other that was female adolescence—a modernity generated largely in the mass media, in which the role of political powers was tangential at best. The choice of *Elle* as the source of the definitions and images of female identity and the exigencies of the female role in the post–World War II era is not a random one: *Elle* was first sold as a supplement to *France Soir,* formerly the clandestine *Défense de la France* during the Occupation, and could thus easily cast itself as representative of the Fourth Republic (1944–58).[2] Indeed, *Elle*'s mixed messages regarding women's role in postwar reconstruction is congruent with the new regime's own equivocality. In the rhetoric of the Fourth Republic, and in the pages of *Elle,* women and girls were called upon to be, variously, wives, mothers, homemakers, professionals, and citizens. Women might be able to "have it all" in the glossy pages of *Elle* and the platforms of Fourth Republic politicians, but these various components of femininity as they were lived in postwar France were fraught with contradiction.

"Douze Millions de Beaux Bébés"

At the end of a suffrage movement begun in 1870 and well after most of their European counterparts, just months before the Liberation, French women acquired the right to vote.[3] Bills for limited female suffrage had been introduced in 1890, 1901, and 1906; in 1919, 1922, 1924, 1929, and 1933 the measure had been defeated in Parliament by alternately left- and right-wing majorities, who warned of the demise of the family and raised the specter of prostitutes at the polls.[4] Finally, on 23 March 1944, the government in exile in Algiers ruled in favor of female suffrage, and the preamble to the new constitution of October 1946 accorded them this right.[5] Practically speaking, the decision to extend the vote to women was less a question of their equal contribution to the Resistance movement than

of the need to complete quorums in municipalities that had been deci-
mated by the war.[6] Fourth Republic politicians were in no hurry to instigate
dramatic social change; while a commission to reform marriage laws was
established, no proposal ever reached the stage of being formally brought
before the National Assembly and the Senate and put to the vote.[7]

Newly acquired civic rights could scarcely topple the Napoleonic *Code
Civil,* which made a woman's submission to her husband a legal reality.
Despite small modifications over time, the Napoleonic Code remained in
place in France well into the 1960s, its effects on women compounded
by depopulation anxieties brought on by two world wars. The *Alliance
nationale contre la dépopulation,* an organization founded in 1899, was
responsible for what sociologist Rémi Lenoir calls the "vulgarization of
demography." The Alliance published the journal *Vitalité française* and
sponsored educational programs through which children in the late 1940s
learned that an increase in the birth rate would automatically revive a
national economy that was lagging behind Germany and the USSR.[8]

In addition to its pedagogical presence, pronatalism had been a linch-
pin of every government from the post–World War I period on, whatever the ideological differences were in other arenas. The law of 31 July
1920 making abortion and birth control illegal remained unchallenged for
thirty-five years.[9] The Vichy legislation that prohibited divorce in the first
three years of marriage, discouraged abortion, and gave financial incentives to encourage couples to have large families bore striking similarities
to the pronatalist policies of the Fourth Republic.[10] Motherhood was the
framework within which women were to understand their newly acquired
right to vote. Both were patriotic duties according to the Fourth Republic's view of women's social role as stated in Article 24 of the October 1946
constitution: "La Nation garantit à la femme l'exercice de ses fonctions de
citoyenne et de travailleuse dans des conditions qui lui permettent de rem-
plir son rôle de mère et sa mission sociale" [The nation guarantees women
the exercise of her functions as citizen and worker in conditions that allow
her to fulfill her role as mother and her social mission]. Women's participation in the political life of the nation was justified as part and parcel of
their responsibility for raising children.[11]

The consensus on the promotion of the family as an instrument of moral,
economic, and social renewal across the boundaries of social class ran
strong across party lines, marked symbolically by De Gaulle's 1945 speech
calling upon the French to produce "douze millions de beaux bébés" for

the good of the nation.[12] Outside the arena of party politics, the social program of *allocations familiales,* or family allowances, was pivotal in promoting a uniquely maternal role for women in the postwar period. Allocations familiales were actually created at the end of the nineteenth century by socially minded business owners, who distributed "family supplements" to employees proportionate to the number of children they had, with the amount of the supplement varying between employers.[13] This private sector initiative inspired a policy during World War I whereby families of mobilized men received governmental allowances and fathers with five or more children were not sent to the front. In the post–World War I years, various financial measures favorable to large families were put into effect, such as tax breaks and cheaper housing. Nationwide, the 1939 *Code de la Famille* established the first comprehensive system of family allowances provided by the state rather than the employer, the amount in direct correlation to a family's number of children. The *Code* was largely absorbed into Vichy policy, but with greater ideological designs. Pétain's *Révolution nationale* extended *allocations* to all families no matter what their income or class, favoring those whose children numbered three or more. Indeed, the family replaced the individual as the basic unit in Pétain's vision of a society where he presided as supreme father figure.[14]

With the instatement of the Fourth Republic, associations with fascism fell away, but the financial incentive for couples to have large families remained, this time in the face of a population decline brought on by war. Rather than relying on ideological exhortations, the government emphasized providing practical economic advantages to mothers. For example, a one-time bonus, the *prime à la naissance,* was rewarded to newly married couples who had a baby within the first two years of marriage, thus encouraging the mother to stay at home. Monthly *allocations* began with the second birth and continued until the children were no longer of school age. 1955 saw the creation of the *allocation de la mère au foyer,* a stipend for the at-home mother regardless of her husband's income.[15] This particular *allocation* was the first economic measure directly aimed at women. It had been preceded by a less drastic measure along the same lines: the *allocation de salaire unique,* paid when only one parent worked outside of the home. Both discouraged women from working and penalized those that did.[16] The antiabortion and anticontraceptive law of 1920, in effect until 1967 despite efforts by the nascent family-planning movement, supplemented the economic incentive for women to have children and stay at home.[17] Incentives to produce ranks of large families could produce social problems of their own; in *Les Petits enfants du siècle*, Christiane Rochefort's 1961 novel about life in an HLM (low-income housing project), children who are too numerous for their parents to keep track of become juvenile delinquents and sexually active at an appallingly young age, and mothers identify their offspring by the home appliance each birth allowed them to acquire. *Les Petits enfants* caricatures this equivalence but stands as sobering social commentary nonetheless.

Public and Private

Even though motherhood dominated the Fourth Republic's definition of women's role in postwar society, French women did much more in those years than stay at home. A significant increase in the visibility of young and mature women in the public sphere accompanied the economically reinforced ideology of domesticity. In the privileged classes, the number of women in prestigious employment and university classrooms increased steadily.[18] Young women writers, as we shall see in the following chapter, were highly publicized and widely read. Alongside the antiabortion and anticontraceptive propaganda, movements for women's reproductive rights, from the right to anesthesia during childbirth to the first family-planning clinics, were beginning to take shape.

Historians who study the separation of public and private spheres have traditionally charted the process in terms of the increasing valorization of work done in the public sphere over domestic work.[19] The actual time frame of this ideological and economic division has been a subject of much debate. Many historians assert that the private sphere came into its clearly defined separate existence as a result of the decline of court society and an aristocratic way of life.[20] In court society, where power depended on birth and not gender, both men and women held powerful positions. It was gender, though, which served as the basis upon which European societies restructured into public and private spheres as industrialization took hold in the late eighteenth and early nineteenth centuries. The division, in its early stages, was not an ideological one. The private sphere meant much more than what today we call housework: work done in the home was and, just as importantly, was perceived to be vital to a family's material existence. The woman's role as manager of the early private sphere was thus a powerful and prestigious one.

Only with the development of a cash economy in the nineteenth century did society begin to value paid work outside the home more and work done in the home less. Attitudes underwent a major shift. What had been power in the private sphere came to mean disempowerment for women, as the economic division between public and private spheres acquired psychological dimensions. In the realm of representation, associations with work and productivity diminished, and domesticity came to signify passivity, dependence, and devalorized feminine emotionality, in relation to the public sphere of male activity, earning power, and worldly wisdom. The narrative of women's emancipation in the twentieth century has been written as a struggle to emerge from the confines of a devalorized private sphere as well as from the confining definitions of the feminine, which came into their own in the nineteenth century.

The 1950s in France represent an ambiguous moment in this progression. The long-awaited acquisition of the vote in 1944 did not trigger a flurry of political activity as it had for women in other national contexts. More French women were receiving university educations, and more women had high-status jobs, but postwar culture was more visibly marked by the revalorization of female domesticity. Domesticity could be revalorized because it was in a sense redefined—by the impact of technology. The home-appliance industry skyrocketed in the postwar years: between 1950 and 1958, production went up a remarkable 400 percent.[21] For those who could afford washing machines, dishwashers, and the like, the time-consuming drudgery of household tasks was transformed, although the number of hours spent on these tasks remained largely the same.[22]

Because the purchasing power of the individual salary lagged behind the steadily rising cost of living, most people could not actually afford the new time-saving appliances before the late 1950s.[23] The redefinition of household tasks was primarily a question of representation: technology did not redefine women's domestic role, but how people *saw* it. In tandem with the industrial boom to which the statistics testify, the advertising industry transformed the home into a fantasy space that women of every social class could experience. In those modern times, as ads showed, washing machines and refrigerators were the ideal gifts for wives (fig. 1). Household appliances signified both modernity and a uniquely feminine desire, one which knew no class bounds. Similarly, in women's magazines, the housewife became a glamorous and stylish figure, the smooth lines of her accessory appliances continuous with her own attractiveness, savvy, and plea-

Fig. 1. The new ideal in gifts for women
Reprinted with permission from Whirlpool France

sure (fig. 2). Such images of ultramodern domestic space were often fake: in the early 1950s, for example, French television commercials for home appliances were filmed in American suburban kitchens.[24] Sometimes flagrantly, sometimes not, it was American-style home life that constituted the fantasy of glamorous domesticity in France.

Beyond the fantasies of American kitchens and pricey appliances, French life in the 1950s was generally not characterized by the luxury of American standards. Under the guidance of Edgar Faure, the Ministère des Finances at the time, the Second Plan (1954–57) attempted to modernize and expand industrial productivity and to make more choices available to consumers, but prices remained inflated until 1957. The gap between media images of homes stocked with appliances and actual living conditions was never fully closed for most people. In the media-generated fantasy of the French woman in her high-tech, American-style home, *Elle* magazine played a major role, placing the new pleasures of the home alongside the equally glamorous novelty of women's expanding public role, as if both were the real and unproblematic components of the modern woman.

"Elle apportait l'Amérique . . ."[25]

Who was the modern woman before her 1950s incarnation in *Elle*? In the late 1930s, the women's magazine that was the voice of modernity was *Marie-Claire*.[26] *Marie-Claire* was launched in 1937 by Jean Prouvost, owner of *Paris Soir*. At a time when the *presse féminine* focused either on women's duties in the home or on personal appearance, *Marie-Claire* de-emphasized such traditional content in favor of a new discourse of personality and independence. Prouvost's cooperation with the Nazis meant that the magazine continued publication during the Occupation years and was banned with the postwar purges. *Marie-Claire* reappeared in October 1954 bearing a new message: now, the magazine told its female readers, the domestic world was to be their only world. In this first issue (which had the unprecedented success in the history of the French press of selling out its 500,000 copies after several hours on the newsstand), the editorial stated: "*Marie-Claire* ne vous parlera ni d'hier, ni d'aujourd'hui, mais du seul jour qui compte pour une femme: demain. Nous laisserons l'actualité des hommes au quotidien et à l'hebdomadaire" [*Marie-Claire* will not speak to you about yesterday, or today, but of the only day that matters for a woman:

Fig. 2. A woman and her refrigerator: elegance and modernity
Elle 21 February 1955

tomorrow. We will leave men's current events to newspapers and magazines]. *Marie-Claire*'s advocacy of such resolutely separate spheres can be seen in the titles of articles and features in the first few issues: "J'attends un bébé pour Noël," the monthly column "Claude Maman" for the expectant mother, "J'ai épousé un G.I.," and "J'ai 25 ans," an article on the plight of the single woman. The once modern *Marie-Claire* had been reincarnated as a voice for women's traditional place at home.

Elle, on the other hand, presented itself as the voice of modernity, taking its cue from the American way of life under the guidance of the magazine's founder, Hélène Lazareff (née Gordon). She was a French woman of Russian Jewish origin who began her career as a journalist in the 1930s, writing the children's page for *France-Soir* under the pen name of "Tante Juliette."[27] Gordon later married the paper's owner, media magnate Pierre Lazareff. At the outbreak of World War II, the couple left Paris for New York City. Unlike her husband, Gordon-Lazareff spoke perfect English and was easily integrated into journalistic circles in New York. Their experiences of exile were quite different. He was part of an intellectual expatriate milieu that included Antoine de Saint-Exupéry, André Maurois, Jules Romains, René Clair, and André Breton. She became an editor of the women's page of the *New York Times Magazine* and also at Harper's *Bazaar.* Upon her return to Paris in 1945, Gordon-Lazareff was able to meet the challenges of bad paper, a shortage of film, and primitive technology; and the first issue of *Elle* came out in October 1945, just a year after the Liberation.[28] One year later, Françoise Giroud joined the magazine and took over as editor-in-chief when Gordon-Lazareff became seriously ill.[29]

Sociologist Edgar Morin has called *Elle*'s role in the immediate postwar years that of a "découvreur de confort" [discoverer of comfort].[30] At first the magazine limited itself to the most basic comforts, making ends meet more pleasantly in the face of the continued shortages of the late 1940s. Staples were in short supply in the modern world of 1945 that *Elle* ushered in. Then, "the old days" meant abundance, and "modernity" was synonymous with hardship. Rationing for food staples like bread, sugar, dairy products, and edible oils continued until 1949. Gas heat was not readily available until 1953, and the limited availability of coal meant that one of the major preoccupations of the early postwar years was trying to stay warm. In the face of ongoing material difficulties, the "*Elle* Cuisine" recipe in the magazine's first issue declared, "Ne vous méfiez pas des oeufs en poudre" [Don't mistrust powdered eggs]; the following week's issue

Fig. 3. The use-value of French elegance
Elle, 1 April 1948

provided suggestions of how to prevent cold from entering the home and recipes for keeping warm. The 12 December *Elle* may have featured the fantasy of a robust woman in a fur coat on its cover, but articles in the 26 December Christmas issue discussed with realistic practicality how to give turkey leftovers and old sweaters new appeal.

Even the hallowed institution of couture received practical treatment: in a 1948 issue, *Elle* showed its use-value to readers (fig. 3).[31] With the foreign sales from dresses by Dior, Balmain, and Balenciaga, France could buy 9,800 bags of wheat, 3,000,000 kilograms of wool, and 789,000 kilograms of meat from abroad. Exported French elegance, the magazine informed its readers, was helping the more practical matter of survival at home, where conversely it was more à propos to do as American women did and wear trousers: "Pourquoi ne porterions-nous pas, dans nos appartements mal chauffés, ce vêtement pratique. Appelons-le «slacks» de son nom américain et personne n'y trouvera à redire"[32] [Why don't we wear, in our poorly heated apartments, this practical item. Let's use the American name, slacks, and no one will find fault with it]. Until the mid-1950s, the women who modeled fashions in *Elle* were uniformly shapely and robust, fantasy bodies in a country that had survived on rations just a few years before. The first issues of *Elle* relied upon American models, whose bodies bore no traces of hardship; their hair and makeup were arranged "à la française" so that French readers couldn't tell the difference.[33]

With its help, the magazine asserted, women would be able to fight the continued shortages and poor living conditions of the late 1940s, to create comfort in their homes, and thus achieve happiness in their lives. In fashions and features, *Elle* showed women in the role of the inventive, efficient housewife. No matter what her socioeconomic status, the reader like the magazine was "la Reine des débrouillardes"[34] [the queen of the make-doers]. The material situation of the postwar housewife was not so very different from that of the *débrouillards,* the men and women who had used their wiles to make everyday life more bearable during the Occupation.[35] The only difference was that after the Liberation, the cheerful make-doer became a uniquely female role. Now that men had returned to the workplace, it was understood that women should take up where they had left off before the war: at home.

While most individuals and businesses were struggling to emerge from the penury and unproductivity of the Occupation, *Elle* was already helping women organize their homes and their personal lives. Just as women continued to use ration coupons for food staples,[36] the diligent reader could cut out the occasional "bons magiques," or magic coupons, in the magazine's pages, to be exchanged in stores for both personal and home-related luxury products, cheaper because they were made for the *Elle* label (fig. 4). In 1951 Paris, the magazine had a stand outside the Bazar de l'Hôtel de Ville (the Parisian equivalent of Macy's) staffed by a young woman whose job was to assist shoppers and answer their home-related questions ("facilitera vos achats, répondra à toutes vos questions «maison», et vous tirera de tous vos embarras ménagers.")[37] The magazine had a radio program, Radio *Elle.* In 1952 *Elle* even ran a contest for the ideal housewife: 27,500 women competed for the prize of one million francs.[38]

From its very first issue on, *Elle* showed all sorts of women leading productive lives in the public sphere but rarely to the exclusion of the traditional sphere of femininity, the home and, by extension, the family.

Fig. 4. "Magic Coupons" made for *Elle*
Elle, 15 October 1948

Actresses, anonymous models, athletes, intellectuals, white collar professionals, and attractive readers were all shown to be briskly, efficiently, and happily managing their cooking, cleaning, and numerous children, in always immaculate and fully outfitted households. By 1955, one out of six French women read *Elle.*[39] By this same time, *Elle's* covers had progressed from showing the prewar fantasy of women in fur coats to its own modern fantasy: women with children, laundry baskets, or even refrigerators—a fantasy that made sense in light of the composition of the nation's adult female population. As the magazine reported in 1956, of fourteen million women voters in France, 13,300 were artists or "intellectuals"; 200,000 were maids; 812,000 owned their own businesses; 900,000 were office workers; 1,125,000 were factory workers; 1,415,000 worked in agriculture; and 9,320,000 were identified as "sans profession," meaning they were housewives[40] (see fig. 5).

Intellectuals React

La liberté de ton de *Elle* était, à l'époque, révolutionnaire. Pensez qu'avant la guerre *Marie-Claire* ne se permettait pas d'imprimer le mot amant. Les femmes n'avaient que des amis, ou des fiancés.[41]

[The liberty of *Elle's* tone was, at the time, revolutionary. Just think that before the war, *Marie-Claire* didn't venture to print the word "lover." Women only had friends, or fiancés.]

While *Elle* largely focused on the pleasures of the home, the occasional articles on frigidity, female hygiene, and extramarital sexuality that do not

Istanbul : Sylviane Carpentier devient Miss Europe.   Palaiseau : Miss Europe redevient Sylviane Carpentier

Fig. 5. Miss Europe: From beauty queen to housewife
Elle, 3 January 1955

look revolutionary today certainly did in the 1950s, as Françoise Giroud remembers from the early years of *Elle*. The magazine's matter-of-fact acknowledgement of female sexuality led authorities in many areas to prohibit its sale, resulting in unimpressive national sales figures. For those who could and did read it, *Elle,* says Giroud, was an "instrument of liberation"[42]—hindsight that runs counter to the scathing criticism the magazine received from intellectuals at the time. The best-known critiques of *Elle* are to be found among Roland Barthes's *Mythologies,* a collection of essays originally published in Maurice Nadeau's left-of-center journal, *Lettres nouvelles,* in the 1950s. In *Mythologies,* Barthes examined in minute and bemused detail new and age-old habits and fascinations of the French public in order to demystify popular pleasures and unveil their ideological dimension. What interested and troubled him about *Elle* was the magazine's power to present luxury as if it were ordinary reality to readers for whom it could only ever be a dream:

> *Elle* est un journal précieux, du moins à titre légendaire, son rôle étant de présenter à l'immense public populaire qui est le sien (des enquêtes en font foi) le rêve même du chic; d'où une cuisine du revêtement et de l'alibi, qui s'efforce toujours d'atténuer ou même de travestir la nature première des aliments . . . Le plat paysan n'est admis qu'à titre exceptionnel (le bon pot-au-feu des familles), comme la fantaisie rurale de citadins blasés . . . C'est, au sens plein du mot, une cuisine d'affiche, totalement magique, surtout si l'on se rappelle que ce journal se lit beaucoup dans des milieux à faibles revenus. Ceci explique d'ailleurs cela: c'est parce qu'*Elle* s'adresse à un public vraiment populaire qu'elle prend bien soin de ne pas postuler une cuisine économique . . . *Elle* donne la recette des perdreaux-fantaisie, *l'Express,* celle de la salade niçoise. Le public d'*Elle* n'a droit qu'à la fable, à celui de *l'Express* on peut proposer des plats réels, assuré qu'il pourra les confectionner.[43]

> [*Elle* is an invaluable magazine, at least in its legendary capacity, since its role is to present to its vast public, which (market research tells us) is working class, the very dream of style. Hence a cookery of adornment and alibi, which is forever trying to extenuate and even to disguise the primary nature of foodstuffs . . . A country dish is only admitted as an exception (the solid, familial pot-au-feu), as the rustic whim of jaded urbanites . . . It is, in the fullest meaning of the word, a pin-up cuisine, totally magical, especially if one remembers that this magazine is widely read in lower-income milieus. The latter, in fact, explains the former: it is because *Elle* targets a truly working-class public that it is very

careful not to take for granted that cooking must be economical . . . *Elle* gives a recipe for fancy partridges, *L'Express* gives one for *salade niçoise*. The readers of *Elle* are entitled only to fantasy; real dishes can be suggested to readers of *L'Express,* in the certainty that they will be able to prepare them.]

Food is not for real in *Elle;* Barthes unveiled recipe pages with their ostensibly practicable lists of ingredients and instructions as little more than fairy tales that whisk readers away from the unsubstantial offerings of their own lives and tables. What he found most significant about the seductive pictures of fancy food that beckoned from glossy pages was their de facto audience: "market research" identified them as working class. In unveiling one kind of seduction, Barthes overlooked another to which he himself fell prey, that of the supposed objectivity of statistics.[44] The market research he referred to was a contemporary myth-maker in its own right whose codes he could have examined along with those of the new Citroën and laundry detergent. Instead, Barthes used statistics as the reified base from which the act of reading *Elle* became relevant as a class indicator alone.

By focusing on social class, Barthes missed the opportunity to complicate this particular analysis of *Elle* with another layer of his contemporary culture's mythology that was particularly obvious for this magazine: femininity. For the appeal of the fantasies that *Elle* offered was first and foremost feminine, cover to cover, from the title on. The magazine's targeted readership was based first of all on gender, not class, its codes primarily those of femininity: what the reader could and should make or wear or buy or dream or be because she was female. No male reader's experience could take this form of identification.

While other intellectuals writing for the French press may have acknowledged that *Elle*'s primary audience was female, they did not all agree with Barthes's assessment of the magazine as a fantasy text for the working classes. For *Le Figaro*'s editor-in-chief Louis Pauwels, the problem with *Elle* was that it was rather *too* real. The magazine's significance lay in its considerable influence on women of all ages and in its status as a sociological artifact: evidence of the contemporary feminine state of mind. "Il n'y a pas de journal plus important que le vôtre. Il exerce une influence réelle sur un nombre considérable de dames et demoiselles. Il reflète avec la plus grande exactitude possible l'état de ces dames et demoiselles. Point question de ne pas lire «Elle» si l'on veut y voir clair"[45] [No magazine is more important than yours. It has a real influence on a considerable number of ladies and young ladies. It reflects with the greatest possible accuracy the state of these ladies and young ladies. Not reading *Elle* is out of the question if one wants to see one's state clearly]. It is clear that Pauwels did not like what he saw. In the magazine's pages, he went on to say, what one saw clearly was a complicity with contemporary culture's demystification of romance and the couple:

> Et l'on y voit clair, en effet. On voit que nous allons à toute vitesse vers un monde extrêmement sec où le dialogue ne s'engage plus qu'entre une caricature de l'homme et une femme-semblant pour qui l'amour n'est que le pince-homme ... [L]a sociologue qui se réjouit, photos à l'appui, de voir Monsieur et Madame devenir des «copains» plutôt que des étrangers éternellement émerveillés de leur mutuelle étrangeté et l'amour se faire par téléphone plutôt que dans ce tremblement sacré.

> [And one does see clearly in its pages. One sees that we're going full speed towards a cold, cold world in which dialogue is only ever exchanged between a caricature of man and a make-believe woman for whom love is only a mantrap ... (One sees) the lady sociologist who, with photos to prove her point, rejoices in seeing Monsieur and Madame become "pals" instead of strangers filled with eternal wonder at their mutual strangeness, in seeing that love is made over the telephone rather than in a sacred fit of trembling.]

Why Pauwels directed his reproach to women and not to men here remains unspoken and understood: sentiment is not only a female pleasure, it is a social identity and responsibility—making "la sociologue" a particularly vivid sign of the "cold, cold world." Pauwels bemoaned the infiltration of technology into ways of living and understanding: so-called advances meant that love no longer stood outside of time. Moreover, he played upon the fact that the magazine's title is also the feminine pronoun "she" and wrote as if he were addressing an actual woman. He acknowledged *Elle*'s/her prominent place in the media, remarking that "des leçons de journalisme, c'est vous qui avez à m'en donner" [you're the one who should be giving me journalism lessons], a condescending and ironic quip, coming from the editor-in-chief of one of the nation's most respected newspapers. It also indicates the very real impact that the upstart *Elle* had on the French press.

In his "Lettre inutile à *Elle*," Pauwels referred to an "attack" on *Elle* by Colette Audry in *Les Temps modernes*. Audry's article made a far more subtle and valid contention: that *Elle* did indeed put a "Modern Woman" on display but always in terms of her counterpart—sometimes in the same person—the Eternal Feminine.[46] Audry, who had been a colleague of Simone de Beauvoir's in the 1930s in her teaching days in Rouen and also went on to become a novelist, essayist, and playwright, was more interested in unmasking ideology than in bemoaning the apparent demise of romance. She went one step beyond Barthes, noting how gender as well as class inflected *Elle*'s matter-of-fact presentation of everyday life.[47]

Audry began her piece by describing some of the features of a particular issue of *Elle:* the exhilarating New York life of a French model; Ginger Rogers's secrets on staying young; voluntary Caesarian births that produced physically perfect specimens for ordinary parents.[48] What she saw underlying the display of glamour and comfort in the modern lives of movie stars, working women, and housewives alike, was a bottom line of bad faith: the ideology of the Eternal Feminine, whereby women must ultimately sacrifice their individuality for the good of the family. The example cited was a sensationalistic two-part article: "énorme titre sur double page, JE SUIS UNE FEMME TROMPEE"[49] [enormous headline spanning two pages, "I'm a wife who's been deceived"]: the "true story" of thirty-three-year-old Yvonne, whose twelve-year marriage has yielded three beautiful children, a comfortable house, evening bridge games, ski and shore vacations, and weekends in the country. All is well until Yvonne finds out that her husband is having an affair. She wants to walk out but has no money of her own. She and the children go to her parents' house, where Yvonne's mother confides that her own husband had done the same thing years ago. She advises Yvonne to do as she did for the children's sake and go back to her husband, which she eventually does. Audry deplored Yvonne's trust in marriage as an anchor in the world, in her own identity as a wife, and in her avowal that she would have preferred to remain unaware:

> Mais qu'une fille puisse à notre époque aborder le mariage sans avoir jamais envisagé l'incident; qu'Yvonne n'ait jamais songé au cours de ses douze années de plat bonheur que douze ans de vie commune peuvent engendrer la satiété; qu'elle n'ait jamais pensé dans son malheur que son bon droit d'épouse ne vaut pas cher . . . qu'elle ne puisse pas concevoir le bonheur sans l'absolue fidélité de son mari, et qu'elle finisse par constater que «l'idéal serait de ne rien savoir, de se refuser à savoir», que tout cela puisse être autant d'erreurs et de petites ignominies accumulées, Yvonne ne s'en avise pas un instant . . .
>
> Une chose saute aux yeux: la brillante féminité des premières pages est bien

loin . . . Le destin et le devoir des femmes n'ont pas changé: comme dans *Le Journal des Demoiselles*, ils ont nom silence et résignation.

[But that a girl these days could approach marriage without ever having foreseen that such a thing might happen; that Yvonne never thought in the course of her twelve years of dull happiness that twelve years of shared life can engender satiety; that in her unhappiness she never thought that her rights as a wife weren't worth much . . . that she couldn't conceive of happiness without the absolute faithfulness of her husband, and that she could end up declaring that "the ideal would be to know nothing, to not let yourself know," that all this might be so many accumulated errors and small embarrassments, Yvonne doesn't seem to notice . . .

One thing is immediately evident: we are far from the brilliant femininity of the first pages. The destiny and duty of women have not changed: as in *Le Journal des Demoiselles*, their names are silence and resignation.]

Audry found Yvonne's willful ignorance and limited perspective unbelievable, her decision to do as her mother had done a sad comment on the stagnancy of the feminine condition in an otherwise changing world. Perhaps Simone de Beauvoir would have explained Yvonne's decision more sympathetically. As Beauvoir saw it, unlike men, women were not, typically, free to choose their destiny, but were trapped in a perpetual state of bad faith that translated as duplicity or complicity with men.[50] Yvonne's decision to go back to her husband illustrates perfectly the ineluctability of patriarchy.

Interestingly, Yvonne does not fear the loss of her husband's love, but of their lifestyle. The word "love" is not even mentioned; it is not Yvonne's heart that is shattered, but the fantasy world of her domestic comfort. Indeed, the lesson for the *Elle* reader was above all a practical one: money is the crucial element of autonomy. This is a coming to consciousness that transcends the opposition Audry saw between the Eternal Feminine and Modern Woman. Unlike the nineteenth-century reader of *Le Journal des Demoiselles*,[51] Yvonne does not have an emotional need for a man, but rather an economic one, and in the process of the fairy-tale life coming apart, she finds this out full well.

The Invisible Man

The male breadwinner was most often invisible in *Elle*, yet he was necessary. The magazine demonstrated to its readers how all kinds of women could successfully achieve self-realization and even fame in the public sphere as actresses, writers, Resistance fighters, politicians, astronomers, and mountain climbers, but never to the exclusion of a reference, however oblique, to the man in their lives. As Yvonne's story illustrates, femininity was at its most complete in *Elle* when it entailed a home and an accessory husband of one's own. This is best seen in Juliette Gréco's transformation from a bohemian public figure into housewife. Gréco, a glamorous actress and singer associated with the jazz clubs of Saint-Germain-des-Prés and the existentialists that frequented them (notably Sartre), was a familiar face to the weekly reader of *Elle*, from its first numbers through the late 1950s. In 1953, the magazine did a detailed feature on her marriage. In the caption under a photograph of Gréco, now Madame Lemaire, serving dinner to her husband, *Elle* enumerated the bride's many new acquisitions, repeating the possessive adjective in quotation marks to emphasize that they were indeed *hers*. She now had: "«son» réfrigérateur, «son» sechoir, «sa» table (et son mari à servir)" [52] ["her" refrigerator, "her" dryer, "her" table (and her husband to serve)]; another caption under a photograph of Gréco in the basement of the house reads: "Mme Lemaire a «sa» cave qui la change bien des caves de sa jeunesse, à Saint-Germain-des-Prés" [Madame Lemaire has "her" basement, which is quite a change from the basement nightclubs of her youth in Saint-Germain-des-Prés]. The new home furnishings may be featured in this equation, but the parenthetical new husband is essential: without him and his salary, none of these domestic objects would be hers.

As the trappings of home technology came increasingly to situate women in the contemporary world, to define not only their place but also their pleasures, fashion took a clear back seat in *Elle*. In the early 1950s *Elle* showed its readers fashions that were economical and simple, as befitted a woman whose home was her passion. According to Françoise Giroud in a 1951 article called "Où en est la haute couture française?" [Where is French haute couture these days?], extravagant fashion was, quite simply, passé:

> Quel que soit son budget, la cliente de 1951 dépense proportionnellement moins pour s'habiller que celle de 1939. Elle préfère acheter et entretenir une voiture personnelle, s'offrir des voyages, une machine à laver, un réfrigérateur. Bref, distractions et surtout confort l'emportent sur la coquetterie pure. Evolution profonde qui ira vraisemblablement en s'accentuant parce qu'elle accom-

pagne une évolution de femmes qu'on ne saurait honnêtement critiquer, au contraire.—C'est la disparition progressive de la femme-poupée uniquement préoccupée de ses chapeaux et de ses robes.[53]

[Whatever her budget, the client of 1951 spends proportionally less on clothing than the client of 1939. She prefers to buy and keep up her own car, take vacations, buy a washing machine, a refrigerator. In short, fun and especially comfort win her over rather than simple coquetry. It's a major evolution that will probably become even more dramatic, because it accompanies a change in women themselves, one that no one would criticize. On the contrary: it's the progressive disappearance of the woman as doll, preoccupied solely with her hats and dresses.]

As Giroud saw it, a major shift had taken place in the realm of female desire: French women were less concerned with their appearance and decorative function than they had been before the war. "Distractions et surtout confort"—the two were interchangeable in her equation. Washing machines, refrigerators, cars, and trips formed a continuous chain that signified independence, ease, pleasure, and integration with the modern world. She thus effaced the real differences between these distractions and comforts, making them equal signifiers, not of the good life, but of maturity. No longer a dress-up doll, the 1950s woman was an adult. But the funding source of so-called adult acquisitions remained unarticulated.

The feminine pleasures of domestic comfort took precedence over fashion, but *Elle* also recognized the reality of women at work outside the home who needed clothing that would suit a public professional lifestyle. In a 1953 issue, models posed as working women in ensembles that would be suitable for an odd array of jobs: writer, doctor, secretary, printer, actress, saleswoman.[54] Less whimsically, it was the secretary who appeared most often in *Elle*. Much of the issue of 7 February 1955 was dedicated to office lifestyle and fashion. According to *Elle,* secretaries were on the cutting edge of new looks:

Les couturiers créent quelques «chocs» de mode: ce sont les secrétaires qui se chargeront d'en démontrer le succès—ou de les anéantir. Cette année, ce sont les femmes travaillant dans les bureaux qui ont lancé (et cela prouve la justesse de leur instinct, puisqu'elles ont choisi par goût, les vêtements qui convenaient le mieux à leur activité): les jupes courtes, les cardigans longs, les escarpins à petit talon . . . La secrétaire est devenue, au XXe siècle, un peu comme le symbole de notre civilisation. C'est un personnage-test, le rouage précieux de la machine industrielle, commerciale, artistique.[55]

[Designers create various fashion "shocks": secretaries are the ones who will make or break them. This year, it's women working in offices who have decided what's in (and this proves how right their instinct is, since they themselves, without anyone telling them to do so, have chosen the clothing best suited to what they do): short skirts, long cardigans, low-heeled pumps . . . The secretary has become, in the twentieth century, something like the symbol of our civilization. She's a litmus test character, the invaluable gears of the industrial, commercial, and artistic machine.]

Domesticity has momentarily become invisible in this equation. Instead of the housewife and mother, the "symbol of the twentieth century" is the secretary: a confident, vital part of the modern economic machine. Yet the Eternal Feminine has not been abandoned: the secretary may be a fashion innovator, but what remains unspoken is that she is the helpmate of her male superior, the executive.

Women in male-dominated professions were also shown to take part in the Eternal Feminine. A 1953 article entitled "Toutes les femmes n'en font vraiment qu'à leur tête" [Women really only do what they want to], presented the careers of several remarkable women: the twenty-two-year-old founder and editor of a small left-wing paper called *Le Soulèvement de la jeunesse* [The uprising of youth]; a judge; a painter; and the youngest female lawyer practicing in Nice, Mireille Martin, who succeeded in having the president of France commute the death penalty for her client. The scene as recounted in *Elle* bears little resemblance to legal protocol:

Monsieur Auriol vit entrer dans son bureau une jeune fille ravissante et rouge de confusion, qui trébuchait sur les mots. Peu à peu, l'avocate s'enhardit. Ce fut un torrent de paroles, et enfin de larmes. Aucun avocat ne s'était ainsi conduit devant le Président . . . qui signa. (ellipsis in text)[56]

[Monsieur Auriol saw a ravishing young woman enter his office, red with confusion, stuttering. Little by little, the lady lawyer became bolder. There was a torrent of words, and finally tears. No lawyer had behaved that way in front of the President . . . who signed.]

No need for a career woman to relinquish her emotionality at work, according to this article. In fact, "femininity," in its pretty, blushing, talkative, tearful way, was shown to still be her most effective tool of all. Unexpected yet expected, such behavior was presented in *Elle* as both unprofessional and innate. In a sense, the anecdote is a belittling one: as an ostensible paragon of modern female self-realization who gives in to the Eternal Feminine, the lawyer is awkward and girlish and even cries. But the message is more ambiguous than that. As the story shows, feminine behavior can change minds and even save lives. Here was a case of a woman with power who used it to make the world a more humane place.[57]

Babies and Books

Elle's image of women who were capable of achieving success in the public sphere without relinquishing their share of the Eternal Feminine extended to features on woman writers. *Elle* found their faces and private lives of more interest than what they wrote. Occasionally the magazine included abridged, easy to read, cartoon versions of contemporary novels, such as Elsa Triolet's *Roses à crédit* and Michèle Perrein's *La Sensitive*. Most of the fiction offerings in *Elle* consisted of either excerpts from English gothic novels or well-respected French realist writers.[58] Colette, who happened to be a neighbor of Hélène Gordon-Lazareff, was the exception: excerpts of her previously unpublished memoirs appeared in *Elle* during the first few months of its publication.[59]

Because of an essay written by Roland Barthes on the subject, even those who had never thumbed through the pages of *Elle* might know of one case where the faces and home lives of contemporary women writers appeared. In the issue of 22 November 1954, *Elle* printed a full-page photo under the title "70 romancières, 300 romans: les femmes de lettres s'imposent" [Seventy women novelists, three hundred novels: women of letters make a name for themselves]. Each of the novelists was listed by name along with any profession she might practice — writing didn't count. Parenthetically, one learned how many children each woman had and how many novels she had written. In terms of production, children came first in the parentheses, novels second.[60] Barthes reacted to this order of things as an instance of the persistence of the Eternal Feminine, circumscribing even the artist's possibilities in the world despite her gifts of self-expression and creativity:

> A en croire *Elle*, qui rassemblait naguère sur une même photographie soixante-dix romancières, la femme de lettres constitue une espèce zoologique remarquable: elle accouche pêle-mêle de romans et d'enfants. On annonce

par exemple: Jacqueline Lenoir (deux filles, un roman); Marina Grey (un fils, un roman); Nicole Dutreil (deux fils, quatre romans), etc . . . [L]'écrivain est un artiste, on lui reconnaît un certain droit à la bohème . . . Mais attention: que les femmes ne croient pas qu'elles peuvent profiter de ce pacte sans s'être d'abord soumises au statut éternel de la féminité. Les femmes sont sur la terre pour donner des enfants aux hommes; qu'elles écrivent autant qu'elles veulent, qu'elles décorent leur condition, mais surtout qu'elles n'en sortent pas . . . Un roman, un enfant, un peu de féminisme, un peu de conjugalité, attachons l'aventure de l'art aux pieux solides du foyer: tous deux profiteront beaucoup de ce va-et-vient.[61]

[If we are to believe the weekly *Elle*, which some time ago assembled seventy women novelists in one photograph, the woman of letters is a remarkable zoological species: she gives birth, randomly, to novels and children. We are introduced, for example, to *Jacqueline Lenoir (two daughters, one novel); Marina Grey (one son, one novel); Nicole Dutreil (two sons, four novels)*, etc . . . The writer is an artist, entitled to a little bohemianism . . . But make no mistake: women must not believe they can take advantage of this pact without having first submitted to the eternal statute of femininity. Women are on earth to give men children; let them write as much as they like, let them embellish their condition, but above all, let them not break out of it . . . A novel, a child, a little feminism, a little connubiality. Let us attach the adventure of art to the strong pillars of the home: both will profit a great deal from the dynamic.]

Barthes viewed *Elle*'s promotion of these women writers as mothers as little more than imprisonment. He dismissed it much as Colette Audry had dismissed the story of Yvonne. But what he didn't account for was the intended audience. Most likely, many were mothers themselves or intended to be. It is exciting now as it must have been then to see assembled in one photograph seventy young women novelists. No matter what came first, babies or novels, the photo makes the fantasy of having them both look feasible.

While the domestic lives of women writers were a source of interest and enthusiasm, *Elle* treated writers who were not young and pretty mothers or mothers-to-be rather differently. In a 1952 *Elle* survey of a hundred women under thirty and a hundred over forty-five, "Voudriez-vous changer votre visage et votre vie contre ceux d'une femme célèbre?"[62] [Would you like to swap your face and your life with a famous woman's?], the choice of the fewest women in both age groups was the forty-eight-year-old Simone de Beauvoir (0/3). This is not surprising. For much of her adult life, Beauvoir lived in hotels, never married, and never had children. Her chosen life-style could only be seen as eccentric in 1954 France, where large families were the norm and most people's impossible dream was to own their own home.[63] Besides her scandalous liaison with Sartre, Beauvoir was known as the author of *Le Deuxième sexe* (1949), noted less for its exhaustive histori-cal research than for a frank and clinical approach to female sexuality that had resoundingly shocked the French public. But by 1954, the shock had faded with the popular and critical success of *Les Mandarins,* a *roman à clef* interweaving the private lives and politics of postwar intellectuals for which Beauvoir would win the prestigious Prix Goncourt. *Elle* interviewed her soon afterwards.

Elle introduced its readers to a Beauvoir who shouldn't intimidate them, who preferred the *Série noire* detective novels to Kant as bedtime read-ing.[64] All associations to *Le Deuxième sexe* were conjured away by invoking the popular caricature of its author and of feminists in general as harm-less historical curiosities: Beauvoir as "la nonne de l'existentialisme, [de] la diaconesse aux talons plats, aux cheveux tirés, ignorant le maquillage, universitaire et pédante, le type même de la féministe, aux temps révo-lus et héroïques des suffragettes" [the nun of existentialism, the deaconess in flats and pulled-back hair, wearing no makeup, academic and pedantic, the image of the feminist, in the bygone heroic times of the suffragettes]. Though she had little interest in couture—a disregard advocated as we have seen in the very same magazine's pages—Beauvoir demonstrated care in her slightly bohemian appearance, in the "femininity" of her dangling earrings and fabrics brought back from Third World travel, "de quelque Guatemala." And as for domestic responsibilities, she did as every woman did and took them on when she "had to":

> Tout comme la suffragette, il est vrai, elle a horreur du ménage. Mettre le cou-vert l'a toujours ennuyée, et quant à la cuisine! . . . Il a pourtant bien fallu s'y faire, pendant l'Occupation, puisqu'elle ne voulait ni ne pouvait fréquen-ter les restaurants de marché noir. «Je ne savais confectionner, raconte-t-elle, que des crêpes de pomme de terre et le pot-au-feu. Le pot-au-feu, c'était ma grande spécialité. Mais il était toujours brûlé! J'en ai, cependant, servi, un jour, à Picasso, Camus et Sartre. Comment l'ont-ils trouvé? Ils n'en ont rien dit, mais le fait est qu'ils l'ont mangé.»

> [Just like the suffragette, it's true, housework horrifies her. Setting the table has always bored her, and as for cooking! . . . But she had to get used to it, dur-ing the Occupation, since she neither would nor could frequent black-market

restaurants. "I only knew how to make potato crepes and pot-au-feu," she re-counts. "Pot-au-feu was my specialty. But I always burned it! I served it any-way, one day, to Picasso, Camus, and Sartre. What did they think of it? They didn't say anything, but the fact is that they ate it."]

Elle's portrait of the "real" Simone de Beauvoir ended up reassuring the reader that even the intellectual sphere was a conservative place where gender roles were maintained. When existentialists got together, it was still the woman who would do the cooking.[65]

While the article may have highlighted Beauvoir's participation in the Eternal Feminine and caricatured feminism, it also precluded any attempt to dismiss her intellectual prowess. Both she and Sartre took the *agréga-tion* exam in philosophy in the same year; Sartre placed first, Beauvoir sec-ond: "Mais que les antiféministes ne se réjouissent pas trop vite: Simone, elle, se présentait au concours pour la première fois" [But the antifemi-nists shouldn't rejoice too quickly: it was Simone's first try (and Sartre's second)]. The interviewer reminded the reader that Beauvoir was more than Sartre's companion—she was his intellectual equal. To merely pass the *agrégation,* historically the most significant hurdle in the process of be-coming an intellectual in France, was and still is a great accomplishment. By French standards, "Simone" deserved everyone's respect.

The Prix Goncourt meant that she deserved everyone's readership. The Goncourt itself does not count for much in direct financial remuneration, but enormous sales to curious readers have always followed a book's re-ception of the prize. This article in *Elle* must have worked well as pro-motional material. Interspersed with the text were succinct quotes from Beauvoir's oeuvre: from *Le Deuxième sexe,* "On ne naît pas femme; on le devient" [One isn't born a woman; one becomes one]; from *Le Sang des autres,* "Chacun est responsable de tout" [Everyone is responsible for everything]; from *Les Mandarins,* "C'est toujours immérité, l'amour" [Love is never deserved]: philosophical statements that doubled as home-spun, even motherly wisdom in this context, but wisdom nevertheless. While *Elle* did compromise Beauvoir's intellectual achievements in order to make her accessible to the average reader, it also succeeded in com-municating that a philosophical relationship to the world was within every woman's reach.

How to achieve autonomy and recognition without, like Beauvoir, ven-turing too far from the primary feminine role as man's mate: this was the modernity *Elle* most often advocated for its readers. The winners of a contest of February 1948, "Envoyez-nous la lettre d'amour que vous n'avez pas osé écrire à l'homme que vous aimez"[66] [Send us the love letter that you haven't dared to write to the man you love], were promised publication. The information for the contest mentioned that two members of the Académie Française would be among the judges. *Elle* went on to note that for centuries women had achieved recognition as great correspondents and welcomed readers to take part in this particularly feminine sector of the "patrimoine littéraire" through the eloquent revelation of their deepest feelings for a man. *Elle* could have run a poetry contest, or a short-story contest, but it did not and never did during this period. The prestige of having the Académie Française judge love letters is incongruous yet significant: as arbiters of distinction, the judges were not so much evaluating the literary talent of the *Elle* reader as they were her ability to express sentiment. The message to women was clear: you can be creative, but you are at your creative best in love—and on that you will be judged. The love letter contest took women momentarily out of the domain of busy domesticity and suggested they stop and reflect upon the man whom they were doing it all for.

Political Involvement

Elle was part of a social fabric that assumed that women thought of the men in their lives first and impelled them to do so. Only several years after women had acquired the right to vote, it was commonly thought that, whether with her husband or against him, it was through him that a woman defined her political opinions. When asked about women and the vote in an *Elle* survey, Béatrix Beck, the second woman to win the Prix Goncourt for her novel *Léon Morin, Prêtre,* was firmly against it. Her reasoning went as follows: "Ou elles sont influencées par leurs maris, et cela ne signifie rien. Ou elles votent différémment, et l'on risque des conflits"[67] [Either they're influenced by their husbands, and it has no meaning. Or they vote differently, and there's the risk of conflict]. Beck was not alone in her surmise that women lacked political savvy; her opinion was held by a majority of the French. What had happened since the first issue of *Elle*, when a reader's letter asking whether she should sacrifice her political preferences to be in harmony with the man she loved was met with a resounding "non!"?

When feminist theorists, historians, and political scientists try to make sense of the discontinuity between women's right to vote and their almost immediate disengagement from political involvement, they tend to attribute it to custom. Women in France were not used to taking part in the political process. After the initial euphoria of receiving the vote at the Liberation, they met this symbolic gesture with uncertainty. The initial rush of women's participation in national politics soon dwindled. From a high of 32 female deputies out of 575 announced in the first issue of *Elle*,[68] by 1955, Françoise Giroud reported with dismay that their numbers were down to 23 out of 627: equally dismaying to her was the fact that 15 of them were communists and few were married.[69] Apathy was certainly not the province of women alone; Fourth Republic politics were frustrating for many in 1950s France. But sociological and media attention was riveted primarily on the novelty of women voters.

Articles in *Elle* spoke out against the trend of women's disinterest in the political process in several issues of 1955. An article of 5 December remarked that "Une Française sur quatre ne vote pas"—although no comparative statistic is offered for men. A month later, *Elle* printed an appeal from former president Vincent Auriol urging women to vote:

> Egales aux hommes dans le travail, participant à la vie active de la Nation, elles doivent l'être dans la gestion des affaires nationales desquelles dépendent le bien-être et le bonheur de la famille.
>
> Coeur du foyer, la femme en a la garde vigilante et si vient le malheur, guerre civile ou guerre étrangère, chômage ou misère, c'est elle qui souffre et saigne le plus. Parmi les survivants, c'est elle surtout la victime douloureuse.
>
> Tels sont, outre les considérations de droit et de justice humaine, les motifs essentiels de l'égalité politique que nous fîmes triompher par l'octroi du droit de vote à la femme.
>
> Je n'ignore pas que très souvent les femmes restent à l'écart de la vie publique, car elles en redoutent la violence, les haines, les déchirements . . . Mais c'est à elles qu'il appartient d'apporter un élément de calme et d'apaisement.[70]

> [Equal to men at work, participating in the active life of the nation, they must be active in the management of national affairs upon which the well-being and the happiness of the family depend.
>
> At the heart of the home, the woman is in vigilant charge, and if misfortune arrives, war at home or abroad, unemployment or misery, it is she who suffers and bleeds the most. Among the survivors, she especially is the suffering victim.
>
> Besides the considerations of law and human justice, these are the essential

purposes of political equality that triumphed by our authorization of women's vote.

I realize that quite often, women stay away from public life, for they fear its violence, the hatreds, the rifts. But they are the ones who have the duty to bring an element of calm and peacefulness to it.]

Auriol's appeal to women to vote as mothers is a familiar one. Feminists in Britain and France in the eighteenth and nineteenth centuries used a similar line of reasoning to argue for women's right to education: in that they were responsible for the formation of their children as the nation's future citizens, women too should be educated.

Auriol reversed the terms to convince *Elle* readers that decisions at the state level would affect life at home. In melodramatic terms which hearken back to configurations of a delicate and dependent femininity, he identified women as the primary victims of political strife, of war, unemployment, and hard economic times. They were the ones who "suffer and bleed the most," so they should vote out of self-preservation. At the end of the article, Auriol responded to what must have been the common protest that women did not vote knowledgeably. In his region of France, he remarked, women did not all vote in line with their husbands or confuse religion and politics. At the end of this appeal, he gave this practical advice to the *Elle* reader, who had magically metamorphosed from victim to go-getter: to vote with confidence, all one needed to do was to go to meetings, read editorials, and get informed. In Auriol's hypothesis that women as voters could redefine the public sphere by contributing "calm and peacefulness" to it, once again the Eternal Feminine surfaces in the configuration of the Modern Woman.

This issue of *Elle* was a politicized one, probably because of the importance of the upcoming elections of 2 January 1956.[71] Algeria was the central question but not the only one. In a December 1955 survey for *L'Express*, 25 percent of the French named North Africa as the major issue in the elections; 15 percent named salaries and purchasing power; for 9 percent it was conflict between east and west; for 5 percent, the housing crisis.[72] Neither communists, socialists, nor the MRP (popular republican party) had been able to mobilize the population with their platforms on the issues.[73] The outcome was very much up in the air, and it was important for political parties to attract new voters. The possibility that formerly disaffected women voters could determine the outcome of the elections was a real one. On the cover of the 2 January issue of *Elle* is a photograph of people lined up to vote, among them two women, one with her young daughter. The summary on the inside reads: "A la mairie de Marnes-la-Coquette, comme dans toutes les mairies de France, aujourd'hui 2 janvier 1956, les femmes aussi bien que les hommes doivent voter" [At the Marnes-la-Coquette town hall, as elsewhere in France, today 2 January 1956, women as well as men must vote]. This cover was surely as surprising in 1956 as it would be on a women's magazine today: then as now, magazine covers typically featured a close-up of a woman so that the reader could scrutinize her makeup and clothing. Here though, the women's appearance does not matter. Their dress does not connote any particular career or social class. Instead, the cover shows women in their active roles as mothers and citizens. Mothers should vote and bring their daughters with them to the polls because they should teach the rising generation that the fate of the nation will be their responsibility too. The issue of the vote and political involvement is an excellent example of how *Elle* called upon women to take part in the modern world while still remaining within the contours of the Eternal Feminine.

One month before the fall of Pierre Mendès-France's government in February 1955, an article in *Elle* gave women readers the opportunity to reconfigure their definition of politics as matters that did, in fact, affect their daily domestic lives. The article, "Trois ministres promettent aux femmes"[74] [Three ministers promise women], is a discussion of the concrete reforms planned by Mendès-France that would be of interest to *Elle* readers: new and improved daycare centers *(crèches),* the problems of working women, a program to fight alcoholism, the improvement of the physical plants of elementary and high schools and universities, changes to the Social Security system, equal pay for equal work, and the strict application of safety and hygiene rules in the workplace. As the one minister commented, "Je n'oublie pas un instant les préoccupations des femmes. Leur compréhension et leur action sont indispensables au succès de la tâche que le gouvernement a abordée" [I don't for a moment forget women's preoccupations. Their inclusion and their action are indispensable to the success of the task the government has begun to undertake].

The publication in a women's magazine of these numerous political promises just before the government's fall is open to interpretation. What is certain is that while articles like this one may have defined a gender-specific sphere of interests, they also gave women the opportunity to recognize that on the national scene, the personal—issues like workplace safety, education, and daycare—was very much political. According to Françoise Giroud, women's disinterest in politics could be attributed to their sense that national and international issues mattered little to them personally, a situation she saw as changing in the mid-1950s:

> Un regain d'intérêt pour les affaires publiques, déclenché par le drame indo-chinois, par la perspective du réarmement de l'Allemagne, par le problème du logement et la question scolaire, par le fait surtout que la politique s'est soudain incarnée en quelques hommes, a provoqué des conversations dans des milieux où jusque-là on ne parlait jamais «politique».
>
> Et puis les problèmes ont paru plus concrets, donc plus accessibles, et plus propres à frapper l'imagination des femmes.
>
> L'esprit féminin est rebelle à l'abstraction, à la théorie... C'est pourquoi, lors-que la politique se personnalise, comme ce fut le cas en France avec M. Pinay, avec Pierre Mendès-France, leur attention est brusquement requise et quel-quefois passionnée...[75]

[A renewal of interest in public affairs, brought about by the dramatic situa-tion in Indochina, by the prospective rearmament of Germany, by the housing shortage and issues in education, especially by the fact that politics has sud-denly become incarnated in a few men, has provoked conversations in milieus where up to now no one ever "talked politics."

And the problems now seem more concrete, more accessible, and better suited to women's imagination.

The female mind rebels against abstraction, against theory . . . This is why, when politics get personalized, as was the case in France with Monsieur Pinay, with Pierre Mendès-France, women's attention is suddenly necessary and sometimes passionate.]

Politics receive attention from women when the issues are concrete, wrote Giroud, and when they involve daily life. For her, it was a question of female nature. Women naturally tended to ally themselves with individu-als rather than political parties, and they did so only when they thought their voices mattered. Although many feminists today would find Giroud's evocation of female nature reductive, her explanation of women's past dis-interest and current involvement in politics can also be seen as encour-aging for those women who might have previously felt left out. Now, for "natural" reasons, their involvement made sense.

It would be wrong to characterize Giroud's position as simply essentialist. She also implied that the apathy of French women eligible to vote was not innate, but the result of the impossibly tangled politics of the Fourth Republic and the French parliamentary system in general.[76] In comparison, American women, as she noted, who could vote directly for the candidate of their choice, were more involved and concerned than their French counterparts. Very much aware of an instability which no voter or body of voters had the power to rectify, women simply shrugged and stayed away from the polls.

There is a subtle idea expressed here: women's disinterest in politics on the heels of their acquisition of the right to vote may have had something to do with female nature, but for them as for everyone else at the time—meaning men—it was just as much a question of context. Giroud's article offered unusual and matter-of-fact insight into what historians and sociologists have always declared to be inexplicable. Quite simply, these new voters had no patience for their own government and its politicians. But disaffection masked potential power: when the charismatic Charles de Gaulle reappeared on the political scene in 1958, it was women's vote, according to sociologist Evelyne Sullerot, that brought him back into office.[77]

Housewives' Rights

Not only was the "American way" better for women in the political arena, according to *Elle,* but in the home as well. Along with the Franco-American comparison, the magazine made the remarkable move in several articles of bringing up the legal status and socioeconomic value of the anonymous female majority who were categorized as "sans profession," or housewives. The French should look to the United States, Françoise Giroud declared, as a model society where the housewife was respected and as a result content with her lot:

> Elles existent en Amérique comme partout, et rien ne permet d'affirmer qu'elles sont moins heureuses que les autres. Le pays leur rend d'ailleurs hommage en toutes occasions et glorifie volontiers le rôle de la femme au foyer. La Mère est sacrée et son autorité semble plus effective que celle du père. . . La grande vague qui, ici comme dans le monde entier, soulève les femmes et les pousse vers les commandes de la nation, ne tend absolument pas à les arracher pour autant à leurs tâches ancestrales ou à les mépriser.[78]

> [They exist in America as elsewhere, and there's nothing that proves that they are less happy than others. Besides, the country pays them homage frequently

and chooses to glorify the role of the housewife. The mother is sacred and her authority seems more effective than the father's . . . The great wave which, here as everywhere in today's world, awakens women and pushes them toward the commanding positions of the nation, absolutely does not take them away from their ancestral tasks or teach them to hate them.]

As Giroud saw it, the qualities of the Eternal Feminine and Modern Woman were in perfect equilibrium in America. Women could achieve in the public sphere and still be housewives who cheerfully performed their "ancestral tasks." This was precisely the fantasy *Elle* had been displaying as a reality for French women from the first issue on. Here Giroud stated it to be the American standard and a worthy French goal. One does wonder where Giroud got her information.[79] No matter how wrong she may have been about the status of housewives in the United States, the effect of the article was to articulate the French housewife's invisibility as a working member of society to many of these women themselves and to imagine the possibility of greater respect.

The improvement of the housewife's social status was one of *Elle*'s short-lived political causes. In their article "Sept Millions de Françaises Epouses au Foyer" [Seven million French women are housewives], Marianne Andrau and Paul Gérin discussed the legal invisibility of the French housewife. For the past ten years, they wrote, women had cast their votes in elections, but still had not managed to obtain legal recognition for housewives. Those who categorized the housewife as a nonworking person, wrote Andrau and Gérin, ought to look closer:

Que font . . . les «inactives»? Mariées pour la plupart, l'ayant été ou devant l'être un jour, elles font la lessive, le ménage, la cuisine, la vaisselle, la couture, le repassage; elles élèvent leurs enfants, les mènent à l'école, leur font réciter leurs leçons. Elles totalisent douze ou quatorze heures par jour au foyer, exerçant les fonctions de mère de famille, de bonne à tout faire, d'infirmière, de blanchisseuse, de cuisinière, de répétitrice, pour le compte d'une famille dont elles sont quelquefois le gouvernement, mais toujours la servante . . .

Ce sont des femmes intelligentes et coquettes, comme les autres, curieuses, exigeantes pour elles-mêmes. Elles veulent rester femmes, être des épouses aimantes et désirées, des maîtresses de maison agréables.

[What do "inactive" women do? Married for the most part, having been married or going to be one day, they do the laundry, the housework, the cooking, the dishes, the sewing, the ironing; they raise their children, bring them to school, help them go over their lessons. They total twelve or fourteen hours of work a day at home in their capacity as mothers, maids, nurses, laundresses, cooks, tutors for a family for whom they are sometimes the government, but always the servants . . .

They are intelligent and coquettish like other women, curious, demanding of themselves. They want to remain women, to be loving and desirable wives, agreeable housewives.]

Gérin and Andrau found certain rumblings of discontent among the two hundred housewives they surveyed as representative of the seven million others. While the scientific value of the sample is dubious, the message conveyed was simple and powerful: women's domestic work was not recognized and deserved to be, with unemployment pay and a retirement plan, just as salaried workers had in France.

Gérin and Andrau's conclusion remained unthreatening to the traditional separation of spheres. All women wanted, they claimed, was to have their work at home recognized as useful in a society whose economy was booming and where productivity, whether public or private, seemed to matter more than ever.

The Generation Gap

Women as politically astute citizens whose involvement mattered because they were mothers; women in careers and on adventures who still groomed themselves carefully and identified themselves primarily as wives and mothers; all sorts of women as inherently domestic beings ensconced at home in technological comfort in a world where feminism's demands were deemed unnecessary: how might girls read *Elle*'s various contradictory components of femininity, reconciled in a fantasized equilibrium between the Eternal Feminine and Modern Woman? Somewhat critically, I would argue: by the middle of the decade, popular representations of femininity had diversified. Images of the home-centered adult woman were supplemented by a new character: the female adolescent, who became increasingly visible in novels, films, and advertisements over the course of the 1950s. In the best-known of these novels, the eighteen-year-old Françoise Sagan's novel *Bonjour tristesse* (1954), the teenage protagonist Cécile leads a carefree existence with her widowed father, Raymond, and his various girlfriends until Anne, a woman he takes seriously, comes onto the scene.

Raymond is oblivious to the tensions between future mother and daughter, which escalate into Cécile's heartless plot to undermine Anne's control. When teenage girls appeared in articles and advertisements in *Elle*, on the other hand, their place was squarely within the magazine's emphasis on domesticity. Two generations were often shown sharing a common domestic end: a linen company advertisement (15 April 1953), for example, promoted the continuum between mother, daughter, and home in side-by-side images of a teenage girl and a woman in her thirties, both dreamy-eyed, their gazes uplifted, one caption a variation on the other: "A quoi rêvent les jeunes filles? A un trousseau plein de draps Solidra", and "A quoi rêvent les femmes d'intérieur? A une armoire pleine de draps Solidra." Once again we are faced with the invisible man via the trousseau or the linen closet, a future husband or one who will be home later than evening. Like most of its advertisers, the magazine initially conceived of the adolescent reader as simply a younger version of her elders. Beginning in 1953, Anita Pereire's weekly column "Nous les jeunes filles" [Us girls] focused on domestic skills for the junior set, presenting girls of all ages as docile creatures on their way to becoming good wives and mothers.[80]

It is in an advertisement for a brand of margarine, whose manufacturers were attempting to create new associations for its use after the shortages of the Occupation, that a familial triangulation between mother, daughter, and father along the seductive and conflictual lines of gender and generation is made startlingly clear. This time, however, the mother is invisible: the father and his adolescent daughter take center stage. The full-page ad for Astra margarine (fig. 6) is a conversational narrative told in the paternal voice, by a man whose wife has left home to visit her sister for a few weeks during the summer. He finds himself alone with his teenager Arlette. She exposes him to all kinds of new products appreciated by the youth of the day, including fish prepared with margarine instead of butter. Margarine is something his old-fashioned wife, daughter Arlette assures him conspiratorially, would have rejected before even trying: "Je voulais essayer depuis longtemps, mais maman est un peu vieux jeu; toi, tu es plus compréhensif" [I've been wanting to try it for a while, but Mom is a bit old-fashioned; you're more open-minded].

The Astra ad communicates on various levels. First, it gently pokes fun at the rigidity of the adult housewife set in her ways, aligning instead with the youthful and "relaxed" approach of the teenage girl taking a spin in the kitchen—thus encouraging women of all ages to do the same. The *femme*

De la margarine ?...
... C'était bien pendant la guerre !

L'ÉTÉ dernier, ma femme partit se reposer quelques semaines chez sa sœur. Au début, seul avec ma fille Arlette, je me sentais un peu perdu. Et puis... Arlette m'initia gentiment à une vie pleine de fantaisie. Danser un swing frénétique avec Arlette devant la radio, décrocher la photo d'un grand-père militaire accrochée à son piton depuis 25 ans, tout cela m'aurait fait bondir en temps normal ; maintenant, je m'amusais follement. En quelques semaines, je modifiai bien des jugements. Tenez, un soir...

...Un soir, comme j'entrais dans la cuisine en sifflant, Arlette me dit :

— Mon petit papa, ce soir, je te fais goûter à un plat fait à la margarine.

Je bondis.

— De la margarine ? Qui t'a donné cette idée saugrenue ?

— J'ai mangé une truite à l'Astra chez des amies, j'ai trouvé ça excellent ; alors, je me suis renseignée... Je voulais essayer depuis longtemps, mais maman est un peu vieux jeu ; toi, tu es plus compréhensif.

(Elle était habile, ma petite Arlette).

— Ta mère a raison, coupai-je, la margarine, c'est un ersatz, c'était bien pendant la guerre ?

— Parce que tu crois que le paquet que tu achètes maintenant chez ton épicier est la même chose que cette margarine que tu touchais pendant la guerre avec des tickets de rationnement ? Eh bien, tu te trompes, mon petit papa. Pendant la guerre, la margarine était forcément moins bonne puisqu'il était impossible d'importer des huiles d'outre-mer, tandis que...

— Comment... Astra est faite avec de l'huile ?

— Mais bien sûr, des huiles comme l'huile d'arachide, l'huile de palme.

— Peut-être, dis-je, mais encore faudrait-il que ce soit bon...

Arlette bondit sur l'occasion.

— C'est pourquoi je t'ai fait une daurade à l'Astra, dit-elle, en me brandissant sous le nez un plat appétissant, ma foi.

J'hésitai un moment puis, poussé par la curiosité et la gourmandise, je goûtai et j'avoue que je trouvai cela excellent.

— Bravo Papa, *te voilà débarrassé d'un préjugé ridicule... qui te coûtait cher !* conclut Arlette...

Non, décidément, ma femme n'allait plus me reconnaître en rentrant.

Vous aussi essayez !

Astra vous convaincra

AIMEZ-VOUS LA DAURADE ? Et les autres plats de poisson ? Alors, demandez à Françoise Bernard sa brochure de recettes de poissons. "A quelle sauce les mangerons-nous ?". Écrivez : 8, Avenue Delcassé, Paris-8e. Elle vous l'enverra gratuitement.

Fig. 6. The Family Romance
Elle, 7 February 1955

au foyer of the early covers of *Elle,* proudly flanked by her refrigerator or laundry basket has, in this formulation, become a quaint relic of the recent past: her absence is what facilitates a newly exciting domestic scenario, where the reader is called upon to do away with old images of femininity and identify with the teenage girl. Along with the housewife on vacation, wartime and the difficult postwar years are also banished—to history. Astra has a new and good "fifties taste" which, as the advertisement claims, has nothing to do with the margarine rationed during the war as a butter substitute. It's up to teenage girls, the rising generation of homemakers like Arlette, who have no memory of margarine's association with war and low-quality substitutes, to integrate this product into modern 1950s cuisine. Nevertheless, modern times continue to hold the Eternal Feminine in reserve—as the ad reassuringly intimates, Arlette's play in the kitchen suggests that she will eventually reign in the home, just as her mother did before her.

But it is not yet Arlette's time: images of the teenage girl in the 1950s may refer to their domestic potential, but they foreground their sexuality. The vehicle of the Astra narrative of modern times and the banishment of war memories is the daughter's seduction of the father. As he recounts the weeks spent alone with his daughter, "Arlette m'initia gentiment à une vie pleine de fantaisie" [Arlette kindly initiated me to a life full of originality and imagination]—a recollection whose sexual overtones are echoed in Arlette's conspiratorial tone when she tells her father that she's been wanting to try it, and she's sure he'll like it too, but the domestic experimentation has been off-limits due to the mother's old-fashioned ways. Yes, the daughter will eventually become a mother in her own right, but for the time being she's making her father's life just a little more lively. The Astra ad shows youth and femininity acting upon each other in neat balance in the teenage girl: youthfulness eroticizes femininity, while femininity domesticates youthfulness. The end result is the pleasure of the adult male consumer.

Domesticity may have been the reigning ideology, but popular culture and real social mutations had other messages to convey. After Françoise Sagan's first novel, 1956 brought the gyrations of the equally young Brigitte Bardot to the French public in Roger Vadim's film *Et Dieu créa la femme*—if it escaped the town censors. In the privileged classes, the presence of girls in higher education was on the rise. By mid-decade, the youthful reader of *Elle* could no longer be simplistically conceived as an aspirant to domestic technology and tranquility. This was a creature whose habitat was not the home and whose desires and relationship to the new technology were not defined by duties. Indeed, the Pereire column was quick to disappear, and *Elle* just as quickly declared that the differences between the desires of girls and those of their mothers had the scope of a generational rift:

Réussir: voilà le mot. La jeune arriviste 1956 ne pense pas bonheur d'abord. Le bonheur lui paraît une idée vieille en Europe. Non, cette adolescente pense réussite personnelle . . . A-t-elle encore le temps de penser en secret au beau cavalier qui troublait Ninette ou Ninon? A peine. Ce qui était grave en 1830 — les amours — l'est beaucoup moins en 1956 . . .

Le règne de l'adolescente commence . . . [S]achant qu'elle peut gagner tant d'argent tout de suite, [qu']elle ne songe plus à se marier coûte que coûte. Au contraire, il faut connaître la vie, n'est-ce pas? Un peu de liberté est si amusant! La jeune fille arriviste est un produit nouveau. Autrefois, Rastignac était un bon jeune homme qui aimait bien Paris. Notre demoiselle 1956 . . . est une personne rouée qui arrive de sa province avec un accent chantant . . . Sa grande soeur, dans l'euphorie de la Libération, lui a appris que l'on n'est que ce que l'on se fait. Elle croit alors que les millions peuvent remplacer le bonheur. Que ferait-elle d'un mari?[81]

[Success: there's the word. The girl go-getter of 1956 doesn't think of happiness first. Happiness to her seems like an old word in Europe. No, this adolescent thinks about her own success . . . Does she still have the time to daydream about the young gentleman who set Ninette or Ninon aquiver? Hardly. What was serious in 1830 — love affairs — is much less so in 1956 . . .

The reign of the adolescent begins . . . Knowing that she can earn plenty of money right away, she no longer thinks of getting married at all costs. On the contrary, one should experience life, right? A bit of freedom is so much fun! The girl go-getter is a new product. In the past, Rastignac was a good young man who liked Paris. Our young miss 1956 . . . is a wily one who arrives from her province with a singsong accent . . . Her big sister, in the euphoria of the Liberation, taught her that one is only what one makes oneself. So she believes that millions can replace happiness. What would she do with a husband?]

After ten years spent offering to its adult readers the fantasy of balancing traditional femininity with modern opportunities and fitting girls neatly into the equation well within these lines, *Elle* announced that a new type of teenage girl was taking the nation by storm. As the magazine imagined the new queen of French culture and her dreams, she was a far cry from romantic heroines à la Musset as well as the home-and husband-centered femininity of her mother. According to *Elle*, the pleasures of domestic comfort looked hopelessly old-fashioned to young women, who lived their modern times in the public sphere alone. These girls didn't want husbands, but success: fame and fortune they dreamed of generating for themselves alone, just like their male counterparts.

Why the change? In way of a historical hypothesis, *Elle* traced this novel desire for self-fulfillment among girls to the *esprit du temps* of the recent past, in particular to existentialism. The assimilation of Sartrian philosophy into popular culture is signaled by the evocation of an intermediate generation of "big sisters" and the lesson they taught: that "one is only what one makes oneself." In *Elle*'s presentation of two female generations who did not identify with the home, the existentialist's ethical call for individual consciousness and action in lieu of passivity is reshaped for the *adolescente* of 1956 as a claim to economic self-realization. No longer did girls bide their time in provincial villages as Romantic heroines had done; instead, they were apt to pack their bags, move to a big city, and set about making their own lives.

The lessons of existentialism were only one piece of the puzzle of the newly ambitious teenage girl. If she read the newspaper, she had seen others like herself, just as young—and almost always, I would add, economically privileged —find fame and fortune: "Elle a découvert son visage dans les pages des quotidiens. Elle sait qu'elle est devenue l'actualité." [She has discovered her face in the pages of the daily papers. She knows she has become the latest news] Françoise Sagan, unmentioned but essential to such a statement, has left her mark, along with other young writers and actresses, making stardom seem feasible for any girl from a good family. With Sagan in the public eye, the present seemed to belong not just to the young, but more specifically to the young female. And if stardom did not await, nor did the life of a housewife:

> La jeune fille d'avant guerre travaillait si elle était obligée de gagner sa vie. En 1956, elle travaillera davantage par plaisir ou par envie: «Que faites-vous, Mademoiselle?»—«Rien!» Elle rougirait de honte en répondant cela. Et c'est bien . . . Tous les métiers s'ouvrent devant elle, il n'y a qu'à choisir. Elle ne fréquentera plus l'école du Louvre, où sa mère somnolait chaque après-midi. Cette école,

affirme-t-elle, ne mène nulle part . . . Elle apprend donc un vrai métier, se spé-
cialise . . .[82]

[The girl of the interwar years worked if she had to earn a living. In 1956, she
works more out of pleasure or desire: "What do you do, Miss?"—"Nothing!"
She would blush with shame if that were her answer. And that's a good thing
. . . All professions are open to her, she has only to choose. She will no longer go
to the école du Louvre,[83] where her mother dozed every afternoon. That kind
of schooling, she affirms, leads nowhere . . . So she learns a real profession, she
becomes an expert.]

As the reference to the école du Louvre makes clear, what *Elle* represented
as the reality of teenage girls belonged more specifically to the middle
classes. Working class girls, as they always have, continued to work out of
financial necessity. New in the 1950s was the fact that an increasing number of girls who didn't have to work were actually choosing to continue
their studies and develop professional identities. They scoffed at the domesticity their mothers had embraced as daily life just as they dismissed
genteel and feminine pastimes outside of the home, for they were not "real
jobs," and yielded neither financial independence nor an identity in the
public sphere. What mattered to the younger generation was economic independence and self-determination. Girls were becoming more like boys,
a process of social transformation that as we shall see in the following chapters, met with lament as well as applause.

There were other factors at work besides the ones *Elle* mentioned in the
conception of the teenage girl that emerged in French culture in the mid-
1950s: along with their increasing presence in university classrooms, there
was the phenomenon of the expansion of technology to a gender-neutral
leisure market, and American cinema's exported images of rebellious teenagers like those portrayed by James Dean and Marlon Brando whose appeal also extended to youth of both sexes.[84] But *Elle*'s particular version of
the teenage girl as an amalgam of the cultural forces of existentialism and
the mass media is truly remarkable when we consider the magazine's own
emphasis on family life and a transgenerational feminine identity forged
in relation to men.

"Voici enfin votre magazine"

Elle's attempts to appeal to an audience of individualistic teenage girls
alongside faithful adult readers never quite worked. If anything, the maga-

zine became less interesting in the beginning of the new decade, with a noticeable absence of polemical features, of calls to political action for voters, mothers, or housewives, or of recognition of the different interests and ideals of the teenage reader. But the latter need had been articulated, and in February 1962, a new magazine appeared on the newsstands: *Mademoiselle* (unrelated to the American magazine). While *Mademoiselle* would be short-lived, its début was triumphant. "Voici enfin votre magazine" [Your magazine is here at last], the cover proclaimed, alongside a laughing young woman clad in slacks and a turtleneck, posed as if in the midst of an energetic dance session. Although the monochromatic backdrop offers no information other than the energy of its color, it was most certainly no one's kitchen (fig. 7). According to this first issue's editorial, the carefree cover girl was the typical young *Française*. She had her father's newspapers as a source of information on politics and the world, and her mother's magazines to learn how to keep up a country house (sic)—situating the "typical French girl" once again as economically privileged. But neither world news nor home decoration met the preoccupations of the teenage girl as *Mademoiselle* imagined her. Like Arlette in the Astra margarine ad, the *Mademoiselle* reader, projected to range in age from fifteen to twenty, was a girl who wanted a life both more comfortable and more exciting than her mother's.

In 1962, however, comfort was no longer defined in opposition to wartime conditions it had been for the readers of *Elle*. Just as in the Astra ad, this *Mademoiselle* editorial does away with unsavory memories by positing an irreconcilable generation gap *au féminin*, valorizing youthfulness in order to move beyond the recent past. The *Mademoiselle* reader, the editors wrote, was a girl who never had to "make do" in the hard times of the Occupation and the immediate postwar years. She was part of a "new generation" who had always lived with television and nylon stockings, a generation for whom "la dernière guerre n'est déjà qu'une page d'Histoire" [the last war was just a page of history]. The typical reader that *Mademoiselle* projected, though, was less a student of history than an object of the current consumer culture, and it was in the latter domain that the magazine envisaged its role: "Vous devenez un phénomène social. Fabricants et détaillants, couturiers et coiffeurs se préoccupent de satisfaire ce nouveau «marché» des jeunes filles. Mais il vous faut un porte-parole"[85] [You are becoming a social phenomenon. Manufacturers and retailers, fashion designers and hairdressers are preoccupied with satisfying this new "market" of girls. But you need a representative].

Fig. 7. The first issue of French *Mademoiselle*
Mademoiselle 1 (1962)

With consumer culture's attention turned to girls, *Mademoiselle* positioned itself as something better than a best friend: a guide, one who could help them make choices among the bewildering assortment of fashions, accessories, hairstyles, and beauty products. As magazines necessarily do, *Mademoiselle* alternately served as a guide to consumer products and as an advertising forum for them: no longer refrigerators and baby formula, but record players, acne creme, and boutiques for teen fashion.

Nevertheless, *Mademoiselle* wasn't just about how to shop. To fulfill its assumed role as a magazine which spoke for French girls, the first issues featured profiles of teenagers' lives in different French towns ("J'ai 17 ans et j'habite Blois"), articles on how to get along with one's parents and how to be appealing to boys—alongside one boy's plaintive averral that in Paris, "girls aren't romantic anymore"—beauty tips, and a short story contest—something *Elle* had never offered—with a trip to Paris as first prize. A surprisingly large amount of space is consecrated to letters of thanks and praise for being a magazine for girls who were, as one reader put it, "real," and not how their grandmothers wanted them to be. Even *Salut les copains,* the magazine for fans of the international popular music scene, had not proved itself to be completely on the mark for the teenage girl audience. As another *Mademoiselle* reader wrote, "Depuis longtemps j'avais perdu l'espoir de trouver un journal qui «nous comprenne» . . . un journal qui s'occupe de nous et non pas de Johnny Hallyday ou d'un pitre quelconque"[86] [For a long time now I had lost the hope of finding a magazine that "understood us," that focused on us and not on Johnny Hallyday or some other clown]. Girls had other things to think about besides popular teenage heartthrobs: most specifically themselves. "Focusing on us," though, generally involved physical appearance alone. For example, in echo of *Elle*'s early postwar innovation of coupons known as "bons magiques," *Mademoiselle* instituted a Club *Mademoiselle,* which earned its readers reductions on the purchase of certain beauty items.

For the most part, *Mademoiselle* concentrated less on following in *Elle*'s footsteps than on defining itself against its elder, often by heralding its own version of pragmatic realism. *Elle* glamorized the secretary in a fashion piece as a "key personality" of the twentieth century; *Mademoiselle*'s version was an article entitled "Dactylo à «Perpete»?" [Secretary "forever"?], comprised of a series of interviews in which many young secretaries talked about the daily tedium of the job. While the home was often the backdrop for fashion shoots in *Elle*, it disappeared in *Mademoiselle*, where at first, as in the initial cover shot, there was no familiar context at all. Against brightly colored backdrops, *Mademoiselle* exhibited "la mode jeune fille": inexpensive clothing available at the local Prisunic that could be worn to school or on dates (figs. 8 and 9). By the third issue of 1963, according to *Mademoiselle*, one out of three girls read the magazine. "Pour la première fois, un journal, notre journal, tente de donner aux jeunes les plus fragiles, les jeunes filles, des armes" [For the first time, a magazine, our magazine, is trying to give to the most fragile of youth—girls—a defense]. Adolescent girls were fragile because they were alone: no longer under the constant surveillance of parents[87] and not yet married and under the protection of husbands. The latter was, however, the end that all *Mademoiselle* readers knew awaited them: "Votre vie sera, pour la plupart, à l'image de ce que sera votre mariage. En l'attendant, vous avez le droit de rire et de rêver, de beaucoup rire et beaucoup rêver."[88] [Your life will be, for the most part, determined by your marriage. While waiting, you have the right to laugh and dream, to laugh and dream a lot].

In what today reads as a rather pathetic evocation of female adolescence as a premarital swan song, *Mademoiselle*'s message just like *Elle*'s was at heart a profoundly contradictory one. By the early 1960s *Mademoiselle* could scoff at "women's magazines" and their sedate, home-oriented brand of femininity. Nevertheless, its own conception of adolescent femininity kept domesticity in the picture, albeit as a future rather than a present state for its young readers. Girls had "the right" to laugh and dream *while waiting* for marriage, that ineluctable destiny which would come as the final punctuation mark of their lives. Marriage was a destiny which in this equation figured above all as dismal: as the end of laughter and dreams. Not only should girls laugh and dream—, they should do so "a lot,"—for it was their last chance.

Most articles and editorials in *Mademoiselle* did not, of course, take on such an unintentional voice of doom. But moments such as these make us view the magazine's self-presentation as being young, fresh, and unshackled by recent history, with a more critical eye. *Elle* was founded by women, for women, to show them how to create comfort at home in a new society where they could and should take part in the political process. *Mademoiselle,* on the other hand, was a creation of marketing savvy, capitalizing on the important and heretofore neglected audience of teenage girls both as readers and consumers. The editor-in-chief, Hervé Lamarre-Terrane, was a man—a problematic choice as "guide" and "representative" for young

Figs. 8 and 9. Teenage fashions
Mademoiselle 1, 4 (1963)

female readers. Under Lamarre-Terrane, *Mademoiselle*'s message was far from a radical one: have fun, purchase widely and wisely, for tomorrow you may be married.

I would like to evoke once again the parable of the Astra margarine ad as an illustration of the relationship between *Mademoiselle* and *Elle*, of the way youthfulness and femininity do ideological battle with each other in media images of teenage girls. In that ad, youthful energy, newness, and even revolt were framed and contained within the domestic norm that was presented as the only ending possible. In this, it was not unlike the rejuvenation that we see in *Mademoiselle* of *Elle*'s mix of the Modern Woman and the Eternal Feminine. The modern girl of the 1950s and early 1960s could revolt, reject romance and sentiment, remain untouched by the past, and indulge in the new as long as she remained a good daughter and kept in mind her domestic destiny. As we shall see in the following chapter, these same standards were applied to young women writers.

2 Fictions of Female Adolescence

MADELEINE CHAPSAL: On pense que vous représentez la jeunesse actuelle. Et vous?

FRANÇOISE SAGAN: Ça, je trouve ça complètement délirant. Je ne suis le porte-drapeau de personne.[1]

[MADELEINE CHAPSAL: People say you represent today's youth. What do you think of that?

FRANÇOISE SAGAN: That's totally crazy. I'm no one's flagbearer.]

The modernity to which *Elle* and *Mademoiselle* each laid claim positioned them in the women's magazine market as distinct generational voices. Underlying the market difference, however, was a common vision: marriage and domesticity as the endpoint of the feminine life trajectory, no matter what else merited exploration en route. *Elle* and *Mademoiselle* imagined and exalted a range of possible experiences for women and girls in the public sphere but remained largely silent on the most private aspect of the private sphere: female sexuality. The sex lives of teenage girls may not have been on French newsstands in the 1950s and early 1960s, but the curious had an ample array of other sources to choose from. Well before the first issue of *Mademoiselle* and the recognition of teenage girls as a consumer group in their own right, the 1950s witnessed a dramatic entry onto the national literary scene of novels about the sexual misadventures of female adolescents written by equally young women writers and a marketing campaign by publishers that capitalized on their sensationalistic value as a new genre. In line with the mode of the literary criticism of the time, which treated fiction as an extension of the author's own life and psychology, reviewers presented these novels to the public as thinly disguised autobiographies, indeed documentaries about female adolescence in the modern world. The result of commercial and critical practices was to construct young women writers themselves as characters. Along with their allegedly equivalent female protagonists, they were both hailed and reviled as representatives of a new breed of femininity: rebellious, precociously sexual, antisentimental, and disdainful of conventional social mores. The writer, her novel, their marketing, and their reception—all took part in an process that was instrumental in generating a comprehensive fiction of female adolescence for public consumption through fictions that were consistently presented as social facts.

The role of the postwar press in calling the public's attention to young women writers cannot be overestimated. In this period that preceded television's domination of the media, the press was one of the sole arbiters of opinion and taste.[2] Because of the continued high cost of new books, many people had to content themselves with reading literary reviews. New and old magazines, journals, and newspapers appeared after the hiatus of the war: from the novelties of *Les Temps modernes* and *Elle* in 1945 and *L'Express* and *Roman* in 1953 to prewar standards like *La Nouvelle Revue Française* in 1953 and *Marie Claire* in 1954. New books were received with great anticipation. "Every novel, every novelist, was an event," said Anne-Marie de Vilaine, today a writer and journalist at *Le Nouvel Observateur.* Sales of her own first novel, *Des Raisons d'aimer,* benefited from full-page coverage in *L'Express,* complete with a photo of the beautiful nineteen-year-old author (fig. 10).[3] Now out of print and forgotten, De Vilaine's novel recounting in three voices a young college student's affair with her married professor and the awareness of his suffering wife won her admiring personal letters and reviews from many of the well-known men of letters of the day in newspapers that were not above punning in their captions, "Elle n'est pas vilaine!" [She's not bad-looking!].

The nineteenth century may have invented the concept of the woman author as a character worthy of fiction, as Christine Planté asserts in *La Petite soeur de Balzac,*[4] but the 1950s witnessed a new development of the type. As the case of Anne-Marie de Vilaine demonstrates, her essential quality became youthfulness—and more often than not, attractiveness. The publishing industry and the press became forums for the exposition

DÉBUTS

Une jeune fille du siècle

● *C'est important d'être aimé. Ce n'est pas suffisant.*

UN jour de 1954, une jeune fille est entrée dans les bureaux de « L'Express ».

Elle était très belle, mais ce détail ne semblait pas l'intéresser.

Rien de la petite Parisienne, charmante et rouée, sachant plaire et tirer parti de ses imperfections autant que de sa grâce.

Plutôt le contraire. Mal mise, abrupte, marchant à la façon des filles qui n'ont pas franchi l'âge ingrat, et comme étrangère à sa beauté, elle était attendrissante. De jeunesse, de maladresse.

Nous connaissions un peu sa famille. C'est pourquoi elle avait osé franchir la porte.

Elle apportait un article intitulé : « Je suis une jeune fille du siècle », qu'elle remit en bredouillant.

Il y en avait vingt pages, dont dix avaient non seulement du style, mais une rare vigueur de ton et de pensée.

Elle voulait, en toute simplicité, refaire le monde. Comment ne pas lui donner raison ?

Coupé, mais non remanié, cet article eut un certain retentissement.

Quelques semaines plus tard, la jeune fille reparut. Toujours belle, toujours bredouillante.

Elle souhaitait abandonner le secrétariat, qu'elle assurait chez un avocat, pour travailler avec nous.

Notre équipe était alors très réduite, si réduite que nous avions seulement deux secrétaires écrasées de travail. Nous en cherchions une troisième, capable, elle aussi, de nous sacrifier ses jours, ses nuits et ses dimanches.

Fut-elle déçue, notre jeune fille, lorsqu'elle comprit que quelques pages bien écrites et sincères ne la qualifiaient pas pour être journaliste, mais que, sténodactylo et parlant bien l'anglais, elle pouvait nous rendre service ?

Je ne crois pas. Elle n'abritait aucune prétention, et moins encore de confiance en elle. Seulement un immense désir de « faire quelque chose », de trouver un sens à son travail.

Son éclat accusait encore une attitude, caractéristique de sa génération, et qui peut se résumer ainsi : bien commode d'être jolie, c'est important d'aimer et d'être aimée, ce n'est pas suffisant.

Une double vie

Cette exigence neuve et douloureuse de vivre à la fois une vie de femme et une vie d'homme, d'exister pour un homme, mais autrement qu'à travers un homme, toute l'ironie facile qu'elle suscite lorsqu'une créature sans attrait l'exprime s'effondrait devant elle.

Donc, elle voulait « faire quelque chose ».

Pendant cinq ans, elle travailla avec fureur, acceptant les enquêtes ingrates et les petits travaux fastidieux, les sollicitant, se décourageant soudain, et trainant les pieds dans les couloirs...

Après deux ans d'apprentissage, elle cessa d'être secrétaire pour devenir officiellement rédactrice. Une victoire.

Le don d'écrire, elle l'avait toujours possédé. On ne l'enseigne nulle part. Mais elle avait lentement appris à discipliner son style, à écouter au lieu de parler, à modérer ses jugements, à juguler ses emportements.

Aujourd'hui, son nom — Anne-Marie de Vilaine — orne la couverture d'un livre mis en vente cette semaine et qui s'intitule : « Les Raisons d'aimer » (1).

Elle a écrit ce livre parallèlement à son travail quotidien dans des conditions morales et matérielles difficiles. Ce qui n'a d'ailleurs aucune importance, ce qui ne plaiderait en aucune façon pour elle si le résultat était médiocre. La littérature n'est pas un travail de force.

Mais voilà que cette entreprise, menée jusqu'au bout, non par volonté de « réussir » ni même par volonté

(1) Éd. Julliard. 184 p. 570 fr.

tout court, simplement parce que la nécessité d'écrire est toujours plus impérieuse que la nonchalance, voilà que cette entreprise révèle un écrivain.

Cette petite fille lumineuse et fantasque, le bébé vamp de « L'Express », voilà qu'il faudra désormais la prendre au sérieux. Anne-Marie de Vilaine, romancière...

Ouvrez son livre. Dès les premières lignes, il s'impose et se lit d'un trait.

Ni impudique, ni complaisante, exerçant à ses propres dépens un

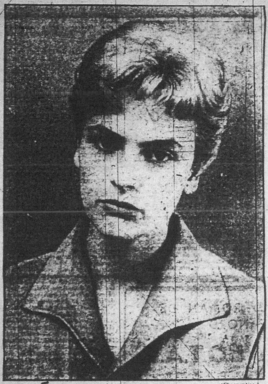

ANNE-MARIE DE VILAINE
Des raisons d'aimer

(Charpentier)

humour fin, parfois cruel, traçant d'une jeune fille bourgeoise, empêtrée dans ses propres contradictions, un portrait impitoyable, Anne-Marie de Vilaine a écrit, dans une belle langue exacte et ferme, l'un des bons romans de l'année.

Elle en écrira d'autres, mieux élaborés peut-être ; mais celui-ci a la saveur des fruits que l'on cueille à l'arbre, tout juste dorés par le premier soleil.

F. G.

Fig. 10. Reviewing young women writers

Reprinted with permission from *L'Express,* 12 March 1959

of the author in seamless juxtaposition with her protagonist: her real life and her fictional creation were presented as equivalent, and both became sources of entertainment and titillation for the reading public. René Julliard, best known for publishing the unknown Françoise Sagan's *Bonjour tristesse* in 1954, was captivated by novelists who had their own "story" to go along with a manuscript. Every Julliard novel contained a one-page insert in which a short biography of the author followed a plot summary. One of his favorites was Anne Huré, author of a first novel entitled *Les Deux moniales* [The two nuns]. Huré, a nun herself in a remote Benedictine abbey, had renounced religious life on the eve of pronouncing her vows. Once back in the secular world, she became implicated in several financial misdealings, which landed her in the Petite Roquette prison. This was where she wrote her novel, whose autobiographical connections as exposed in the insert made the title itself sufficiently piquant for a potential reader.[5]

The press picked up on publishers' tactics of romancing the young authors, in many cases putting a face on them. In a 1953 issue of *Elle,* a photograph depicts the pastoral scene of a girl surrounded by goats, absorbed in her reading. The caption states that the young shepherdess, age seventeen, had just written her first novel, *La Poupée de Chine.*[6] Much of the press coverage of young women writers came from the Right.[7] *Arts,* a newspaper of cultural and literary trends, which positioned itself against the dominant postwar mood of *engagement,* habitually featured photographs and spirited biographies of authors along with critical summaries of their novels. One novelist to receive this treatment was Claude Martine, whose distinction in the world of letters was to be the wife of *Arts'* owner and editor-in-chief, Jacques Laurent.[8] *Arts* presented Laurent's wife as if she were describing herself through the form of a pseudo-questionnaire: a cunning tactic resembling more contemporary advertisements for brand names in which glamorous people reveal their idiosyncrasies and private lives to the ordinary reader turned voyeur. In the case of Claude Martine, one would necessarily learn about the private life of Jacques Laurent:

PROFESSION: Femme d'écrivain

VIE: Epouse, en 1949, Jacques Laurent

AIME: Ecrire, parler (avec Jacques Laurent), les endroits célèbres (parce qu'ils ont raison d'être célèbres), Rome, le restaurant Lapérouse, la forêt de Fontainebleau, Cannes et Versailles; l'automobile, comme jeu d'adresse . . .

N'AIME PAS: Ne pas écrire, trop parler, la vitesse, le désordre, les fenêtres modernes, les mensonges de politesse, la radio des voisins, le manque de conscience professionnelle, le nylon, les jeux de société, la contradiction de pensée.

PARTICULARITES: Vie si heureuse qu'elle lui a laissé le loisir de plisser le front sur ses problèmes.[9]

[PROFESSION: writer's wife

LIFE: marries, in 1949, Jacques Laurent

LIKES: writing, talking (with Jacques Laurent), famous places (because they have a reason for being famous), Rome, the restaurant Lapérouse, the forests of Fontainebleau, Cannes and Versailles, the automobile as a game of skill . . .

DOESN'T LIKE: not writing, talking too much, speed, disorder, modern windows, polite lies, the neighbors' radio, lack of professional conscience, nylon, board games, contradictions in thought.

PARTICULARITIES: A life so happy that it has left her the leisure to furrow her brow over her problems.]

What is striking in this biography-as-questionnaire is how self-effacement takes the form of objective self-description: in the context of her own creativity, Claude Martine presents herself not as a writer, but as a writer's wife who writes. Claude Martine may be worldly and the *Elle* shepherdess provincial, but for both of them writing is represented as secondary, a hobby for the bourgeois sophisticate or a pastime for the country lass. In the collective imagination of the publishing world and the press in the 1950s, women writers were identified as members of a family and were most interesting if they could be presented as girlish daughters. For the female novelist lacking the eminent connections of a Claude Martine, youthfulness was the strongest selling point she could have. Young authors were much in demand in the newly commercialized publishing industry, especially in the house of one of the principal innovators of the postwar publishing industry, René Julliard.

Marketing Youth

The unprecedented number of young women writers published in the 1950s was a result of changes that had begun in the book industry after World War I with Bernard Grasset's promotional tactics for the seventeen-year-old Raymond Radiguet's *Le Diable au corps* [Devil in the flesh] (1923), a novel in which the schoolboy protagonist has an affair with a young married woman while her husband is at the front. Instead of limiting himself to the literary press, Grasset sent copies of *Le Diable au corps* to actors, politicians, and journalists and put advertisements into religious weeklies and dailies, banking on the interest in the author and his book that could be elicited by one elliptical line: "Il a 17 ans."[10] Julliard followed through on Grasset's innovations, quickly making his mark by becoming the first publisher in France to practice an intensive commercial policy.[11] Unlike the previous generation of publishers, Julliard came to the industry not as an intellectual, but as a businessman. From 1922 to 1940, he operated the first book club, the "sélection Séquana," distributing French books in Poland, where he had done his military service.[12] During World War II, as a reserve officer, he supervised publications at the *Commissariat Général de l'Information,* directed by Jean Giraudoux. After editing several books in Vichy, Julliard moved to Monaco in 1942, where he started the Editions de Monaco. Three years later, after the Liberation, he moved to Paris, married the well-connected journalist and socialite Gisèle D'Assailly, and changed the name of his publishing house to the Editions Julliard.[13]

In Julliard's first three years in the Parisian publishing world, his authors won the Prix Goncourt three times, as well as a host of other literary prizes. He created the journal *Lettres nouvelles* with Maurice Nadeau and became the publisher of *Les Temps modernes,* which had been founded in 1945 by Jean-Paul Sartre, Simone de Beauvoir, and Merleau-Ponty.[14] In fifteen years of publishing, a total of 450 first novels came out under Julliard's distinctive white cover with the green trim. According to Julliard, he only made a profit on ten of them.[15] Clearly profits interested him less than the commercial process in its entirety. Massive advertising campaigns, attractive catalogues, book signings—Julliard would stop at nothing to get a face and a title noticed.

Julliard's philosophy was to publish fast and prolifically. Traditionally, in this industry that most still considered artisanal, a manuscript only appeared in book form a full year after being accepted for publication. In the Julliard house it took a mere three weeks.[16] Julliard's quantity-oriented approach was not the only innovation in the publishing industry at the time. The postwar years also saw the advent of mass production in the form of the *livre de poche,* or pocket edition, introduced in France in 1953 by the Hachette Group's Henri Filipacchi. With the cheaper pocket edition, more people could buy books than ever before.[17] These two new aspects of the commercialization of reading were actually quite different: whereas classics and proven best sellers found their way into the livre de poche the novels Julliard chose for publication had in common their commercial potential as novelties, which quite often went hand-in-hand with the youthfulness of their authors. It was a tactic that earned Julliard the nickname "Monsieur Jeunes Auteurs."[18]

Julliard published both young male and female authors. But as publisher Christian Bourgois puts it, this elegant and seductive man had a reputation as a great appreciator of women.[19] An anecdote in Victoria Thérame's *Journal d'une dragueuse* (1990) which recounts her attempts and eventual success in getting Julliard to publish her first novel, *Morbidezza* (1960) provides an apt illustration. Thérame accepts her publisher's invitation to accompany him to a concert at the renowned Salle Pleyel. Acutely aware that she is the object of stares both curious and envious, she wonders why Julliard would want to seduce an ordinary-looking girl like herself and then comes upon the answer. It is obvious to the Pleyel habitués that she is simply the latest of the new "recruits" in the Julliard "stable," as the press dubbed his bevy of young writers:

> C'est vrai que c'est excitant, un nouveau poulain, même pour le public, va-t-il perdre, tomber, se retrouver à tirer la charrue, transformé en viande de boucherie, ou sera-t-il un gagnant, le crack du siècle? . . .
> Le récital terminé, René Julliard et moi, nous séparons devant Pleyel.[20]

> [It's true it's exciting, a young colt, even for the public, is he going to lose, fall, end up pulling the plow, changed into horsemeat, or will he be a winner, the crack of the century? . . .
> At the end of the recital, René Julliard and I part in front of Pleyel.]

As Thérame suggests, Julliard's publication of young women writers involved an entire ritual of public display and seduction, whether or not it was consummated.[21]

Julliard's initial success was Françoise D'Eaubonne's *Comme un vol de gerfauts* (1950), followed by Françoise Mallet-Joris's *Le Rempart des béguines* (1951), a novel about the sadomasochistic relationship between the sixteen-year-old narrator Hélène and Tamara, her father's Russian mistress. Despite the shocking subject, *Le Rempart* did not get much attention at first. Reviews were mixed. In *Les Temps modernes,* Jean-Louis Curtis— himself a Julliard "recruit"—may have called Mallet-Joris "la révélation de cette année littéraire," but *Le Figaro Littéraire,* a much truer barometer of the public mood, was far from laudatory. Buried among short reviews of dismissable recent novels is this short dismissal of *Le Rempart des béguines:*

> L'auteur, qui a vingt ans, présente le plus scabreux sujet et l'expose avec hardiesse et impudeur—ce qui n'est pas assurément la bonne voie vers une oeuvre valable. Il faut un haut et pudique talent pour aborder à ces terres condamnées. Mme Françoise Mallet-Joris n'y a mis qu'une triste violence.[22]

> [The author, who is twenty years old, presents the most scabrous of subjects and analyzes it with fearlessness and immodesty—which is surely not the right approach to a worthwhile literary work. One needs a great and decorous talent to venture into such damned lands. Madame Françoise Mallet-Joris merely employs an unfortunate violence.]

With or without the sensationally negative review in *Le Figaro*, in two years time *Le Rempart* had been translated into thirteen languages.[23] By the end of 1956, close to 30,000 copies had been sold.[24]

Because she was a young author of an audacious work, Mallet-Joris's youth was emphasized to the point of caricature. A sketched advertisement that appeared in *Le Figaro Littéraire* two months after the poor review depicts the author as a pigtailed schoolgirl in a prim white-collared dress over which is scrawled, "Les débuts sensationnels à 20 ans de Françoise Mallet, *Le Rempart des béguines.*" The exceptionally positive *Temps modernes* review is cited in this ad (fig. 11).[25] Clearly, ideas were churning at Julliard as early as 1951; what they were marketing in Mallet-Joris was the schoolgirl image of the author in contrast to the shocking content of her work.

Mallet-Joris received much more attention from the press after the *Bonjour tristesse* media phenomenon of 1954. Critics went back to this earlier Julliard novel in order to compare Mallet-Joris to Sagan. The comparison was natural, albeit superficial: two young and pretty girls named Françoise from respectable bourgeois families (Mallet-Joris was twenty in 1951, Sagan was eighteen in 1954), both first-time authors of scandalous novels. But four years had passed, and Mallet-Joris, at age twenty-four, was no longer a shocking girl novelist. Despite their closeness in age, she was not, newspaper critics hastened to assure their readers, an ally of Sagan. Sagan led the racy lifestyle of jet-set youth; Mallet-Joris chose motherhood. As she quipped in one interview, "J'aime la vie, j'aime faire la cuisine, faire des enfants, et écrire des romans"[26] [I love life, I love to cook, have

Fig. 11. The schoolgirl-author

Reprinted with permission from Editions Julliard and *Le Figaro,* 16 June 1951

children, and write novels]. By her early twenties, Mallet-Joris had joined the ranks of housewives who happened to write, of those for whom, as Roland Barthes had noted, babies came before books. For women whose time was taken up by children and domestic responsibilities, a seedy neighborhood café, Mallet-Joris suggested, was the best place to write. Such advice, the interviewer observed ironically, would probably go unheeded by two of the other female "boarders" in Julliard's stable: Sagan and Minou Drouet—because they were, so to speak, "still" childless.

Minou Drouet was the youngest and perhaps most notorious Julliard author, an eight-year-old visually impaired girl poet—or so it seemed. Julliard "discovered" her and published her verse in a volume entitled *Arbre mon ami* [My friend the tree] (1955). Critics such as André Rousseaux in *Le Figaro Littéraire* greeted the gifted Minou with reviews whose rhetoric was no less than ecstatic: "Où cette petite fille a-t-elle pris une telle maîtrise des mots et de leur musique?"[27] [Where has this little girl gotten such a mastery of words and their music?] Sensing a story, *Elle* magazine sent journalist Michèle Perrein to Minou's home, where she was prevented from being alone with the girl (who did not recognize her own verses when they were cited to her). Perrein thus concluded, in the issue of 13 November 1955, that the girl-poet was a fraud.

News of the "Minou Drouet Affair" could be found throughout the French press in 1955.[28] *L'Express* refuted the story in four sensationalistic pages of a "Dossier de la querelle Minou Drouet" (15–16 November 1955), where Perrein and the *Elle* photographer were discredited for being "young" (Perrein was in her twenties) and "suspicious-looking." Four witnesses were cited in Minou's defense. Ten days later, in *Le Figaro* of 26 November, another witness, the R. P. Lelong, a Dominican priest and personal friend of Julliard's (who had already written a study of Minou for the Catholic journal *La Vie Intellectuelle*), asserted that he, too, had gone to see Minou and that Perrein was lying.[29] To prove to the press and the public that Minou could be a true poet without her mother's help, the Julliards took charge of the young girl for five days. The headline in *L'Express* evidences the continued market value of the story: "Isolée de sa mère, Minou Drouet écrira-t-elle?" [Isolated from her mother, will Minou Drouet write?] The poem she ostensibly wrote at the Julliard's—the "proof of truth," as *L'Express* called it—was published on 30 November in *Le Figaro*. But it proved to be a fake: Minou had given a *Paris-Match* reporter the same poem a full three weeks before its publication in *Le Figaro* and had simply memorized it. Julliard, however, always ready to capitalize on opportunities opened up by the media, published the young *Elle* journalist Michèle Perrein's first novel, *La Sensitive*, shortly after the Minou Drouet affair.[30]

Case Study: The Selling of Françoise Sagan

Through the publication of numerous young authors, René Julliard's dream of becoming the postwar Bernard Grasset or Gaston Gallimard[31] had an unmistakable feel of big business to it. His house rejected the first manuscripts of Christiane Rochefort and Marguerite Duras because they were too intellectual.[32] When he added Françoise Sagan to his roster of young "Françoises"—Françoise D'Eaubonne and Françoise Mallot Joris (he would soon call them "Les 3 F's," much as Grasset had his "4 M's"—Maurois, Morand, Montherlant, Mauriac), he knowingly constructed a marketing phenomenon. Julliard had the idea of putting a photograph of the young Sagan, "avec son regard de petit écureuil effarouché" [with that scared-squirrel expression on her face], on the band around the book (which prevents one from opening it before purchase). In echo of the advertising blitz for *Le Diable au corps*, the band was printed to read, "Le Diable au coeur" [Devil in the heart].[33]

One can only hypothesize about the initial reception of this new object that was the 1950s book, complete with the tantalizing paratext of photo and band that is now a standard purchasing ploy of French publishers. What is traceable is the media attention both novel and novelist received. Radiguet may have been more important than his novel to Grasset (especially after his death from typhoid several months after the scandal of his success), but never before Sagan had an author's face been so visible to the public. As one obituary of Julliard, who died in 1962, commented, "Une chose est sûre, c'est qu'il a bouleversé les moeurs de l'édition. L'auteur, avec lui, est descendu de son piédestal, sorti de sa chapelle pour devenir un des héros de l'actualité"[34] [One thing is certain: he overturned the standards of behavior of the publishing industry. With him, the author came down from his pedestal, emerged from his chapel to become one of the heroes of current events]. Julliard's strategy was to publish a novel, not because of its literary value, but because of its author's potential to generate media interest—as the cases of Minou Drouet, Michèle Perrein, and Françoise Sagan so aptly illustrate.[35] The typical reader of a Julliard novel, one might imagine, was someone who was just as curious about the author as character as he or she was about the book.

Françoise Sagan was an eighteen-year-old girl from a respectable bourgeois family when Julliard orchestrated her dramatic entrance onto the literary scene. In *Bonjour tristesse*, seventeen-year-old narrator Cécile vacations on the Côte d'Azur with her widowed father Raymond, a good-natured playboy and ad executive in his early forties, and Elsa, his current young girlfriend. As such a configuration indicates, Raymond has been less of a parental figure than a "vieux complice," as he calls himself, to Cécile, just two years out of boarding school and pigtails, who has come to prefer late nights out with his friends and the inappropriate dresses he buys for her to company her own age. Father-daughter complicity is threatened with the arrival of Anne Larsen, the closest friend of Cécile's deceased mother. Elegant, reserved, and intellectual, Anne quickly eclipses Elsa and wins over Raymond, who proposes marriage, and Cécile's summer under the easy-going, pleasure-oriented reign of the father gives way to the reign of the mother-to-be.

For the first time in her life, Cécile finds herself under surveillance: Anne makes her eat more and study for a second attempt at the *bac*, forbids her to see her boyfriend Cyril after discovering the young couple lying half-dressed in the woods, knows uncannily that Kant and Bergson are not what occupy Cécile's hours in her bedroom, and one day locks her in. Even though Cécile realizes that Anne herself feels unsuited to such a role, it is "elle" versus "nous" in Cécile's mind. She realizes that Anne is a threat to her "anciennes complicités" with her father. Each humiliating insight or action of her future stepmother elicits a reaction from Cécile. At first, they are emotional, then they become nefariously practical: her concoction of a plot whereby Cyril and Elsa—for their own reasons all too eager to take part—pretend to be lovers and make themselves ubiquitous in order to arouse Raymond's jealousy and desire to prove his virility; the sexual initiation she prompts with Cyril one torrid afternoon after a particularly heated confrontation with Anne; the orchestration of a moment where Elsa and Raymond can be alone.

Cécile tries to prove herself as a "thinking being" to her future stepmother—and to herself—via a plot where the humiliation would this time be Anne's. A thinking being, Cécile is not really sure how she feels. Up to the end of the novel, she is emotionally and narcissistically divided: recognizing that, with Anne in charge, she could be part of a normal family;

raging inwardly under Anne's critical and contemptuous eye. She does, however, know what she wants: to force Anne to accept the lifestyle and moral code she and her father have shared. As Cécile reasons with self-consciously specious logic: "si elle voulait à tout prix avoir raison, il fallait qu'elle nous laissât avoir tort" (137) [if she wanted to be right at all costs, she would have to let us be wrong]. But the future family lunches Cécile imagines will not come to pass: with the immediate and devastating discovery of Raymond's betrayal, Anne speeds off to a semi-accidental death in a car crash.

Along with the discomfort of Anne's surveillance, the formerly carefree Cécile discovers a new side of herself: the thinking side—which happens to be her dangerous side. "Ce rôle de metteur en scène ne laissait pas de me passionner" (139) [The director's role was endlessly exciting to me], she realizes as she recalls the exulting power of pinpointing and manipulating human weaknesses and desires. In Sagan's protagonist, the *enfant terrible* has found the voice of first-person narration, and it is the voice of ambivalence. Cécile is simultaneously amazed, terrified, and proud of her capacities: "Je me sentais dangereusement habile et, à la vague de dégoût qui s'était emparée de moi, contre moi . . . s'ajoutait un sentiment d'orgueil, de complicité intérieure, de solitude" (82) [I felt dangerously clever, and along with the wave of disgust that took hold of me, came a feeling of pride, of complicity with myself, of solitude]. Like Cocteau's Elisabeth, she isolates herself as mastermind, "seule contre tous." In the face of her father's concern, she pretends to think that Anne is unquestionably right; in Anne's presence, the poisonous thoughts that infest her and the accompanying shame she feels only escape in Cécile's unreadable but troubled gaze.

Yet Cécile desperately wants Anne to coax those thoughts out of her. After she returns from Cyril's house no longer a virgin, she finds Anne reading outside on a lounge chair. Ready to offer lies, she gets no questions and sits down next to her future stepmother. She tries to light a match, with no success, then another, then another. Anne finally looks at her, unsmiling, attentive:

> A ce moment-là, le décor, le temps disparurent, il n'y eut plus que cette allumette, mon doigt dessus, la boîte grise et le regard d'Anne . . . Je laissai tomber la boîte par terre, fermai les yeux . . . Je suppliai quelqu'un de quelque chose, que cette attente cessât. Les mains d'Anne relevèrent mon visage, je serrai les paupières de peur qu'elle ne vît mon regard. Je sentais des larmes d'épuisement,

de maladresse, de plaisir s'en échapper. Alors, comme si elle renonçait à toute question, en un geste d'ignorance, d'apaisement, Anne descendit ses mains sur mon visage, me relâcha. Puis elle me mit une cigarette allumée dans la bouche et se replongea dans son livre. (103)

[At that moment, place and time disappeared, there was nothing but that match, my finger on it, the gray box, and Anne's gaze . . . I dropped the box and closed my eyes . . . I begged someone for something, for this wait to end. Anne's hands lifted my face, I squeezed my eyes shut so she wouldn't see my gaze. I felt tears of exhaustion, of awkwardness, of pleasure escape. Then, as if she were giving up every question, in a gesture of ignorance, of calm, Anne lowered her hands from my face, let me go. Then she put a lit cigarette in my mouth and went back to her book.]

In this exquisitely choreographed scene, Cécile's wordless fumblings, incommensurate tears, pleasure, and closed eyes are matched only by Anne's silent gaze and the intimate gestures she quickly abandons. While each is incapable of asking or telling, Cécile's first-person perspective reveals that she wants both. She will get neither from Anne, for whom a sullen teenage girl is an incomprehensible exotic species. More generally, Cécile wants love: the absence of dialogue between daughter and stepmother creates a moment of plenitude where Cécile senses the possibility of letting go, of giving in, of merging with Anne, a possibility that Anne abruptly cuts off. In her desire for Anne to take over, Cécile also recognizes, with pitiless lucidity, her own passivity. In silence "begging someone for something," she is instead left alone.

Raymond mourns Anne, then eventually goes back to his former play-boy ways. Once back in Paris, Cécile dispassionately realizes that her attachment to Cyril was merely a function of the pleasure he gave and follows her father's example. Nevertheless, at the end of the novel, just as in the beginning, she admits to being haunted by *tristesse,* a wistfulness for the family life she might have had with Anne as a mother. The underlying message of conservatism went unacknowledged when *Bonjour tristesse* came out in 1954. Much to the contrary, the literary establishment declared it to be shockingly new. The first to do so was François Mauriac in an essay that appeared on the first page of *Le Figaro* on 1 June 1954. Mauriac's melodramatic assessment of the novel as profoundly linked to its historical moment merits quotation at length:

Enfants Terribles

Le choix d'un jury littéraire engage donc la conscience? Oui, et gravement si l'on est chrétien. Voici par exemple ce Prix des Critiques décerné, la semaine dernière, à un charmant monstre de dix-huit ans . . . Le jury du Prix des Critiques a-t-il eu tort de couronner ce livre cruel? Je n'en déciderai pas. Le mérite littéraire y éclate dès la première page et n'est pas discutable. Mais toute considération autre que littéraire devait-elle être écartée? Et par exemple la conjoncture historique? La France vit des jours d'angoisse; son destin se noue en ce moment; il va être déterminé pour des générations peut-être. Qu'est-ce que cela a à voir avec le roman d'une petite fille trop douée? Ceci à mon avis: que le choix d'un jury littéraire devrait manifester au monde, et d'abord à nous-mêmes, que nous nous sommes réveillés de notre assoupissement, que nous n'ignorons plus ce qui se trouve en jeu, fût-ce lorsqu'il s'agit de couronner un ouvrage d'imagination. notre devoir est alors de proposer, à mérite littéraire égal, une oeuvre qui rende temoignage à la vie spirituelle française, brûlante encore, et plus que jamais, nous le savons bien, nous qui demeurons en contact avec la jeunesse de ce pays.[36]

[Does a literary jury's choice then engage the conscience? Yes, and solemnly so if one is Christian. Take for example the *Prix des Critiques* given, last week, to a charming monster of eighteen . . . Was the jury wrong to award a prize to this cruel book? I will not determine that. Its literary merit shines forth from the first page and is not debatable. But must every consideration other than the literary one be put aside? For example, that of the historical moment? France is living days of anguish; her destiny is now being formed; it is going to be determined for generations, perhaps. What does this have to do with the novel of an overly gifted little girl? In my opinion, this: that the choice of a literary jury should show the world, and show us first of all, that we have woken from our somnolence, that we are no longer unaware of what is at stake, even if it be at the moment of giving an award to a work of imagination: our duty, then, is to propose a work of equal literary merit that bears witness to the French spiritual life, still impassioned, now more than ever, as we well know, we who remain in contact with the youth of this nation.]

Mauriac's review of Sagan's novel of youthful misdeeds and a world of privilege in Saint-Tropez was singular for a number of reasons. Before and after the publication of *Bonjour tristesse,* literary critics did not present young women writers in terms of their historical moment, except in the rare case of an overtly political work such as *Une société anonyme,*

Christine Peyre's autobiography of a year spent as a factory worker.[37] From the hallowed page one of the nation's bastion of conservatism, on the contrary, Mauriac called upon his readers to heed Sagan, a "charming monster of eighteen," not for the literary qualities of *Bonjour tristesse* (to call it just as good as any other novel under consideration for the Prix des Critiques was more like affirmative action than praise), but for its spiritual qualities. And French spirituality, he wrote, was crucial "more than ever" in light of the nation's situation in the mid-decade.

On 1 March 1954 the United States government released the H-bomb on Bikini island; the French lost the battle of Dien Bien Phu on 7 May; the Laniel government dissolved on 12 June; and Pierre Mendès-France took office on the 18th. In such days of anguish, Mauriac averred, literature that expressed the spirituality inherent to national identity ["la vie spirituelle française"] deserved recognition first and foremost. Essentially reading Cécile's narration as a confession, Mauriac identified *Bonjour tristesse* as a sign of the renewal of the tradition of the Catholic novel that his own work exemplified.

As the following chapter will discuss, literary critics in the same years detected a renewal of the *esprit français* in a different sense, that of the tradition of verbal acuity spanning seventeenth-century salon conversation and the rapier wit of Proust's duchesse of Guermantes. *Esprit* characterized the writings of the *hussards,* Gallimard's group of young male writers fascinated with the military and disdainful of Sartrian *engagement* as a literary imperative: Roger Nimier, Antoine Blondin, and Jacques Laurent.

Sagan's narrator is similarly insolent and witty, but Sagan was never a member of the resolutely male hussard band. Like the hussards, however, she was treated by the publishing industry and the press as an eloquent representative of a disaffected generation. The distinction would remain in place through the late 1950s when *L'Express* would interview Sagan as the only female public persona to speak for the age category it dubbed "La Nouvelle Vague." By 1962, 840,000 copies of her book had been sold in France, and 4,500,000 abroad in translation.[38] Mauriac was alone in tying Sagan's narrator to sociopolitical crisis, but other critics joined him in hailing *Bonjour tristesse,* "ce livre cruel." The book also became an economic phenomenon. The sales figures for *Bonjour tristesse* were most certainly related to the passing of a key term from the American book industry into common French parlance: *le best-seller.*[39] Less than a year after the publication of Sagan's novel, *L'Express* in April 1955 published the first bestseller list ("liste des meilleures ventes") in France, a list where *Bonjour tristesse* figured prominently.[40]

Sagan received an overwhelmingly positive response from the fathers of journalistic literary criticism, many of whom associated her with other writers canonized as voices of previous generations. Echoing Julliard's marketing ploy, Emile Henriot in *Le Monde* compared Sagan to Raymond Radiguet; Robert Kemp in *Le Figaro* compared her to the Romantic Benjamin Constant; Michel Déon in *Paris Match* compared her to Colette. Today a novel for the preteen set, *Bonjour tristesse*, at the time of its publication, reached a public well past the *bac* years. As Jacques Laurent put it in an article in *Arts* entitled "Sagan et les vieillards":

> Le fameux conflit de générations est bien fini. Du moins en littérature. Pas un vieillard lettré qui ne s'éveille en sursaut dès qu'on lui parle d'un écrivain de moins de vingt ans . . . Lire soigneusement un moins de vingt ans c'est également s'instruire. Nos vieillards en faisant le mot à mot du texte de Françoise Sagan s'informent comme devant un documentaire des nouveaux rites de leur tribu. Je les soupçonne de prendre des notes; ils apprennent que les jeunes ne se rencontrent plus dans des caves.[41]

> [The notorious generation gap is no more. At least not in literature. There's not one lettered elder who doesn't jump with a start as soon as someone speaks to him of a writer who's less than twenty . . . Careful reading of one of the under twenty set is also instructive. Our elders, by parsing Françoise Sagan's text, inform themselves as if they were watching a documentary of the new rites of their tribe. I bet they take notes; they learn that young people no longer meet in nightclubs.]

In the same vein as Mauriac but with a humorous twist, Laurent asserted that the value of *Bonjour tristesse,* and of novels by other young writers in 1950s France, was less literary than socioanthropological. As documents or testimonies of teenage behavior, these novels were of greatest use to adults as a point of access to the mystifying ways of a generation they eagerly sought to understand. Moreover, the Biblical title—*Suzanne and the Elders*—for the picture Laurent evokes of old men peering at novels penned by adolescents adds a prurient dimension to their interests as well.

With *Bonjour tristesse* required reading for parents and grandparents, Sagan herself became a character in the media, where she was accorded a singularly sustained attention. There were countless interviews, and the

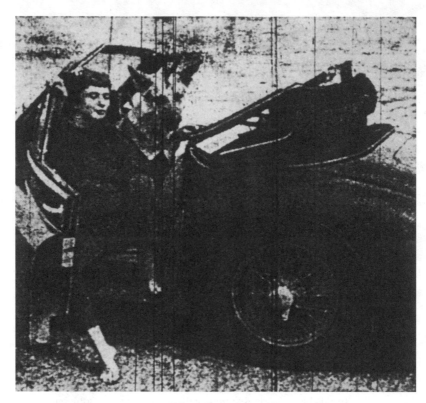

Fig. 12. Francoise Sagan: a girl and her car
Reprinted from *Paris-Match,* 26 May 1956, with
permission of Hachette Filipacchi Associés

press ceaselessly scrutinized her private life——true to her novel, she shuttled between Paris and Saint-Tropez and had a sensational near-death accident in her Jaguar sports car (fig. 12). She was also a travel writer herself for *Elle,* the glamorous locales she described further fueling public curiosity as to her whereabouts. Because she had been identified as a generational spokesperson, Sagan represented the rare case of a young woman asked to express her political opinions in the popular press, including her thoughts on the continued French presence in Algeria. Surely her responses elicited a much greater interest than the political opinions regularly aired by Simone de Beauvoir in *Les Temps modernes.*

Sagan's initial success as the voice of a generation paved the way for other young women writers whose novels the press would, instead, review as primers on femininity. The critics' focus on the writers' gender did not function as a means to limit potential readership: exposure in well-respected newspapers and magazines like *Le Monde, Le Figaro, Arts,* and *L'Express* meant that novels by young women found their way into the hands of many more—and male—readers.[42] Critics had previously treated women writers as exceptional for their century—Madame de Lafayette, Madame de Sévigné, George Sand, Colette—no matter how numerous their actual ranks. But in the 1950s, the publishing industry and the press presented women writers as a veritable force to be reckoned with. A 1958 headline in *Arts* exclaimed that "one out of three novels is written by a woman";[43] a 1956 issue of *La Table Ronde* entitled "Psychologie de la Littérature Féminine" opened with a title page advertising "Deux ans de littérature féminine chez René Julliard" that listed thirty-eight women novelists and forty-six of their novels.[44] Along with recognition came a good dose of paternalism: critics tended to see young women writers as daughters, even when they were "bad girls." As Jacques Chardonne indulgently commented about Sagan: "Cette jeune fille est de bonne famille, la famille des grands écrivains . . . Quand on est de cette famille, on peut écrire ce qu'on veut"[45] [This girl comes from a good family, the family of great writers . . . As a member of this family, one can write whatever one wants].

The Antisentimental Novel

This brings us to the central question of what young women did write about in the 1950s. Theirs were not romance novels in the traditional sense—one of the reasons, one can hypothesize, that they could appeal to a diverse readership. While none of Sagan's female peers achieved her renown, the media attention they were accorded follows the trajectory of the bestseller, whose success, according to Pierre Nora, can come unexpectedly, in violation of what he calls its "natural sociological space." For Nora, the bestseller merits sociological study in that it is less revelatory of literary tastes at a given historical moment than it is of a collective mood.[46] The case of Sagan reveals a cultural fascination with youth in the mid-fifties, specifically in a context of privilege from which politics were effaced. The result was that the "natural" readership of youth expanded to include adults, intellectuals, and readers abroad; a hypothesis reinforced by the fact that today, *Bonjour tristesse* has returned to its "natural space" as a novel that adolescents read.

It was less a generational space than a gendered one that other young women writers violated, a space defined by cross-cultural tendencies to associate certain genres with certain readers. We assume that men read and write about war, adventure, and politics, while the female literary realm is that of romance. Indeed, with few exceptions, women have traditionally written within this genre, which men have largely ignored and which has thus been devalorized. More broadly termed the genre of "sentimental literature," it consisted of what was written "by, for, and about women."[47] In the 1950s, what the French called "littérature féminine" broke with the conventions of the genre. In critic Jean-Claude Ibert's analysis of the corpus, the typical novel recounted a loss of innocence particularly disturbing in its practicality: the young female protagonist's gradual realization that amorous relationships were not founded on pure, noble, and disembodied sentiment, but on physical pleasure as well as economic arrangements. As Ibert wrote, "Ce ne sont point là des héros de roman, au sens qu'on leur prête habituellement, mais des héros de la vie quotidienne, qui partagent lucidement—et non sans courage—la médiocrité échue au plus grand nombre"[48] [What we have here are not heroes of the novel, in the sense usually given to the term, but heroes of everyday life, who share lucidly—and not without courage—the mediocrity that has fallen to most of them].

Underlining their rupture with the heroines of traditional sentimental literature, protagonists of the 1950s were instead "heroes of everyday life," in that theirs was a battle with the real world and its banalities rather than a fantasy of foreign lands, of torrid affairs ending in equally torrid marriages in some imagined historical past—the sort of fiction found in women's magazines at the time. Instead of exalting physical love through euphemism, they described it methodically, minutely—just as they described the city streets, workplaces, and living rooms that serve as their novels' settings. The graphic description of sexual encounters in the context of contemporary life is a crucial aspect of this corpus. Was this the stuff of literature? Ibert had his doubts; according to him, the novel must aspire to render more than the everyday. Yet as he simultaneously acknowledged, within what he saw as the limited aspirations of young women writers, "elles font preuve d'une autorité que nul ne saurait contester"[49] [they demonstrate an authority that no one could contest]. For Ibert, such authority did not emerge from the protagonist's intellectual domination of her world, but as a result of her inglorious survival. "Survival," though, as analyses of some of the key novels of the period will reveal in the following pages, is an ambiguous condition.

As they struggle towards survival, young female protagonists do not discover romance, but the ambivalences of sexual pleasure, a deromanticization that is their most obvious departure from their sentimental predecessors. Critics at the time noted that a new corpus was in the process of formation: what I will call the antisentimental novel. As Mathieu Galey commented in *Arts:*

> Les femmes-écrivains ne sont plus ce qu'elles furent: sages, convenables et bien-pensantes. Fini, le temps des Zénaïde Fleuriot, des comtesses de Ségur nées Rostophchine, des Gyp. Maintenant, elles osent. Les livres de femmes ne sont pas toujours à recommender aux jeunes filles, quand ces dernières écrivent des romans à faire rougir leurs aînées.[50]

> [Women writers are no longer what they once were: wise, decent, and God-fearing. Gone are the days of the Zénaïde Fleuriots, of the Countesses of Ségur nées Rostophchine, of the Gyps. Now, they dare. Women's novels are not always to be recommended to young girls, when young girls write novels that make their elders blush.]

Critics in the 1950s both admired and berated young women writers for not following in the footsteps of their sentimental elders, for replacing love and romance with frank narration of sexual experience. With the propensity of these novels to feature female narrators who were as young as their authors, reviewers usually assumed that the titillating details of sexual experience were unsubtly autobiographical.

First-person narrations led to such assumptions: for example, singer-poet Nicole Louvier's *Qui qu'en grogne* is a first-person narrative written in the form of a sexually frank love letter from Adrienne to Gabrielle, in which she announces her dual realization that while she finds other girls attractive, it is a novelty and a relief, "une chose nouvelle et apaisante," to be in a heterosexual couple.[51] Lucette Finas's *Les Chaînes éclatées* recounts in diary form the fascination of a young teacher in a small town for her teenage female student.[52] Critics were shocked by the lengthy clinical description of paternal sexual abuse as well as the lesbian liaison in Suzanne Allen's *La Mauvaise conscience,* an autobiography of girlhood and adolescence in the 1930s and 1940s. The narrator France's coming of age takes place in terms of the slow emergence from a provincial Catholic childhood as well as from the political and sexual empire of a tyrannical father, "ce père universel," with whom she identifies nonetheless: government employee, autodidact, alcoholic, and Maurrasian. France's affair with a woman is but an interlude; like Louvier's Adrienne, she realizes it is easier to be with a man.[53] In Violette Leduc's *Ravages,* a novel whose opening scenes of lesbian lovemaking were so graphic that Gallimard excised the entire section, Thérèse passes from an unsatisfying affair with a woman to an unsatisfying marriage with a man, all the while longing for her boarding school lover of the absent prologue, Isabelle.[54] The autobiographical component of other novels was more ambiguous. For example, reviewers debated whether it was Geneviève, the sexually addicted narrator of Christiane Rochefort's *Le Repos du guerrier,* or a secondary female character to whom Geneviève herself is attracted, Rafaële, who could be identified with the author. Rochefort herself confided to Françoise D'Eaubonne that she actually identified with Renaud, the cynical male antihero.[55] Just a few years after Simone de Beauvoir had written about lesbianism in *Le Deuxième sexe,* a significant number of writers presented the attraction of young women to each other as an integral aspect of female sexuality, whether episodic, a conscious choice, or innate.

Sometimes critics praised these novels; just as often they dismissed them as purely sensationalistic confessions, for many lacked the tone of remorse that Mauriac had detected in *Bonjour tristesse.* Claudine Chonez, herself a poet and novelist, berated the "troop," to use her term, for relying on personal revelations rather than imagination, for writing novels that seemed to her to be no different than diaries:

> A vrai dire, elles n'en sont plus aujourd'hui à l'aveu ni au défi, mais à l'audace tranquille (ou qui se voudrait telle). Le ton général n'est plus celui du lyrisme (qui exalte ou justifie), mais celui du défoulement méthodique et pour ainsi dire hygiénique, de la lucidité que rien n'arrête — surtout pas l'hypocrite pudeur des aînées escamotant toujours le striptease sous un dernier voile.[56]

> [In truth, today they are no longer at the point of avowal or challenge, but tranquil audacity (or what would like to be). The general tone is no longer lyrical (which exalts or justifies), but one of methodical and even hygienic release, of a lucidity that nothing stops — especially not the hypocritical modesty of their elders, always conjuring away the striptease under a final veil.]

In a word, Chonez is hostile to "women's writing" as a category: she expresses equal disdain for earlier generations, with their feminist challenges and proclamations and coyness, and for her own contemporaries' unadorned and untheatrical accounts of sexual encounters. But Chonez herself does not interrogate the category: she does not look beyond gender, for example, to possible links between the methodical lucidity of "littérature féminine" and the tradition of the realist novel. Chonez's observations made her part of the critical apparatus that kept the age-old division of genre along the lines of gender virtually intact—but also identified the oppositional concept of antisentimentality that tested those very same lines. Critics who might dismiss sentimental novels had much to say about fictional renditions of young women's unapologetic sexual experimentation when they could hint at a connection to the writer herself.

Sagan and her protagonists furnished critics and the public with archetypes of the precociously sexual and antisentimental female adolescent. Romance, education, and family seemed to mean little to them. Contrary to traditional images of both writer and daughter, Sagan's jet-set lifestyle flanked by wealthy and famous friends, her fast cars and even faster success, made an appropriate media double for the narrators of the two novels that quickly followed *Bonjour tristesse: Un certain sourire,* and *Dans un mois, dans un an.* Critics looked to Sagan's media persona to explain the absence of sentimentality in her fictional adolescents. As Dominique Aubier commented:

> [D]ans l'aventure, c'est le sentiment qui perd . . . Le sentiment s'en va mourir dans l'ennui. Françoise Sagan l'enterre dans ses petits romans étriqués qui n'ont su donner vie qu'aux quinquagénaires, qu'aux amoureux désaffectés. D'ailleurs, elle ne les aime pas. Elle les laisse faire.[57]

> [In the process, it's sentiment that loses . . . Sentiment dies away in boredom. Françoise Sagan buries it in her cramped little novels which have been able to give life only to fifty year-olds, to disenchanted lovers. Besides, she doesn't like her characters. She lets them do what they will.]

Aubier reproached Sagan for stifling any possibility of emotional warmth in the space of her short novels. In her reading, only the secondary characters came to life in these minimalist spaces, middle-aged men and disappointed lovers. And even they, she added, were unlikable. Aubier's evaluation of Sagan is typical of the two-sided critical system based on gender: literary history may be replete with unlikable characters in desolate settings, but women writers should remain within the realm of sentiment, portraying good and kind people for whom love will conquer all.

Many antisentimental novels were more disturbing than anything Sagan had to offer, portraying young women as masochists in situations where the psychological stakes were much higher than bourgeois ennui. Elisabeth Trévol's *Mon amour* is a novel written in the form of a young secretary's lengthy suicide note addressed to "Monsieur," her middle-aged boss and lover. The narrator Elisabeth (sic) is innocent to such an extent that after her first intercourse, she is unaware of no longer being a virgin—but neither does she have any shame once she makes the connection between word and deed, announcing with satisfaction that she has committed "le premier acte irréparable de ma vie."[58] The second and final one will be her suicide, when she gets pregnant and "Monsieur" does not leave his wife. One has to wonder about a culture in which a novel like this could be so successful that after its 1954 publication by Julliard it was reprinted by the Club français du livre, the French equivalent of the Book of the Month Club. The popular and widely disseminated image of adolescent girls as masochists in postwar France, combined with the simultaneously disapproving and titillated reception of the equally young authors of these novels, communicates the ambivalence within 1950s' French culture regarding the sexual freedom of young women, an ambivalence in which these writers participated as well. Novels where adolescent girls explore their sexuality while the world around them reacts never end triumphantly and often come to tragedy: senseless death, loveless marriage, terrifying solitude, emotional and psychic crippling.[59] The fact that these are typically first-person narratives further compounds the ambivalence. Inexperienced and naive, yet passively willing to have experience imprinted on them in dubious circumstances, and in possession of the precise language that lets them tell of it all, these narrator-victims inspire in the reader a complicated admixture of admiration and pity, identification and repugnance.

Sixteen-year-old narrator Hélène of *Le Rempart des béguines* is a good example of such a narrator-victim. Bored with life as a schoolgirl in provincial Belgium (reputedly the most conservative European francophone culture at the time), one day she seeks out her widowed father's Russian lover Tamara in a seedy part of town, on the eponymous street of the title. The older (all of thirty-six) woman's curiosity is piqued. She kisses Hélène and orders a second encounter which immediately turns sexual, though Hélène's language remains elliptical: "elle ne se contenta pas de m'embrasser"[60] [she did something more than kiss me]. A sexual innocent in search of nineteenth-century-style romance, what she gets instead is mistreatment, both psychological and physical. The word lesbian is never pronounced in *Le Rempart des béguines*. It is enough that Tamara is an attractive woman living alone—an oddity at the time—for Hélène to believe in her exotic singularity, as well as that of the nature of their relationship.[61] When the confused girl attempts to confide in a doctor friend of her father's, he is titillated and amused but brings her no closer to knowledge. Tamara, of course, from the moment she orders Hélène into bed with her, possesses not only knowledge, but complete control, and her pleasure is to alternate domination with nurturance. She makes Hélène cry, then appeases her with caresses. At one moment she makes her kneel and beg for forgiveness, which leads to Hélène's most intense sexual pleasure. In the novel's most violent scene, the drunk and hallucinating Tamara beats Hélène savagely after an evening at a caricatural lesbian bar, then while Hélène's father looks on approvingly, nurses her back to health at home. Hélène's bruises are compounded by scarlet fever, an appropriate affliction for an adolescent heroine nostalgic for an experience of romance from another era.

Tamara's month of dutiful maternal performance leads to the only possible reconciliation of this triangle in which she can be both heterosexual and homosexual lover and omnipotent mother: marriage. As she tells Hélène, she is thirty-six years old, tired of financial insecurity and the fear of losing the looks that have guaranteed her attention from a string of wealthy men.[62] The epiphany comes for Hélène when she overhears Tamara talking to the man who is now her husband, Hélène's father René:

> Cette intonation faussement indignée de femme heureuse qu'on la violente un peu, je la reconnaissais! C'était exactement la mienne, quand elle me prenait dans ses bras malgré ma résistance . . . A ce «non René . . . » languissant, j'avais pensé que Tamara et moi avions peut-être changé d'âme . . . J'étais libre enfin. Même mon vieux désir de vengeance disparaissait . . .
>
> En bas, une porte se ferma, qui devait être la porte de leur chambre à coucher. Dans l'obscurité, je me mis à rire.[63]

[That intonation! It was the pretended indignation of a woman happy to be roughed up a bit. I recognized it! For it was precisely my own intonation when she took me in her arms despite my resistance . . . That "No, René," pronounced in her languorous voice, made me think that perhaps Tamara and I had exchanged personalities . . . I was at last free. Even my former desire for revenge had disappeared . . .

On the floor below, a door closed. It had to be the door to their bedroom. And alone in the darkness I began to laugh.]

The novel closes with the bitter laugh that follows Hélène's moment of recognition and detachment. The masochistic position in pleasure that was hers has now been taken up by Tamara in her marriage. Hélène feels relieved that she and Tamara have "exchanged personalities," liberated, as if she were free to reinvent her life and identity. Hélène does indeed survive, and the novel, told in solemnly disillusioned and deromanticized retrospect, is her testimony. But Hélène's solitary mirth is troubling, for it does not as much confirm her freedom as it does her twisted understanding of the couple as a fundamentally sadomasochistic dyad.

In Christiane Rochefort's *Le Repos du guerrier*, narrator Geneviève, law student and former "good girl," also discovers sadomasochism as the only route to sexual pleasure. In this first novel of Rochefort's, Geneviève finds herself in a small town where she has come to collect an inheritance and ends up saving a man named Jean-Renaud Sarti from attempted suicide. Intrigued by Renaud's slightly dangerous and sardonic manner, she passively lets him determine the nature of their relationship: an all-consuming world of sexual pleasure where he is in control all the time. With Renaud, Geneviève has her first orgasms, but she is never able to fully let go. The quest for pleasure becomes her obsession: she abandons her studies, her family, her friends, and her taste for order and measure. Matters are complicated when Renaud's drinking habit turns into alcoholism. Geneviève tries to sabotage Renaud's drinking, and he, in turn, beats and humiliates Geneviève—wheedles her into unbuttoning her blouse in public and into having a sexual encounter with another woman while he watches. Geneviève submits to all of this in order to be rewarded, in her passive formulation, with the sexual pleasure he has been the first to give her. As she explains her masochism, "J'étais de plus en plus anesthésiée, je ne sentais quasiment rien. Parfois j'allais aux lavabos, vomir un peu: comme les Romains au milieu du banquet, pour pouvoir continuer à avaler les mets délicats, à la saveur toujours nouvelle." [64] [I was becoming more and more anesthetized, I felt almost nothing. Sometimes I'd go into the bathroom and vomit a little: as the Romans did during their banquets, so they could go on swallowing delicacies, each one with a new taste]. The new, sexual Geneviève feels superior to friends who to her eye look repressed. But the sexual knowledge in which she preens is troubling in that submission and debasement are its prerequisites.

Geneviève does manage to find sexual pleasure elsewhere—most threateningly for Renaud, in the lesbian adventure he himself orchestrates—but what puts an end to his escalating abuse, in a conclusion which recalls *Le Rempart des béguines,* is marriage. With a strange 1950s logic, Geneviève's doctor informs the dysfunctional couple that the only way to "save" Renaud from the physical self-destruction of alcoholism would be for Geneviève to marry him. For Renaud, a more palatable pretext for an offer of marriage comes when Geneviève announces she is pregnant. And so he proposes, although it may not be recognizable as such: "Enchaîne-moi. Je veux des chaînes, le plus de chaînes possible, et lourdes, que je ne puisse plus bouger" [Chain me to you. I want chains, as many as possible, and so heavy I can't move].[65] Renaud's proposal turns the tables on their relationship: now it is he who clamors to be the masochist, although for him it is submission of a social rather than sexual sort: "Je veux être rien qu'un homme, je veux dire Bonjour Comment allez-vous Très bien merci et vous, je veux aller moi aussi dans la grande Machine à Laver, aide-moi, toi qui sais cela" [I want to be nothing but a man, I want to say 'Hello, how are you, very well, thank you, and you?' I want to enter the Great Washing Machine; help me, you know how it's done].[66] Just as Renaud has opened up the world of sexual sensation to Geneviève, now he pleads with her to instruct him in the niceties of bourgeois life and conversation. Renaud manages to express contempt for Geneviève even as he asks her to be his savior.

Renaud even volunteers to enter a rehabilitation center for his alcoholism, and the novel ends at the moment he and Geneviève part in front of the center's gate. Geneviève suddenly realizes that Renaud has actually internalized the bourgeois values she has always touted. In horror, she disavows her role in Renaud's transformation: "[J]e ne suis qu'un instrument, je joue le rôle qu'il m'a donné. C'est lui qui fait tout, pas moi. Moi je ne fais rien, je n'ai rien fait, ce n'est pas moi, ce n'est pas moi, je le jure" [I'm only an instrument. I'm playing the part he's assigned to me. It's all his doing, not mine. I'm not doing anything. I never have, I didn't do it, I swear I didn't].[67]

With this denial, Geneviève's testimony of survival comes to double as an avowal of her passivity. She tries to convince the reader that her performance has been imposed, bad faith in stark contrast to the lucidity of Sagan's narrator Cécile in her role as "metteur en scene." Nevertheless, even for the contemporary feminist reader, Geneviève remains a plausible character—less for her struggles with Renaud than for those with herself. Awakened to a sexuality she did not know existed, in trancelike wonderment Geneviève allows herself to be reduced to her sexuality. Yet she never quite abandons her sense of propriety. Older than Mallet-Joris's Hélène and not a social or sexual innocent, Geneviève and her limits are more firmly in place. Her discomfort at the scrutiny of the concierge when she brings Renaud home for the first time, her recurrent nightmares of public self-exposure, the shame underlying her self-satisfaction when the "new" Geneviève faces her mother, and most literally, her sense that the heights of pleasure are just out of her reach, all subtly testify to the guilt and self-consciousness that prevent Geneviève from fully taking part in her sexuality.

A young woman's total submission for male pleasure is indeed her own pleasure in Pauline Réage's *Histoire d'O,* a novel that generated surprisingly little media attention before 1975 when excerpts were printed in *L'Express* and a film version appeared. When *Histoire d'O* first came out in 1954, what most interested the reviewers was not the novel's sadomasochistic content, but the identity of its pseudonymous author. Was Pauline Réage really a young woman writer? Or was the author actually Jean Paulhan, who had brought the manuscript to Jean-Jacques Pauvert, editor of the works of the Marquis de Sade, and who had written the introduction? Eventually, the author revealed herself to be Dominique Aury ("O rit," or O laughs), a respected intellectual in her fifties: journalist, professor of literature, translator, reader at Gallimard, and friend of Paulhan's. In 1955 she was preparing an anthology of religious poetry.[68] Though *Histoire d'O* was not the work of a young woman writer, the reading public's desire to see it as such highlights the problematic nature of making facile connections between author and protagonist. Besides exposing the speciousness of the automatic link between author and protagonist, *Histoire d'O* tested the limits of the depiction of female masochism. Like Geneviève in *Le Repos du guerrier* and Hélène in *Le Rempart des béguines,* O goes through a series of tests of violence and humiliation as proof of affection for her lover René. But in O's case, partly as a function of the narrative voice, the psychological dimension of such tests is presented as negligible. In marked contrast to the first-person voices of Hélène and Geneviève as survivors, the voice of the effaced narrator here, in an incongruously even tone, describes the increasingly invasive acts and mutilations which mark O's body and its orifices. Open to all who would desire her (thus her name), O's body becomes a map upon which all men, and not only René, can read their potential ownership.[69]

Physical pain is involved in the literal branding and reshaping of O's body, but the narration effaces even the visceral: "Yes, it hurts," one can almost hear her say, "but that's okay." Her lack of voice is part of O's transformation from subject into object, culminating in her willing self-enslavement to an Englishman, Sir Stephen. With Sir Stephen, submission to pain for love turns into a desire for submission in and for itself. The face of submission is all the more disturbing in that O is not a sexual innocent or a student, but a young professional woman, a fashion photographer. Significantly, though, the narrator notes how much she looks like a schoolgirl who could pass for Sir Stephen's niece or daughter. This visual contrast is reinforced by the fact that he addresses her in the familiar *tu* form while she uses the formal *vous*. We are not so very far from Bardot's screen persona here. Clad in blue and white, in stripes or polka dots, pleated skirts and bolero jackets, her hair loose, eschewing hats and makeup, "elle avait l'air d'une jeune fille sage"[70] [she looked like a good girl]—which is, after all, not completely off the mark, since O's foremost characteristic is her obedience.

O is "freed" towards the end of the novel, but she chooses to remain Sir Stephen's sexual slave. The final scene, at a party, is the culminating image of her dehumanization. Clad in a costume that is the brainchild of Sir Stephen, O has become completely unrecognizable. Her head is covered with an ornate, feathered owl's head mask, whose only openings are for her eyes and mouth. Her body is nude and hairless. On a dog leash attached to one of the rings clamped through her labia, and led by a fifteen year-old girl who will soon embark on a similar trajectory, O causes a stir upon entrance. Couples approach the strange creature, half animal, half human, hold torches up to her, in order to get a better look. The host leads O to a stone bench at a slight remove from the party. Slowly, the other guests gravitate toward her:

O les fixait de ses yeux cernés de bistre sous la plume, large ouverts comme les yeux de l'oiseau nocturne qu'elle figurait, et si forte était l'illusion que ce qui paraissait le plus naturel, qu'on l'interrogeât, personne n'y songeait, comme si elle eût été une vraie chevêche, sourde au langage humain, et muette.[71]

[O stared at them with her eyes ringed with charcoal under the feathers, wide open like the eyes of the night bird she figured, and so powerful was the illusion that what seemed most natural, that people ask her questions, no one thought of doing, as if she were a real owl, deaf to human language, and dumb.]

At the end of the novel, the absence of O's voice becomes a literal silencing in her transformation into a creature no longer human, an invention of the erotic and violent fantasies of her male masters. Her "survival," if one can call it that, comes in the form of the infinite violations, "tour à tour," one after the other, with which the novel ends.

In the cases of Hélène and Genevieve, the masochism of the survivor-narrator is an identity she tries on and, in time, sheds: a stage in her psychosexual development recounted with the lucidity of hindsight. But lucidity does not make their narratives any less disturbing. In that the masochistic position is not one they freely seek out and consciously choose, but one that comes across their paths and happens to choose *them,* it is the consummate act of bad faith. The fact that Hélène and Geneviève can narrate their survival is an après-coup; up until the novels' conclusions, they are pliant characters in stories whose unorthodox sexual components, among them lesbianism and masochism, they cannot, or do not, even name. *Histoire d'O* is disturbing for other reasons. O is conscious of the sense of her acts and of those of her tormentors at every step of the way. She agrees, then she chooses. The novel tries to convince the reader of O's good faith by presenting a character who submits docilely and entirely, at first for her lover's pleasure, ultimately for her own. By gradually revealing a network of underworlds where O is just one of many women who have chosen the same fate, "Pauline Réage" makes the appalling suggestion that sexual enslavement is what women ultimately want.

On the opposite end of the spectrum from the masochist, a second type of adolescent protagonist found in novels by young women writers is the precocious femme fatale. Aware of her ability to seduce boys her own age as well as adult men, she devises intricate plots, whether for revenge or simply to get what she wants, all in maintaining an appearance of innocence. Like her masochist counterparts, she survives in the end, but it is an ambiguous moment, in which her manipulations, even her guilt, are dissimulated but always intimated. Cécile in *Bonjour tristesse* is the arche-

Enfants Terribles

type, indirectly responsible for what may have been the suicide of her soon-to-be stepmother. Nathalie in Anne Marie de Vilaine's *Des raisons d'aimer* is another example, expressing contempt for her mother as a victim, a condition she defines as giving more than one receives.[72] In her affair with her professor Jérôme, she feels triumphant, superior, and powerful in her capacity for pleasure—a sentiment she defines as "masculine," although we learn from Jérôme's section of the novel that he feels the conquest to be all his. *Lolita* comes readily to mind, and indeed, Nabokov's novel, first published in France in 1955, is contemporaneous with the corpus presently under consideration. It is less the novel's playful modernist irony than the character of Lolita herself, the "nymphet," to use Nabokov's term, that merits comparison with the bad girls in French novels like *Bonjour tristesse* and *Des raisons d'aimer*. Despite the age difference, what is crucial to both the underage nymphet and the young woman in her late teens or early twenties is the combination of innocence and sexual power they may or may not know they have.

While it can be argued that the girlish capacity to seduce, with or without awareness of the full implications of the words and gestures of seduction, is not limited to a particular time or culture, the accelerated growth of consumer and media society was certainly an important catalyst in the formation of the nymphet as a cross-cultural type of the 1950s. As Nabokov described Lolita, she was "a modern child, an avid reader of movie magazines, an expert in dream-slow close-ups":

> She believed, with a kind of celestial trust, any advertisement or advice that appeared in Movie Love or Screen Land—Starasil Starves Pimples, or "You better watch out if you're wearing your shirttails outside your jeans, gals, because Jill says you shouldn't." . . . If some café sign proclaimed Icecold Drinks, she was automatically stirred, although all drinks everywhere were ice-cold. She it was to whom ads were dedicated: the ideal consumer, the subject and object of every foul poster.[73]

Consumers of subliminal advertising, of movies and magazines, beauty products and fashion that were perhaps originally intended for adult women but well within the reach of the adolescent gaze and wallet, Lolita and her French counterparts schooled themselves to perfection in the theatrical art of seduction. In the 1950s, Cocteau's Elisabeth became a recognizable literary and cultural type. Indeed, as novels as well as films about nymphets demonstrated, such self-education within consumer society was pleonastically all-consuming. Despite the keen intelligence to which the narrative always alluded, the character of the nymphet neglected her studies, cut class, dropped out of school, and turned up her nose at both current events and preparation for a career, to the despair, frustration, or titillation of all who necessarily remained exterior to her internal machinations and motivations, never predictable and often astonishing. The hybrid nature of the nymphet was such that not only was her physical appearance simultaneously knowing and innocent, but her machinations were as well. In the absence of extensive life experience, she borrowed from what she had seen and read in order to precociously play the role of femme fatale, to seduce easily credulous adults, and to get what she wanted. The credulous adult also played his role, never as mercilessly unmasked as in Nabokov's Humbert Humbert: ". . . I knew I could kiss her throat or the wick of her mouth with perfect impunity. I knew she would let me do so, and even close her eyes, as Hollywood teaches."[74]

Just as Nabokov created the archetype of the nymphet, he unmasked her as well: Lolita does indeed have firsthand sexual experience, acquired mechanistically and banally at summer camp. To the ultimately debatable and playful question of knowledge and innocence, of who seduces whom in *Lolita*, we must add the scene where Humbert Humbert sees his nymphet for the last time, where much to the horror of this effete European intellectual, she has become the rather colorless wife of a car mechanic, a caricature of white-trash America.

As the banality of Lolita's adult existence shows, one cannot be a nymphet forever. The same holds true for her French counterparts: in these novels, once the machinations have been taken to their (il)logical conclusions, all that remains are feelings of guilt or loss and the dispassionate option of marriage. In Michèle Perrein's *La Sensitive, ou l'innocence coupable*, a novel that unfolds as a series of letters never sent, the charismatic if abrasive law student Odile becomes involved with one young man, Jacques, as a way to recover from the rejection of her childhood sweetheart, José. When she, in turn, rejects Jacques, he kills himself. Through the epistolary form of the novel, Odile matter-of-factly exposes her machinations to the reader, who can only observe with horror as she manipulates the unsuspecting young men in her milieu. Sexual pleasure is not her goal; when Odile has sex for the first time with José, she refers to the experience as an "operation," taking more pleasure in the clandestine nature of the act than in sex itself. One of the few intellectuals found in this corpus of novels, Odile is inspired less by popular culture than by highbrow reading material. As a way to recover the upper hand after the breakup with José, she reads and rereads Jean Anouilh's *Medea* to plot a revenge in which she would make someone suffer as she had. Dispassionately, Odile decides on Jacques Vielmas, who has scrutinized her with interest over the course of the school year.

With their first sexual encounter, Jacques declares his love for Odile; he is emotional, happy. Odile doesn't say a word. Her pleasure comes rather from the realization of her power over him: "Je tenais à cette puissance, donc je tenais à Vielmas"[75] [I wanted that power, thus I wanted Vielmas]. True to the nymphet's hybrid psyche of knowingness and innocence, maturity and immaturity, she feels nothing but resentment toward Jacques for being a better lover than José. When Jacques shoots himself, he does so by holding the gun at arm's length—as if, Odile induces, it were she and not himself who was responsible. Nor does the novel end in this melodramatic moment: Odile goes on to reject and humiliate Glop, her kind, well-to-do, and marriage-minded friend and suitor, by sleeping with a young man they both know to be a womanizer:

J'ai essayé de lui expliquer que j'en avais marre du grand amour. Que je ne voulais ni du mien ni de celui des autres. Je lui ai dit que j'avais tué le sien, exprès, en tuant en moi ce qu'il y restait de naïf . . . Je ne voulais plus qu'on rêvât de moi. Je voulais être une femme tout court.[76]

[I tried to explain to him that I was tired of true love. That I didn't want my own nor anyone else's. I told him that I had killed his, on purpose, by killing in myself what naïveté was left . . . I didn't want anyone to dream about me. I simply wanted to be a woman.]

What exactly do these final words mean? Odile makes a conscious, cold-blooded decision against true love, "le grand amour," against the all-consuming sentiment that society has deemed to be life- and self-defining. Her act of self-determination is, at the same time, one of self-punishment. Odile's way to make the transition from nymphet to adult, to "be a woman," is to savagely reject the relational identity required within a couple or a family. A latter-day Renée Néré without Colette's *vagabonde*'s heady desire to write in communion with nature, Odile, a one-time nymphet, stands alone at the end of the novel, destruction behind her and nothing, it would seem, ahead.

Odile, with her nihilistic choice against a happy ending, must surely—much like Françoise Sagan's Cécile—have perplexed readers in 1956. In a new preface to the 1986 reedition of the novel, Perrein shed light on the cold conclusion by linking it to the "guilty innocence" of the title, itself inspired by a botanical curiosity: the *sensitive,* the common name for the *Mimosa pudica* that is native to the Midi region. The sensitive is a hardy and colorful flower, but when there is a disturbance in the environment of strong sun and frequent rainfall in which it thrives, it closes its petals and produces a strong-smelling, poisonous oil. The tropism of the sensitive, Perrein wrote, recalls the inner workings and behavior of Odile. Thirty years after exposing in print a character she conceded to being very close to her own adolescent self, Perrein offered a new paratext, a reference to Odile's childhood, for those who sought to understand Odile and others like her:

> Odile, petite fille, avait très bien pu craindre de blesser les autres, demander pardon au chat, serrer avec enthousiasme les moignons brûlés d'un vieil ami de son grand-père, acheter des chaussures trop grandes pour ne pas decevoir une vendeuse et se laisser embarquer dans un trolley-bus qui l'emmenait où elle n'allait pas, cela ne l'avait pas empêchée, à l'heure où le sexe se met à compter, de se révéler dangereuse.[77]

> [Odile, as a little girl, was quite able to fear hurting others, to beg the cat's pardon, to enthusiastically shake hands with the sunburned stump of an old friend of her grandfather's, to buy shoes too big so as not to disappoint the saleslady, and to agree to get on a trolley taking her where she wasn't going. That did not stop her, when sex began to matter, from proving herself to be dangerous.]

Unlike Nabokov, Michèle Perrein asserts an unequivocally presexual history for Odile, an innocent childhood which resembles that of Beauvoir's "jeune fille rangée" and which also contains the grains of her psychosexual adolescent self. But Odile's girlish self-effacement and anxious desire to please take a different shape when she becomes sexually active. Hélène and Geneviève implode, continuing obediently to accommodate the desires of others even as they harm themselves. Odile, on the other hand, explodes: she consciously takes advantage of the vestigial image others have of her; she manipulates the desires of which she is the object. To use Perrein's term, Odile is "dangerous" to those who love or desire her.

Perrein's new preface is subtle in the causality it establishes. Not only does Odile's status as a good girl "not stop her" from becoming a dangerous adolescent; in a sense, one leads to the other. Odile's destruction of others and of herself is less mystifying if we see it as a rebellion against herself, against the good girl who defined herself in terms of others, in terms of their choices and desires. This is less the terrain of Nabokovian irony than of feminism, albeit of an immature variety. Much like Cécile in *Bonjour tristesse,* Odile only knows how to rebel by destroying: to return to the counter-example of Colette's *Vagabonde,* one must have positive desires of one's own in order to move beyond those of others and to create a self that is whole.

The annihilatory rebellions of Cécile and Odile are, however, not to be dismissed, first and foremost for their cultural shock value. Their fictional rejection of appropriate suitors represents a dramatic negation of the mentality of a high percentage of teenage French girls at the time. Despite the much-heralded increased opportunities for them in the public sphere, young women across the spectrum of educational level and class difference continued to see marriage as their only possible "happy ending" in real life. While it may not be surprising to hear this from *employées* and workers, many girls who were bourgeois and/or educated also saw university studies, even their careers, as a way to pass the time until Prince Charming or, at the least, a provider, came along to take them away.[78] The enormous success of *Bonjour tristesse* and *La Sensitive* (a version of the latter appeared in *Elle* in easy-reading *bande dessinée* format) is very much an expression of this ambivalence. For fictional heroines who choose against a "happy ending," against the couple or the family, can only scandalize those who never dreamed of such a choice.

Perrein, a young novelist who was "discovered" by the writer and editor Jacques Chardonne and eventually became his wife, was a naturally titillating object of the media's attention when placed side by side with Odile in *La Sensitive.* No such slippage between author and character was possible for Lise Deharme, the author of *Laissez-moi tranquille* and *Carole ou ce qui plaît aux filles.* Deharme, associated with the Parisian circle of surrealists, recounted in this pair of novels the picaresque adventures of a fourteen-year-old who is ostensibly a "vraie jeune fille," a well-brought up young lady and a virgin, but instead lives by night, frequenting an underworld filled with shady characters. Deharme's novels are primarily significant as a commentary. By 1959, evidently, it was already possible to satirize the genre launched by Sagan, Rochefort, Mallet-Joris, Perrein, and others, and to let Lolita speak with the acuity of Humbert Humbert. For in Deharme's surrealist hands, the alternating self-seriousness and nihilism of the female adolescent becomes fodder for modernist farce.[79] As the heroine Carole explains herself, "non, je ne suis pas tout à fait libre physiquement. Je ne peux pas remuer ma mâchoire supérieure."[80] [No, I'm not completely free physically. I can't wiggle my upper jaw]. An avant-garde Lolita in a white trench coat, first in her class, Carole gaily deceives her parents, seduces her schoolgirl friend Gisèle, and baffles her would-be adult seducers, men and women alike, who whisk her away in big cars. Deharme sets the tone with brisk wordplay and self-ironization that are absent from the novels previously discussed, as in this post-seduction dialogue between Carole and an unnamed man:

> Il regarda Carole, ses yeux s'incrustaient en elle. Il resta longtemps sans parler, puis, posant son visage dans les mains de l'enfant:
> —Quatorze ans, . . . fit-il, quatorze ans . . .
> Il se hasarda à dire:
> —Je t'aime.
> —Bien sûr. Moi, pas . . . Je resterai avec toi pendant ces trois jours . . . Je n'envoie jamais de cartes postales.[81]

> [He looked at Carole deeply. He stayed silent for a long time, then, putting his face in the child's hands:
> —Fourteen years old, he said, fourteen years old . . .
> He ventured to say:
> —I love you.
> —Of course. Not me . . . I'll stay with you for three days . . . I never send postcards.]

Rather than cloak the scene in an aura of interdiction, Deharme takes her cue from Nabokov: the adult male seducer is overcome with emotion and desire, the pubescent girl remains blasé, unmoved and unmarked by the transgressive exchange that has just taken place. Only in *Lolita* the narrative builds on the increasingly claustrophobic relationship between Humbert Humbert and the nubile object of his obsessions. In Deharme's surrealist universe adults are nameless, numerous, and infinitely replaceable.

The best-known nymphet in 1950s France was not the invention of a novelist but was a character nonetheless: the screen actress Brigitte Bardot. A voluptuous young woman, Bardot was nevertheless dubbed B.B.

(*bébé*). The Bardot phenomenon drew no boundary between her screen role and her private life[82]—not so very different from the fictions of female adolescence generated by the publishing industry and the press. The "B.B." born with Roger Vadim's *Et Dieu créa la femme* (1956) was instrumental in fixing an image of the nymphet whom not even marriage could really tame. Along with a forgettable *Bonjour tristesse* that brought Jean Seberg to the screen as Cécile, the fiction of female adolescence expanded to draw young actresses and their screen personae into the scripted confusion between author and protagonist, giving the type a full physical presence—the movements of a body, the sounds of a voice—that went well beyond the already seductive press photo.

Simone de Beauvoir was particularly intrigued by the blurring of Brigitte Bardot and B.B., by the star's public display of a frank attitude toward sex and her own sexuality: not a willfully scandalous immorality, but an instinctive, impulsive "amorality," as Beauvoir put it in a 1959 *Esquire* magazine article entitled "Brigitte Bardot and the Lolita Syndrome."[83] Just as she considered such frankness a healthy change, Beauvoir saw the invention of the nymphet as the expression of an ideological struggle: a means for postwar culture to maintain the "feminine mystique," despite the demystification of femininity that was under way. With the increasing participation of adult women in a public sphere previously reserved for men, the intimation of sexual knowingness in an adolescent evoked a femininity that could still be titillatingly dangerous and enigmatic.[84]

Besides being troubled by the eroticization of girlishness, Beauvoir was uneasy with the reduction of Bardot/B.B's identity to her physicality, in the hands of her director-producer-husband Roger Vadim. In *Et Dieu créa la femme*, not only does the character of Juliette lack a personal history, but the world is absent as well. Bardot is never "in situation": "Elle est sans mémoire, sans passé," wrote Beauvoir. Deprived of memory and a personal past, incarnating a purely physical, immanent presence, Bardot offered paternalistic seducers on screen as well as her audience a way out of history.[85] As we saw in the previous chapter, *Elle* and *Mademoiselle* imagined the carefree female adolescent in opposition to a maternal figure burdened with war memories. Bardot added immeasurably to the fiction of a youthful femininity free from the shackles of the past, free—momentarily—to explore her sexuality.

Beauvoir herself is not to be neglected in a consideration of fictions of female adolescence, although she was well past that biological age. Ten years prior to her article on the "Lolita syndrome," in *Le Deuxième sexe* (1949), she had written about the theatricality of femininity as a question belonging to history, philosophy, and contemporary culture. While it wasn't until the late 1960s that *Le Deuxième sexe* came to play a role in the burgeoning feminist movement,[86] the publication of the book was a media event in France. A remarkable 22,000 copies were sold its first week out. It was not Beauvoir's historically exhaustive and philosophically rigorous approach to the study of the female condition that drew such attention but the clinical explicitness of the book's tone and content, abetted by its condemnation by both the Communist Party and the Vatican.[87] *Le Deuxième sexe* was discussed across the spectrum of the French press, and with her work, Beauvoir herself became a media character separate from her status as Sartre's ubiquitous companion. *Paris-Match* devoted seven largely sympathetic pages to the book, but the bastions of serious journalism thought otherwise. Beauvoir's American lover Nelson Algren noted that the French press made a constant mockery of her, sometimes gently, sometimes cruelly.[88] In *Le Figaro littéraire* François Mauriac wrote, "We have literally reached the limits of the abject. This is the ipecac they made us swallow as children to induce vomiting." In a personal letter to a staff member of *Les Temps modernes*, he offered: "I've learned all there is to know about your boss's vagina."[89]

Published reviews were somewhat less graphic. As Beauvoir recalled in *La Force des choses,*

> J'étais une «pauvre fille», névrosée, une refoulée, une frustrée, une déshéritée, une virago, une mal baisée, une envieuse, une aigrie bourrée de complexes d'infériorité à l'égard des hommes, à l'égard des femmes, le ressentiment me rongeait . . . Armand Hoog se surpassa: «Humiliée d'être femme, douloureusement consciente d'être enfermée par les regards des hommes dans sa condition, elle refuse à la fois ce regard et cette condition».[90]

> [I was a "pitiful girl," neurotic, repressed, sexually frustrated, sexually deprived, a shrew, a jealous bitch, a bitter woman full of inferiority complexes about men, about women, resentment gnawed away at me . . . Armand Hoog outdid himself: "Humiliated to be a woman, distressingly conscious of being imprisoned in her condition by the male gaze, she refuses both this gaze and this condition."]

By writing in a frank and deromanticized style about female sexuality, Beauvoir shocked the French bourgeoisie resoundingly. She became notorious overnight—a character—much as young women novelists did in the following decade. As Deirdre Bair writes in her biography of Beauvoir, "When she sat in cafés with Algren, people snickered or pointed at her in derision. She took him to dine on the outskirts of Montparnasse, where she had not gone in years, and a large family from the neighborhood stared openly and giggled loudly all through dinner. It was then that she realized how notorious she had become, because these were ordinary people, citizens of the quarter who were not likely to recognize anyone but film stars or other celebrities."[91] Beauvoir offers an excellent example of how the public attention paid to a woman writer of the 1950s obtained from her incursions into the taboo subject of female sexuality.

Matters changed with *Les Mandarins*, which won the Prix Goncourt in 1954. Smug critics pointed to this second novel of Beauvoir's as a prime example of the sentimental tradition, of "littérature féminine." *Paris-Match* called it her most tender book: "Théoricienne de l'amour, Simone de Beauvoir en est devenue la romancière"[92] [Theorist of love, Simone de Beauvoir has become its novelist]. In the eyes of Robert Poulet, *Les Mandarins* was also responsible for Beauvoir's fall from the dubious grace of being an intellectual woman to a similarly dubious, albeit appropriate, place among women novelists. As he wrote in the right-wing satirical journal *Rivarol*, *Les Mandarins* was yet another offering from the domain of the "ritual woman's novel": "la confession arrangée et camouflée, toujours désespérément la même, qui paraît être le seul moyen d'expression dont disposent la plupart des modernes femmes de lettres"[93] [the altered and camouflaged confession, always desperately the same, which appears to be the only means of expression that the majority of modern women of letters have at their disposal].

The reviewer for *L'Express* also saw *Les Mandarins* as a novel with a traditional feminine sensibility:

Aucun des livres de femmes parus ces dernières années n'est une oeuvre aussi pleinement féminine que *Les Mandarins* . . . Ce gros roman est une succession d'histoires de femmes dont les existences pivotent autour de l'amour et de l'homme, et d'histoires d'hommes envisagées du point de vue non de l'héroïsme, mais du sentiment.

Rien de révolutionnaire dans cette vision affectueuse du monde.[94]

[None of the books by women published in recent years is as fully feminine a work as *The Mandarins* . . . This hefty novel is a succession of stories about women whose lives revolve around love and men, and stories about men envisaged not from the point of view of heroism, but that of sentiment.

There's nothing revolutionary in this affectionate vision of the world.]

In this review, Beauvoir's Left credentials are summarily conjured away. With *Les Mandarins*, Beauvoir could be identified as more of a "woman novelist" than the entire troop of women novelists in the 1950s, who had strayed from their proper domain of sentiment into the uncharted terrain of sexual experience. It was not sex, but love and men that took their rightful place at the center of the women's lives depicted in *Les Mandarins*. After the iconoclastic *Deuxième sexe, Les Mandarins* was a reassuring novel for the critics: even an intellectual woman like Simone de Beauvoir would come back to a male-defined view of the female self.

Le Deuxième sexe was not the work of an adolescent or even a post-adolescent: Beauvoir was forty-one when her book came out. She had, though, been tenaciously and somewhat wrongly associated with youth since the Liberation, specifically with the youth culture rumored to roam the streets of Saint-Germain-des-Prés. While the media showed a prurient fascination with the literary production of young women writers, in their treatment of youth as a collective phenomenon the danger of female adolescent sexuality becomes practically invisible. This was possible, as the following chapter demonstrates, because the media always figured the general category of youth as male. Thus unmarked and desexualized, "youth" became a cipher for the social and political mutations France was undergoing in the postwar years. Mauriac may have hailed *Bonjour tristesse* as an expression of a generation in crisis, but by and large, the critics did not see the crises and revolts in fictions of female adolescence in light of postwar social change. The nymphet and the masochist could titillate or repulse the critics and the public, but never were these novels perceived as anything more than harmless diversion. Youth as a historical category, on the other hand, could be downright dangerous.

3 The *Mal du Siècle:* Politics and Sexuality

It is admittedly odd to set up a paradigm characterizing girls as victims and survivors in novels written by young women after World War II when war memories are nowhere in sight. When recent history and current events figure at all in the corpus, they are the province of fathers, brothers, boyfriends, and occasionally adult women. As we have seen, the female adolescent's status as victim or survivor is an expression of her submission to or rebellion against the trajectory assigned to her as a dutiful daughter within the family and within patriarchy. Once the same terms are evoked in relation to young men in the postwar period, on the other hand, the trauma of the Occupation comes immediately to the fore. This chapter examines the inflection of gender on the meaning of "victim" and "survivor" within the age category of youth.

A young man's life is saved at the beginning of Christiane Rochefort's novel *Le Repos du guerrier.* After meeting with her lawyer in the provincial town where she has come to discuss details of an inheritance, narrator Geneviève opens the wrong hotel room door and comes upon an attempted suicide. While the novel never elucidates the suicide attempt, a kind of note was provided by the Editions Grasset press release, in which Renaud's situation as an adolescent in recent history doubles as his psychological portrait:

> Le 6 août 1945, Jean-Renaud Sarti vient d'avoir vingt ans, la guerre va finir, et, pense-t-il, la vie va commencer, une vie véritable car cette fois tout le monde a compris. Il est plein d'espérance, comme ceux de sa génération. Il voit la lumi-

ère au bout du tunnel de son enfance; il court—et la lumière éclate, éblouit; il est jeté au sol. Il ne s'en relèvera plus. A onze mille kilomètres de distance Hiroshima a tué le germe de toute espérance. Renaud écrit un dernier poème . . . Puis il le brûle, avec tout ce qu'il a, et va se saoûler au pastis, tout seul; et il entre en enfer.

[On August 6, 1945, Jean-Renaud Sarti has just turned twenty, the war is about to end, and, he thinks, life is about to begin, an authentic life, for this time everyone has understood. He is full of hope, as are those of his generation. He sees the light at the end of the tunnel of his childhood; he runs—and the light explodes and dazzles him; he is thrown to the ground. He will not get up again. Eleven thousand kilometers away, Hiroshima has put an end to all hope. Renaud writes a final poem . . . Then he burns it, with everything he has, and goes off to drink himself into oblivion, all by himself; and he enters hell.]

Renaud is a victim of historical circumstance: the Occupation deprived him of an "authentic life," of growing up in the sort of ethical world where "everyone understands"; the release of the atom bomb in Hiroshima elimi-nated his hopes for a future moral order. The future instead consists of a self-generated hell of alcoholism, nihilism, and a sadomasochistic co-existence with Geneviève, ten years his junior. In addition to this psycho-historical diagnosis of Renaud, the press release cast the critical eye on Geneviève that her first person narration cannot render. Too young to have been disillusioned by recent history and current events, Geneviève re-mains uncomprehending of Renaud's sardonic bitterness and mercurial temper, his unwillingness to be saved again, from alcoholism and writer's block, and settle down with her in bourgeois comfort and reasonability.

While the age gap between Renaud and Geneviève presented by the press release as the source of their differences is interesting enough, the factor of gender should not be discounted. Geneviève takes "le Bonheur personnel" [personal happiness] and "une heureuse sécurité" [lucky, happy security]—code words for a good marriage—more seriously than her studies in law. Renaud, on the other hand, in the wake of World War II and the hypothetical imminence of nuclear war, no longer believes in the couple or in keeping up appearances. As late in the decade as 1958, the postwar generation could still be described in terms of the nefarious ef-fects of the Occupation on the psyche and world view of a young man in contrast to a young woman's imperviousness to politics and history. But politics are not just current events in *Le Repos du guerrier:* the roles of victim, survivor, and savior shift when it is a question of sexual politics. Geneviève may have dramatically saved Renaud from suicide, but as she sees it, Renaud goes on to save her from her uptight, nonsexual self. In her ongoing quest for the pleasure Renaud metes out, Geneviève allows herself to become his victim, making herself available to abuse and manipulation. She survives to tell the tale, but it is a survival that produces his destruction: the meek shadow she leaves at the gates of the rehabilitation center as her future husband is frighteningly unrecognizable—and no longer desirable—even to her. The conclusion is a troubling one: traumatized by wartime, young men are bound to be victims once again—of the self-serving schemes of the bad girls who were the *enfants terribles* of the 1950s and '6os.

Le Repos du guerrier was more subtle than most texts in its depiction of the aftershocks of the Occupation on French youth. Sensationalism was the general rule. Most direct was the conversion of the wartime food ration category for ages thirteen to twenty-one into an all-inclusive generational label, "J-3." As imagined by novelists, journalists, sociologists, and filmmakers, the J-3 generation became what *Arts* editor-in-chief André Parinaud termed "l'événement français de cette seconde moitié du siècle"[1] [the most important event in France in the second half of this century]. Morally, politically, and psychologically shaped by the trials of adolescence in the context of wartime France, the J-3s fascinated the public, providing a way to speak about the Occupation years and the new fears brought on by the Cold War.

In the published proceedings from a 1947 conference on the subject of postwar adolescence, *L'Adolescence de l'après-guerre et ses problèmes*, Robert Garric identified what was unique to the J-3 generation across the usual class lines. Rather than learning right from wrong in their formative years, the J-3s had seen what children were usually spared: "le sentiment tragique de l'insécurité quotidienne"[2] [the tragic sense of daily insecurity]. Regardless of social status, fathers were away from home; in the country and in the city, the young witnessed how trafficking on the black market was easier and more profitable than an honest job. Even the end of the war and the beginnings of reconstruction did not bring disorder and material difficulties to an end. Conflict was everywhere: at home and on the political scene, in the newspapers and on the radio. With the years of childhood thus circumscribed, adolescence was no longer an idealistic time of hopes and dreams:

S'il y aujourd'hui un "mal de la jeunesse", ce n'est plus un mal romantique d'illusions, ce n'est plus de l'euphorie, du sentimentalisme: c'est, au contraire, un sentiment de réalité dur, exact, strict, un sentiment presque trop dur de la rudesse de la vie.[3]

[If there is an ennui particular to youth today, it is no longer a romantic ache of illusions, it is no longer euphoria, sentimentalism: it is, on the contrary, a hard, exact, strict awareness of reality, an awareness of the difficulty of life that is almost too hard-hearted.]

A hard awareness of reality, exact and strict: Garric's choice of words itself froze youth in the mold of the social. Even the rise in juvenile delinquency was attributed to the moral chaos of both family and nation during the Occupation. In 1938, 13,000 youth under eighteen were charged with crimes. The numbers rose to between 32,000 and 34,000 in the course of the year following the Liberation.[4] In addition to crossing class lines, the concept of a J-3 generation and their *mal de la jeunesse,* or *mal du siècle,* was one which could be mobilized by both Right and Left. In Paris, two ideologically opposed images of youthful ennui emerged in the late 1940s, blending intellectual trends with popular and media culture: on the Right, the literary group known as the *hussards;* on the Left, the so-called existentialists of Saint-Germain-des-Prés. As for gender, when the specificity of the feminine occasionally comes into play in the image of a traumatized generation, whether J-3s, hussards, or existentialists, it follows the paradigm witnessed in *Le Repos du guerrier:* the young male victim of history encased in a self-protective nihilism is traumatized yet again by the machinations of a young woman whose demure facade falls away to reveal an enfant terrible. Discourses about the politicized yet apolitical and ultimately male mal du siècle posit the sexualized deviousness of female enfants terribles as one of its external causes. Removed from the notion of a generational sensibility, female misbehavior, this chapter argues, merits reappraisal as an essential component of the 1950s' mal du siècle.

Mal(e) du Siècle

The disaffection of youth was a long-familiar concept in France. The mal du siècle, a metaphysical ache with a historical cause, dates from the Romantic movement of the beginning of the nineteenth century. Early Romantics, François-René de Chateaubriand, Germaine de Staël, Benjamin Constant, and Etienne Pivert de Senancour, were passionate young writers drawn to the Middle Ages, rather than the Greek and Roman cultures favored by the Napoleonic regime. Chateaubriand first coined the term *mal du siècle* in *Le Génie du christianisme* (1802). In novels like his *René* (1802) and Constant's *Adolphe* (1816), the melancholic young hero, overcome with ennui, became a recognizable literary type who doubled for the Romantic writer himself.

Whereas the mal du siècle of the early Romantics was a reaction against Napoleon, the collapse of the Second Empire and the enstatement of the July Monarchy (1830–48) led to youthful nostalgia for him. The generation of "orphans of Napoleon"[5] found their spokesman in Alfred de Musset's *Confession d'un enfant du siècle* (1836). For Musset, the mal du siècle originated in two dates: the Terror of 1793, and Napoleon's abdication and self-exile in 1814, both tremendous disappointments for his generation, "enfants pleins de force et d'audace, fils de l'empire et petit-fils de la révolution"[6] [children full of strength and audacity, sons of the Empire and grandsons of the Revolution]. Musset claimed to speak for a generation, but very clearly spoke for young males and their dashed hopes of military might. Boys who saw the Napoleonic wars from afar came of age in a world where joy, glory, and death were all confounded in exotic adventure.

When the glorious battles were over, the men did not return as godlike warriors, but as war-ravaged mortals. Instead of a national glory in which they could participate, boys found themselves in a present so feeble that even its ghosts had ceased to move: "Ils le trouvèrent assis sur un sac de chaux plein d'ossements, serré dans le manteau des égoïstes, et grelottant d'un froid terrible."[7] [They found it seated on a sack of lime full of bones, wrapped in the cloak of egotists, and shivering from the terrible cold.] The disappointment of inheriting a desolate present gave rise to a generation of nihilists, believing in neither God, love, nor country. Young men melodramatically proclaimed their unhappiness—and literary young men like Musset wrote book after book about it—as the only passion possible when politics were banal and culture bourgeois: "Il est doux de se croire malheureux lorsqu'on n'est que vide et ennuyé."[8] [It is sweet to believe you're unhappy when in fact you're just empty and bored.]

From Chateaubriand to Musset, the Romantics were the first generation of youth to be characterized as socially maladjusted in bourgeois culture, the first to overtly distance themselves from the politics and culture of their parents, themselves veterans of the Revolutionary period.[9] The Romantic position was not, however, simply generational. As Margaret Waller notes, the supposedly universal mal du siècle belonged very much to the *mâle*.[10] And, I would specify even further, to the male literati. One of the only novels to figure the mal du siècle hero as a woman was George Sand's *Lélia* (1833).[11] The glories of battle are twice removed from her female protagonist's version of the mal du siècle. As Lélia explains her experience of Romantic angst, patriarchal culture had denied her much more than the experience of battle and military glory. The public sphere in general was closed to her. For recognition came in only one form for women: the realization of their relational potentials as wives and mothers: "Homme, j'eusse aimé les combats, l'odeur du sang, les étreintes du danger; peut-être l'ambition de régner par l'intelligence . . . Femme, je n'avais qu'une destinée noble sur la terre, c'était d'aimer"[12] [If I had been a man, I would have adored battle, the smell of blood, the closeness of danger; perhaps the ambition of reigning through intelligence . . . As a woman, I had only one noble destiny on earth: to love.] Lélia's personal response to this imposed identity is to withdraw entirely from it: she decides to negate her body and lead a life purely of the mind. Frigidity, a typical side effect of Romantic (male) discontent, becomes in Sand's version a conscious act of feminist resistance.[13]

What we see in the post–World War II period is a distinct reversal in the way in which the mal du siècle in its feminine form manifested itself. Even though it also contained the generic elements of ennui, of contempt for family and society, the malaise of the female adolescent translated, not as frigidity, but as precocious and shocking sexuality. Popular texts consistently show that sexual rebellion was the only means available to the female adolescent of the 1950s to challenge the bourgeois norms that dictated her place in her family and in society, a rebellion which constructed her as bad, if not evil: an enfant terrible. These texts often positioned dangerous and sexually precocious enfants terribles alongside sensitive young men whose pensive angst and apathy were diagnosed as political—the effects of war memories, the Occupation, and the threat engendered by the Cold War. Though teenage girls might manifest the same sullen attitude as boys in their sexual behavior, novelists, filmmakers, and journalists intimated that girls did not *feel* the angst and apathy their male counterparts did. Experienced as duplicitous by sensitive young men, this characterization of teenage girls eventually came to stand on its own as an ostensible social fact, the girls' unsentimental sexuality becoming, in turn, one of the reified causes of the male mal du siècle.

The postwar heirs of the Romantic mal du siècle were the young writers known as the hussards, although they themselves rejected the comparison and looked to the seventeenth century for their literary models. A 1952 article in *Les Temps modernes* identified and labeled the hussards as a group, based on their shared fascination for the splendor of the uniformed military and the times of courts and kings and their ties to the *Action française*.[14] The hussards provide an essential point of contrast to the category of *littérature féminine* discussed in the previous chapter. "Littérature féminine" was the term that critics deployed to sensationalize young women writers but also to dismiss their social significance. Any connection between attitudes toward sexuality expressed in these novels and the current situation of postwar France was unthinkable: the critics' assumption of a strong autobiographical identification between author and protagonist served merely to reprimand the author for her lack of imagination and to further titillate potential readers. Critics focused on a very different autobiographical dimension— antirepublicanism—in the writings of the hussards, even though their novels often turned to questions of male sexual initiation and anxieties.[15]

Like many young intellectuals in the interwar period, Antoine Blondin, Roger Nimier, Michel Déon, Stephen Hecquet, and Jacques Laurent had all been aligned with Charles Maurras's extreme right *Action française*, either as members or fellow travelers. Though unrepentant about collaboration, they never expressed pro-Nazi views in print and could thus write freely after the Liberation. The hussards' enthusiasm for the Right, however, was less political than it was cultural. Their forum was the literary and intellectual reviews and publishing houses the hussards created and dominated: *La Table ronde,* a publishing house as well as a review, *Opéra, La Parisienne, Rivarol,* and *Arts,* which was the most successful and long-lasting of the lot, where, as we have seen, the novels of young women writers were such a constant source of fascination and titillation.[16] Hussard reviews attracted some important centrists as well, namely François Mauriac, who found refuge from the witch-hunt mentality of the postwar purges as a member of the editorial board for *La Table ronde* until he left for *L'Express* in 1954.[17]

The ideology of the hussard esthetic was one of reaction against the ethos of seriousness, *engagement,* and ethical responsibility incarnated during the same period in the dominant figure of Sartre. Uncommitted art of the Jean Cocteau *Boeuf sur le Toit* genre was their mode. They perpetuated the spirit of 1925 in what Laurent's ally historian Raoul Girardet called "l'école de frivolité."[18] Cocteau's *Les Enfants terribles* is an important intertext for hussard novels in their emphasis on childhood, playfulness, and rejection of the adult world.[19] Their nostalgia for classicism and distaste for Romantic existentialism was political incorrectness for postwar times. Indeed, Nimier, Blondin, Laurent, et al claimed that the Fourth Republic had been put into place by the corrupt forces of the Resistance and brought with it the persecution of all elements of opposition, namely the Right. Peacetime profiteers, they argued, had little in common with France's real patriots—fervent members of the Resistance and equally fervent members of the Milice, a blurring of ideological differences that marks a typical strategy of the French Right.[20] Although the hussards' own right-wing politics were the underlying source of their dislike of both the Fourth Republic and *littérature engagée,* the autobiographical dimension of their novels and criticism was never a subject of critical conjecture or reproach. With support behind the scenes from older allies such as Jacques Chardonne, Paul Morand, and Marcel Aymé, understandably less visible in the 1950s in the wake of their Vichy connections (Morand, for example, was a Vichy ambassador), the members of the "école de frivolité" were, conversely, taken seriously in their various roles as writers, editors, and publishers.[21]

To write against littérature engagée in the late 1940s was, of course, deeply and incendiarily political. And with or against them, in light of the political sympathies of the hussards, the French press took them seriously as writers and cultural actors. Oddly enough, what made possible their actual impact was a novel that had nothing to do with fantasies of military glory or regal might, but instead followed many of the rules of the traditional "women's novel." Written by Vichyist Jacques Laurent under the pseudonym of Cécil Saint-Laurent, *Caroline chérie* (1947) is a historical romance following the picaresque adventures of its spirited heroine from her adolescence during the Revolution through the Directory.

Published in the same year as *La Peste,* at first *Caroline chérie* did not sell nearly as well as Camus's novel.[22] But, in the early 1950s, as nostalgia for a more remote past took hold of a public who no longer wished to be reminded of the Occupation, sales of Laurent's novel improved dramatically. At a time when French film production was also dominated by "tradition de qualité" adaptations of nineteenth-century novels and evocations of the Ancien Régime, *Caroline chérie* eventually became one of the best-sellers of the postwar years, generating the capital necessary for Laurent to create a forum in the media for the expression of his own hostility towards the enthronement of the Resistance in postwar culture.[23] Laurent founded the magazine *La Parisienne* in 1953, bought out the weekly *Arts* in 1954 and named himself editor-in-chief, and continued all the while his column in *La Table ronde.* Other young writers who shared the view that literature should be everything but *engagée* followed him.

The hussards painted themselves as victims—of the Left's domination of the postwar cultural arena, of a status quo that their ally at *Le Figaro* Louis Pauwels compared to the Terror, "avec ses conspirations du silence, ses censures anonymes et ses calomnies savamment vagues"[24] [with its conspiracies of silence, its anonymous censorship, and its savvily vague betrayals]. But the hussards did not take on the existentialists in debate; as Jacques Laurent wrote in *La Table ronde*, "on ne hait pas une époque dont les saints ressemblent à des clowns"[25] [how can you hate a time whose saints were more like clowns]? Indeed, for them the absurd was characterized by "les gens sérieux d'en face," their solemn neighbors at *Les Temps modernes.*[26] Whether or not they were victimized by Left conformism is debatable; what is clear is that the hussards enjoyed great social and financial success during their short reign over the Parisian literary scene. As in the case of the Romantics, their fiction and essays were taken as testimony of a generational disaffection, always situated in terms of the current political and esthetic climate—terms rarely evoked to understand young women writers: the Occupation, the Cold War, existentialism, and the *embourgeoisement* of French culture.

The best-known hussard was Roger Nimier, part literary James Dean, whose Jaguar sports car toted the six-volume Littré encyclopedia of the French language in the trunk, part salon fascist, whose iconoclastic politics ruffled the feathers of the liberal Left status quo.[27] Nimier was an admirer of Maurras and the Action française, but primarily in a personal equation of fascism and royalism with adventure, with a spiritual and esthetic order rather than a political one. As developed in the essays that comprise *Vingt ans en 1945*, his version of the mal du siècle borrowed heavily from Chateaubriand's analysis put forth in *Le Génie du christianisme:* the imbalance between an impoverished existence and an excess of culture, the fermentation of passions in search of a proper outlet, the aspiration to a metaphysical existence.[28] Nimier positioned himself as a reluctant spokesman for his peers, a generation of latecomers both in relation to the war and to the Left culture put into place in its aftermath: what he called the "académie de la révolution."[29] They rejected both Gaullism and collaboration, and while they admired the Romantics, their direction and tone had changed: "En comparaison, notre génération semble chargée de tous les péchés du monde. Elle indigne par sa légèreté. Après tant de ruines, on réclame des constructeurs" [In comparison, our generation seems to be charged with all the sins in the world. We offend by our light-heartedness. After so many ruins, people want builders]. The *école de frivolité* as a literary trend wanted to look nothing like the esthetic of *engagement*, but both arose from the experiences of World War II and the new threat of the Cold War. Hiroshima had taught young men that the world was "ni sérieux, ni durable,"[30] which made them at the very least the ideological interlocutors of the existentialists, for in their radical difference, both were literary responses to the same political and historical circumstances.

Hussard novels are replete with young men who neither build nor destroy, who find no place for themselves in the reduced political spectrum of their times. For example, Nimier's *Le Hussard bleu* is divided into a depiction of military service with the French First Army during its advance into Germany in 1944–45 and the regiment's ensuing occupation of an unnamed German town. As one of the young soldiers in the regiment describes his own wartime trajectory, he was able to pass from one ideological extreme to the next out of utter apathy: at first signing up for the Resistance, "par manque d'imagination" [out of a lack of imagination], followed by a brief flirtation with the Milice, and finally joining the Gaullist forces: "Les Anglais allaient gagner la guerre. Le bleu marine me va bien au teint. Les voyages forment la jeunesse. Ma foi, je suis resté"[31] [The English were going to win the war. Marine blue is a good color for me. Travel forms young minds. So I stayed]. Believing in nothing, bored in the peaceful German countryside, Nimier's young soldiers consciously court danger with their pleasure, albeit of an ideological sort, in conquests of local German women.

Though aware of the implicit scandalousness of liaisons with the vanquished enemy, the young soldiers themselves find their amorous adventures ultimately meaningless. For unlike the acts of Marguerite Duras's girl from Nevers in *Hiroshima mon amour* who falls tragically in love with a German soldier, the exploits of Nimier's fictional hussards are just as loveless as those of the female narrators of the antisentimental novel. There remains, however, a significant difference. In the antisentimental novel, it is the act of consummation that is essential, a scandalous turning away from love and romance, whether for sexual pleasure or as an efficient means to other ends. The fictional hussards, whiling away the hours in the wake of a war in which they did not believe, were more interested in the narrative of seduction—a more languorous process, it must be said, than the sexual act itself.

In hussard fiction, lack of desire is the primary symptom of the male characters' lack of political fervor and convictions, the autobiographical reference to politics providing a ready-made ideological frame for their studied sexual passivity. The female characters function as signifiers of the bankruptcy of the contemporary world: sexual frankness and detachment in young women disappoint young men who assert their apathy but are, in fact, in search of love and purity. In Michel Déon's *Les Gens de la nuit*, for example, Jean Dumont, bourgeois son of an aspirant to the Académie Française, returns to Paris from the Foreign Legion where he had sought refuge from a great romantic disappointment and takes a meaningless job in public relations. He falls in with a nocturnal underworld of young people whose connections to the Milice and drug trafficking belie their clear-headedness, sense of loyalty, and ethics. Despite his better judgement, he falls in love with one of the girls, Gisèle, who goes to bed with him, comes and goes in his daily life, and then leaves him definitively just when it looks as though she'll stay, all in a most undramatic way.[32]

Inappropriate behavior for a jeune fille. Reflecting the hussard view of modern girls who lose their virginity without sentiment or ceremony, the young hero of Jacques Laurent's novel *Le Petit canard* laments that "les jeunes filles d'aujourd'hui sont en réalité des jeunes gens"[33] [girls today are in fact boys]—a satirical jab and at the same time an acknowledgement of the social content of sexual behavior. Laurent's is a formula worth retaining. For critics writing about young women writers did not offer such provocative if elliptical theories about the blurring of gender lines, did not explore the relationship of fictions of female adolescence to the changing times. They chose instead to bring the protagonists' precocious and unsentimental sexual activity back to the author herself, a one-to-one equation noted by hussard critic Stephen Hecquet when he dryly remarked, "Mlle. Sagan [qui] s'appelle Cécile pour ses lecteurs."[34] The principal question for the critics remained that of feminine nature. Their interpretive grille never went beyond that of sexual psychology, recognizing the character of the female adolescent as a subject, yet placing her, titillatingly, outside of history, outside of the disturbing process of disappearance of a long-intact French way of life.

With the critics relegating the candid first-person narration of female sexuality to the domain of immanence, it is not surprising that numerous essays written in these years on the particularity of being young in the mid-century were inspired by the hussard state of mind, if not their real politics.[35] Following Nimier, Déon, and company, the critics equated generation and generational consciousness with masculinity, an equation whose coordinates were politics, current events, and history, and whose consistent yield was apathy. The causes of apathy can no more be neatly plotted than can those of sexual behavior. Both are a complicated amalgam of individual experience, psychology, and context. But the shocking first-person voice of sexual experience in the antisentimental novel could be summarily dismissed as immanent, as purely physical, and consigned to the realm of female psychology.

The hussards also practiced first-person narration, but they simultaneously said "we." Wise with their experience in journalistic and political circles, they took for themselves the privilege of speaking for their generation. Fictions of female adolescence defined the enfant terrible in terms of her sexual precociousness and dangerousness—inappropriate behavior for her age. In contrast, the writings of the hussards depict young men reluctant to leave the innocence of childhood behind, even though they are well beyond that biological age. Nimier, Blondin, and others claimed a place for their generation in history and current events as eternal children, as the narrator François Saunders explains on the first page of *Le Hussard bleu*:

> J'appartenais à cette generation heureuse qui aura eu vingt ans pour la fin du monde civilisé. On nous aura donné le plus beau cadeau de la terre: une époque où nos ennemis, qui sont presque toutes les grandes personnes, comptent pour du beurre. Votre confort, vos progrès, nous vous conseillons de les appliquer aux meilleurs systèmes d'enterrements collectifs . . .[36]

> [I belonged to that happy generation who will have turned twenty when the civilized world comes to an end. We will have been given the best gift on earth: a time when our enemies, who are almost all grownups, don't count for beans. Your comfort, your progress, we advise you to apply them to the best methods of collective burial.]

In 1956 many others followed up on Nimier's observation that young men lived in a world where nothing and no one mattered. Such an attitude exhibited a patent disregard for the dramatic shifts on the international political scene of the same year, events which sparked new ideological divisions in intellectual communities and in the French population in general: the Soviet invasion of Hungary, the publication of the Khrushchev report on the realities of Stalinism, and Prime Minister Guy Mollet's unexpected extension of military service to twenty-seven months, the latter affecting the very group the hussards spoke for, young men. In light of the official status of the "Algerian situation" as a euphemistic "war without a name," it is not surprising that essays about being young (and male) in postwar France made no mention of possible military glory in North Africa.[37] On the other hand, some simply found the war not worth fighting. Uninterested in whether or not Algeria remained French, Nimier wrote to his friend Antoine Blondin of an FRN (Front Roger Nimier, a pun on the FLN, the Algerian Front de Libération Nationale), and conceded with his best disrespect two years later that the return of De Gaulle was good for the nation, for at least he was a writer.[38]

Instead of focusing on current politics, the hussards spoke for a generation lost to history—thus inscribing them in history. In Antoine Blondin's *Les Enfants du bon dieu*,[39] the protagonist Sébastien is a thirty-year-old history teacher equally bored with his syllabus and married life. His solution: to invent and teach an imaginary national past. As the hussards saw it, their generation was condemned to waste their youth in the desert of contemporary culture. Paul Van Den Bosch followed the example of Roger Nimier and used the first person plural freely in his essay *Les Enfants de l'absurde*, whose title became yet another media label for postwar youth. Unlike Raymond Radiguet's adolescent protagonist François in *Le Diable au corps*, for whom World War I meant "quatre années de grandes vacances" [four years of summer vacation], Van Den Bosch situated young men as victims and survivors. Cheated and traumatized by the experience of the Occupation, they were "revenants" à la Musset, phantoms returning from a war in which they were too young to have participated.

More than any previous generation, he claimed, the postwar generation stood as children of the absurd, having experienced the dramas and disappointments of the Occupation and the Liberation together with the emotional turbulence of adolescence.[40] Disillusioned by the debunking of the national myth and the confessions of cowardice by members of the French army and the Resistance, boys saw their present as fragile and senseless.[41]

Ten years after the Liberation, they had become politically disaffected city dwellers (according to Van Den Bosch, the mal du siècle is always urban, a "mal de la ville" [42]). They believed in neither God nor country. For them, the world was a two-dimensional place where even one's own friends had lost their individuality and sex had become banal [43] —the very same ingredients of Romantic malaise described in Musset's *Confession d'un enfant du siècle*.

When hussards wrote about their contemporary culture, it was usually to comment on its vapidity and empty sensationalism. The goal of Michel Déon's *Lettre à un jeune Rastignac* was to expose a *tout-Paris* all too eager to have angry young men in its midst.[44] Written as a satirical manual for the young provincial newcomer to the capital, Déon's *Lettre* advised all Rastignacs to arrive bearing political opinions that conformed to the dominant Left—"Le rouge-clair se porte bien" [45] [a light red looks good]—and to become a writer, a profession requiring more savvy than talent. He went on to lampoon the 1950s publishing world, where a first novel should question man and country and highlight the anguish of being young and male. Above all, it should be written in order to shock:

> Vous n'êtes pas là pour plaire, mais pour créer un certain malaise, frôler la nausée. Cette société que vous méditez de conquérir a besoin d'avoir peur. Consciente de son embourgeoisement profond, elle aime que les fils de famille lui crachent à la figure. Insultez votre mère, faites de votre père un odieux tyran qui lutine la bonne et court à la messe après. Inventez un curé qui dit merde à son évêque, un sous-officier qui couche avec la colonelle.[46]

> [You're not here to please, but to create a certain malaise, to approach nausea. This society you dream of conquering needs to be scared. Aware of its profound embourgeoisement, it likes its sons to spit in its face. Insult your mother, make your father out to be an odious tyrant who fools around with the maid then runs off to Mass afterwards. Invent a priest who says shit to his bishop, an NCO who sleeps with the colonel's wife.]

The young Rastignac, one can assume, was not a hussard—at least not as the hussards presented themselves.

The provincial whom Déon lampooned was too energetic, too eager in his desire "not to please" in order to make a name for himself. The essential quality of hussard fiction is, rather, the absence of such eagerness: nothing much happens, there are no strong emotions, no tyrannical parents or

Enfants Terribles

passionate romances. Two years later, Déon developed this contrast between these two types of young men in his novel *Les Gens de la nuit:* the Americanized public-relations man pushing his account who works side by side with the insolent cynic. In a world where there was nothing to be angry about, the angry young man was a fabrication, Déon suggested, intimating that the authentic sentiment of apathy could be found among the depoliticized heirs of the political Right.

In a capital seeking sensation, which the hussards claimed not to desire to provide, the young Rastignac should himself aspire to become a subject of interest in the news, since the press had become a form of communication more important than ever before. Déon reflected upon a cultural moment in which literature had effectively become dependent on the popular press: "En 1956, Proust n'écrirait plus à Jacques Rivière, mais à Françoise Giroud. Il solliciterait une notule dans *Paris-Match* ou dans *Elle.* Il offrirait un extrait de son roman à *France-Dimanche* et souffrirait d'y être présenté de façon incongrue"[47] [In 1956, Proust would no longer write to Jacques Rivière, but to Françoise Giroud. He would solicit a small article in *Paris-Match* or *Elle.* He would offer an excerpt of his novel to *France-Dimanche* and suffer for being misrepresented]. Of course, reviews like *Arts, Rivarol,* and *La Table ronde* were just as active in circulating the names, faces, and writings of young authors. The hussards were very much part of the media world Déon satirized.

While Michel Déon signaled the media's pivotal role in determining the success of young writers, in *Les Garçons,* Stephen Hecquet noted that it was young men in general who had become omnipresent in contemporary media culture.[48] Hecquet, a lawyer whose polemical texts in *Dimanche matin* and *Bulletin de Paris* were greatly appreciated by the hussards, railed against a generation which had no sense of the specificity of their identity as young Frenchmen. Nevertheless, they were ubiquitous in the press, which seized upon their every move and word:

> Vous avez conquis un nom, une place. Je lis vos déplacements dans les journaux, j'entends vos émissions à la radio . . . A seize ans, l'on vous voit monopoliser les routes; à dix-huit ans, la littérature, le théâtre, la radio; à vingt ans, s'il vous plaît, le pouvoir est à vous![49]

> [You have conquered a name, a place. I read of your comings and goings in the newspapers, I hear your shows on the radio . . . At sixteen, we see you take over

the highways; at eighteen, literature, the theatre, the radio; at twenty, if you want it, power is yours!]

The energy of Hecquet's young men, like that of Déon's Rastignac, is a sure sign of the author's ironic distance from them. As in the case of Jean Dumont's jovial colleagues at the American-style public relations firm in *Les Gens de la nuit,* some young men could be perfectly integrated into the society the hussards found so empty and repugnant. Writing as heirs of an ideological school, the hussards spoke for a generation disaffected from ideology. But the literary aspect of their self-proclaimed outsider stance was only one piece of a cultural puzzle that communicated the sense of postwar youth, just as Déon and Hecquet both acknowledged. Along with the forum of the mass media and their tendency to sensationalize youth as "news," the "new science" of sociology and its requisite tool, the survey, approached the mal du siècle through the would-be objectivity of field research, leading to a sensationalism that asserted its indisputable truth-value. The ingredients of adolescent malaise in the post–World War II period had changed little from the time of the Romantics; the novelty lay in the mass media's power to disseminate this malaise as news to every sector of the French population, and the sociological claim to quantify it, putting adolescence in a radically different category from the lyrical and personal texts of Chateaubriand, Constant, and Musset, or even the insolent novels of disillusionment of the hussards.

Existential Style

The notorious stance of the hussards set the stage for identifying the mal du siècle of the postwar generation along the lines of a dramatic binary division: if not passively against Sartre, then with him. The fiction and essays of the hussards advocated facing the new mal du siècle with frivolity; the popular press linked the same malaise to existentialism and the unconventional way of life of certain young people who frequented Saint-Germain-des-Prés. What did it mean in the popular imagination to be with Sartre, to be an existentialist? It had little to do with the politics and esthetics of *engagement,* and everything to do with late nights out—for teenagers of both sexes. Devoid of its philosophical content, existentialism was the first postwar youth culture, in which, in the eyes of the French press and their reading public, young men and women took on the personae of survivors.

On 3 May 1946, *Samedi-Soir* headlined an interview with Prime Minister Charles de Gaulle, who had just announced his departure from office. Even more eye-catching than the headline was a photograph, three columns wide. Two young people stand at the top of a decrepit stairwell. The disheveled young man holds a candle; the young woman stares away from him vacantly. The enigmatic caption reads: "Je voudrais renaître en catastrophe de chemin de fer" [I would like to be reborn in a railroad accident].[50] The photograph and accompanying article by Jacques Robert, "Voici comment vivent les troglodytes de Saint-Germain-des-Prés" [Here's how the troglodytes of Saint-Germain-des-Prés live], launched Saint-Germain-des-Prés by equating it, quite wrongly, with existentialism.

Whereas the pair in the *Samedi-Soir* article, filmmaker Roger Vadim and actress Juliette Gréco, were unknown at the time, another image of a couple in defiance of bourgeois norms had already been associated with Saint-Germain-des-Prés: Jean Paul Sartre and Simone de Beauvoir. By 1947, the "existentialist offensive," as Beauvoir called the sudden surge of public interest in Sartre and herself,[51] was well under way. It was not as much the first issue of *Les Temps modernes* of October 1945 that had triggered the couple's status as it was a lecture Sartre gave in the same month: "L'Existentialisme est-il un humanisme?" Sartre's lecture, an inquiry into the possibilities of a nonpartisan, philosophical relationship to Marxism and the political role of the intellectual, drew a standing-room-only crowd, and was the cultural event of the year.[52] In response to the turnout if not to the subject, the next day's papers, from highbrow to lowbrow, treated the lecture as if it had been a rock concert, starring Sartre.[53] In the competition for readership in the postwar press (thirty-four new dailies appeared in 1945), Sartre became the first media personality of the period and his October lecture, one of the first media events.[54] Some critics hailed Sartre as a genius; others warned that he was destroying the tradition of the French bourgeois novel and—just as significantly—that he was a corrupter of young minds.[55]

Samedi-Soir was the first paper to link existentialism and Sartre himself to youth and their postwar malaise, and the equation was a hostile one. As one journalist wrote in 1945, "To the hairy adolescents of Saint-Germain-des-Prés, he is the 'master.' For all right-thinking citizens, he is a murderer."[56] In *Les Gens de la nuit*, Michel Déon referred to the ridiculous tendency in the popular press to accuse Sartre of third-degree crimes where unhappy youth were involved. The narrator reads an article in an unnamed magazine that claims that the suicide of a young woman was the philosopher's fault when, in reality, she was involved with drug running: "Maggy s'était tuée parce que la rongeait le «mal du siècle». Elle était une victime de Sartre sans l'avoir lu"[57] [Maggy killed herself because the "mal du siècle" was destroying her. She was a victim of Sartre without having read him]. With its hysterical tone, *Samedi-Soir* was instrumental in creating an image of a band of wild Left Bank youth with Sartre at their helm at odds with the bourgeois status quo. Before the publication of *Le Deuxième sexe* in 1949, Beauvoir's notoriety obtained primarily from her defiantly antibourgeois status as the female companion, and not the wife, of such a figure.

Jacques Robert's article was more lighthearted, a tongue-in-cheek ethnography. He described everything and everyone he encountered as "existentialist"; a map of the area accompanied the article, along with the daily schedule of the typical existentialist, as he or she wandered from café to bar to café to *cave* to bar, and a physical description of the male and the female of the species. Heterosexuality and gender parity were the necessary but unexamined bases of Robert's presentation of the existentialist world, making it a recognizable and unthreatening society. Others — Déon's novel *Les Gens de la nuit,* Marcel Carné's film *Les Tricheurs* — would evoke bisexuality, homosexuality, and transsexuality, truly the stuff of the underworld for the 1950s and not subject material for the daily papers.[58] Robert did not aim to shock, but to entertain: his playful association of young people, Left Bank Paris, existentialism, and an aimless daily life, nevertheless, became one of the origins of a cultural myth of postwar youth that continues to hold today. But the *engagement* the hussards found so pointless in literature and in life is nowhere to be seen in this image of "existentialist" youth. Instead, they displayed a listlessness and an absence of purpose, which, much like the hussard attitude, was at odds with the energetic mood deemed necessary to *le redressement national,* the social, economic, political, and above all moral recovery from wartime.[59]

In an interpretive leap, Robert characterized the incongruous combination of mania and lethargy he saw in Saint-Germain-des-Prés clubs as the attitude of those who lived their lives "sans doute dans l'attente de la bombe atomique qui leur est chère"[60] [undoubtedly waiting for the atomic bomb that is dear to them]. In obvious ignorance of Sartrian thought, he declared his existentialists to be paralyzed by the sense that nuclear war was imminent:

Certaines nuits, les existentialistes, qu'on n'aperçoit plus qu'à travers un brouillard, se lancent en hurlant dans des jitterbugs et des boogie-woogies forcenés. Mais le plus souvent, complètement prostrés, ils restent assis, en regardant fixement leur verre d'eau tiède. Alors on est frappé de voir leurs jeunes visages si pâles, leurs regards fanés, le découragement de chacun de leurs gestes. La plupart d'entre eux n'ont pas mangé.[61]

[Some nights, the existentialists, whom you can only see through the fog, throw themselves shrieking into deranged jitterbugs and boogie-woogies. But most often, completely despondent, they stay in their seats, staring at their glass of lukewarm water. Then you're struck by their young faces that are so pale, their wan expression, the despondency of every gesture. Most of them haven't eaten.]

Robert went to Saint-Germain des Prés seeking a survivor mentality generated by recent events and located it in tired and broke club-goers. His description of Parisian youth who punctuated their nuclear pessimism with occasional wild dancing, the likes of which had never before been seen in France, was funny and generally harmless. The one glaring error was to call them existentialists and Sartre their *maître à penser*. Sartre insisted, in vain, that he had nothing to do with "those young people," and that they had nothing to do with him. Many were bourgeois; some of them were or had been members of the Communist Party. Others were more influenced by surrealism than by phenomenology.[62] In the view of Anne-Marie Cazalis, one of the "muses" of Saint-Germain-des-Prés, young people had never been less philosophical.[63] But even she resorts to the facile label to describe the *cave* ambiance: "Le jitterburg (sic) plut aux existentialistes parce que c'était une danse violente et abstraite, qui rapproche et repousse pour rapprocher encore. Mais sans équivoque et sans passion"[64] [Existentialists liked the jitterbug because it was a violent and abstract dance in which two people come together, then separate, then come together again. But without equivocation or passion].

With the assimilation of existentialism into youth and Left Bank club culture, it quickly became a "look," a style of dress rather than a way to live or think.[65] In a very different register from Robert's article in *Samedi-Soir*, psychologist Georges Amado set out to both diagnose and document the existentialists in a 1951 issue of *La Nef* devoted to the so-called mal du siècle. References to philosophical argument are noticeably absent. Along with describing the mal du siècle as if it were the symptoms of an early stage of mental illness, Amado painstakingly documented for his readers what young people were *wearing* in Saint-Germain-des-Prés—a style that, according to his analysis, served the purpose of mutual recognition. His detailed description merits quotation at length:

> Les garçons portent les cheveux longs et volontiers la barbe, leur col ouvert laissant apercevoir une chaîne ornée de médailles et beloques. Leurs blousons, leurs vareuses et leurs pantalons retroussés proviennent de stocks américains ou ont été empruntés ou donnés. Leurs pieds sont souvent nus dans des sandales découvertes, ou bien ils portent des bottines de toile, autrefois chaussures de sport, aujourd'hui de danse.
>
> Les filles laissent leurs cheveux raides, sans artifices apparents, et n'usent pas de fards, à moins qu'elles n'en fassent un usage excessif. Elles sont vêtues d'un pantalon étroit et affectionnent la couleur, noire, qui en ajoute à la tristesse de leur teint blafard, de leurs yeux battus, de leur maigreur et de leur moue désabusée. Nous ne saurions trop faire remarquer l'aspect lamentable de ces jeunes gens, leur regard insaisissable, lointain et inaccessible, qui n'est pas toujours seulement affecté.[66]

[The boys have long hair and beards, their open collars reveal chains decorated with medallions. Their leather jackets, their pea coats, and their rolled-up pants come from American stocks or were given to them or borrowed. Their feet are often bare in exposed sandals, or they wear canvas shoes, at one time athletic shoes, today dance shoes.

The girls leave their hair straight, and don't style it in any obvious way. They don't wear makeup, or they wear too much. They dress in snug pants, and are fond of the color black, which adds to the sadness of their pale complexion, the circles under their eyes, their thinness, and their disillusioned pout. We couldn't overestimate how pathetic these young people look, their elusive gaze, far away and inaccessible, which is not always only affected.]

Again we witness the importance of gender-inclusiveness, this time to lend a tone of authenticity to the ethnological description. Amado's article appeared in the very moment that the discourses of sociology and anthropology were becoming increasingly present in the intellectual field. Claude Lévi-Strauss's *Structures élémentaires de la parenté*, where he developed the notion of the binary division between nature and culture and the principle of the exchange of women, was published in 1949. In 1950, the Presses Universitaires de France (PUF) created the Bibliothèque de sociologie contemporaine series, edited by Georges Gurvitch, with Marcel Mauss's

Sociologie et anthropologie and Gurvitch's *Vocation actuelle de la sociologie* among the first titles. In 1951, PUF published Germaine Dieterlen's *Essai sur la religion bambara,* the first systematic description of the rituals of a specific populace. In the same year, Louis Dumont applied ethnographical methods to the study of local folklore in his book *La Tarasque.*[67] Amado's article is a popularization of this sort of discourse but, nevertheless, one that takes itself seriously, presenting the male and the female of the species who distinguish themselves from mainstream society, among other ways, by their dress. The "existentialist look" was in direct opposition to the norm: for young men, open-collared shirts and sandals at a time when ties and suits were still de rigueur, and for young women, an intentional disregard for traditional feminine attractiveness: straight hair instead of teased, pants instead of skirts, black instead of pastels, gauntness instead of curves.

Amado's interest in fashion was decidedly ethnological, as were his observations of everyday life in the quarter. In *Samedi-Soir,* Robert's article was tongue-in-cheek; Amado took himself for Lévi-Strauss or Dieterlen and described young people as if they were a tribe in a far-off land. On their eating habits, he observed, "Il est . . . bien vu d'exhiber, en entrant dans un café, une baguette de pain, représentant tout le repas, et dont chacun se servira au passage" [It is well looked upon to exhibit, upon entering a café, a baguette, which represents the entire meal, and from which each person will serve himself in passing]. On the custom among bourgeois youth turned beggars of selling their clothing to each other, he went as far as to develop his own theory of exchange: "la vente ou l'échange de ses propres vêtements réalise dans le groupe une sorte de mouvement de permutation circulaire" [the sale or exchange of one's own clothing within the group creates a sort of movement of circular permutation].[68] For the contemporary reader, the ethnological terminology that Amado used to ascribe a tribal meaning to the daily behavior of Latin Quarter youth makes his comments funny in spite of his scholarly intentions. In view of the fact that *La Nef* was a reputable journal, one can hypothesize, however, that his ethnography of the mal du siècle was taken as seriously by his readers at the time as he seems to have taken it himself.

For Georges Amado, the young existentialists' style of clothing, their taste in music, the way they danced, and their everyday life, expressed the morose world view of survivors expecting the next disaster: a desire to believe in nothing, to remain passive, to have no hopes or goals. Nihilism was the only admissible way to think and live—a far cry from the *engagement* with which the denizens of Saint-Germain-des-Prés were first associated, and while lacking their frivolity, an attitude remarkably close to the hussards. As French culture imagined the new mal du siècle, it transcended ideological division of Left and Right, all in remaining vaguely political.

Amado viewed Saint-Germain-des-Prés as a psychologically dangerous place for young people; as late as 1958, Marcel Carné would make the association between Left Bank youth and criminality in his film *Les Tricheurs*. The media brought together existentialism, youth, and Saint-Germain-des-Prés in a category that could accommodate all that was considered deviant, marginal, dangerous, and anarchic.[69] However wrong the label as the media used it may have been, it nevertheless kept the subjects of the Occupation and its aftermath in circulation—subjects which were still too ideologically divisive to take on in the context of the nation as a whole.

The equation of existentialism with youth culture ended as quickly as it had begun. With the appearance of an article in *Life* magazine, Saint-Germain-des-Prés no longer belonged exclusively to the young or to the French. Adults and tourists descended upon the quarter and into the nightclubs, and the reign of youth there came to an end.[70] By 1952, *Elle* was surveying young people to see whether existentialism was passé.[71] In 1953, *Marie-Claire* reported that a police squad had received several letters denouncing Beauvoir and Sartre for having perverted the youth of Saint-Germain-des-Prés. When brought in for questioning, the young people had never even heard of the famous couple.[72] The media was just as capable of separating youth from existentialism as it was of linking them.

The J-3 Affair

The image of existentialist youth as survivors did not remain gender-inclusive for long. The association of the mal du siècle with criminality brought with it the sense that young men were particularly victimized by wartime trauma and the new threats of the Cold War, while their female counterparts were capable of generating new forms of danger and disillusionment in the emotional realm. This formulation of the post–World War II mal du siècle culminated in a notorious *fait divers*. The actual event took place in 1948, but served as fodder for the popular imagination well into the mid-decade. The "J-3 affair," as it was named in the press, was a murder committed by a group of adolescents. The facts of the case are minimal. In Melun, sixteen-year-old Claude Panconi shot and killed his classmate Alain Guyader, on the advice of Bernard Petit and with the consent of Nicole I. (as the only minor, her last name remains off the record), a girl both Panconi and Guyader were courting. The reason for the shooting was that Alain had kissed Nicole. Panconi admitted to the murder the next day.

Faits divers, what we call in English human interest stories, are the small curiosities and tragedies in the lives of ordinary people grouped together in the newspaper. They include strange suicides, murders, and crimes: *"chiens écrasés,"* as the French slang goes. Far from front-page news in every way, faits divers nevertheless capture the attention of readers; minimal explanation and background information allow for all sorts of conjecture and everyman theories. They intrigue intellectuals as well. As facts without context, comprehensible without need for outside knowledge, faits divers in their narrative components were a useful corpus for structuralism; for historians on the other hand they are signs of the specificity of a cultural moment.[73] Faits divers inscribe themselves in the interstices of events and institutions, compete with them as a source of history and social memory. Because of the superficial information relayed and the ordinariness of the people involved, the reader's experience is one of an uneasy identification. We can and cannot recognize ourselves in what happened: "It could have been me . . . I couldn't have done that." The J-3 Affair was a fait divers through which this sort of uneasy identification transpired on a national level, making it into a front-page event. The Melun youths' testimony brought to the cultural surface fragments of the recent unsavory past in which 1950s France could not and would not recognize itself, and the media followed through. The Melun murder was converted into the narrative of a generation warped in childhood by the experience of the Occupation, who as adolescents were making the contemporary world a dangerous place to live in.

The coverage of the J-3 Affair and trial in its most minute detail can be found in a book by French Academy member Joseph Kessel, tellingly entitled *Le Procès des enfants perdus.*[74] Kessel recounted how Panconi's initial confession to the murder was full of dramatic references to the war: arms traffickers, Resistance fighters, espionage and counter-espionage, statements quickly revealed to be false. When pressed to further explain their deed, Panconi and Petit told how Guyader, their victim, had been embroiled with Nazis, collaborators, black market millionaires, and other shady wartime characters, which also turned out to have been pure fabrication. But the boys had actually believed Guyader's tales. The fantasized yet deadly serious connections to the Occupation, and not the actual murder, was what made the J-3 Affair an especially provocative fait divers for its time. According to Kessel, the case signaled a profound change in the inner life of the nation's youth. Instead of make-believe cowboys and Indians peopling their fantasies, there was now the nightmare of history, the world they had witnessed as children during the Occupation.

When the case came to trial in 1951, the Occupation was at center stage in the courtroom and in the media. Lawyers for the defense argued that the moral chaos of the Occupation was to blame for the otherwise incomprehensible crime of the Melun youth. In the oblique references that newspapers made to the recent shameful past, an uneasy identification is clearly at work. "Society" and "the times" were euphemistically deemed causal factors of the crime. In *Le Figaro*, Pierre Seize commented that even if the Melun youth were not representative of their generation, "ils sont tout de même le produit d'une époque" [even so, they are a product of their times]. In *Arts*, Benjamin Peret expiated the Melun youth, whom society, he wrote, had taught to be assassins.[75]

Novelist Maurice Descotes suggested much the same thing when he wrote in *La Nef* that the sentencing of the Melun youth was proof that "the century" did not know how to explain the attitude and behavior of its own youth, for whom it was, nevertheless, responsible.[76] Descotes, author of a 1951 novel whose plot bears a strong resemblance to the J-3 Affair (one boy shoots another who brags about having fought in the Resistance),[77] had the following theory about the effects of the Occupation on youth: as ten year olds in 1940, they had passively witnessed horrors that adults on all sides committed. By 1945, Resistance fighters, whom they had learned were heroes, had once again become ordinary people, and the overturning of values was complete. Soon after, newspapers, books, theatre, and films proclaimed the next apocalypse: the menace of nuclear war.[78] From past trauma, youth were catapulted into present fear. But the judge and the jury did not give credence to the Occupation or the Cold War as a defense of the J-3 murder. Panconi ended up serving a ten-year sentence, and Petit five.

In the transition from ration category to fait divers to national event, J-3 became a generational condition, psychology emerging from history in a one-to-one relationship: "children of the absurd" born of the Occupation and the Cold War. Victims of the moral, political, and psychological disorder that adults had put into place, they were now making victims of each other. The J-3 Affair made it possible to elliptically evoke the effects of recent history and current paranoia on the nation as a whole. Was France a victim of Germany or an accomplice? What were the psychological, political, and moral repercussions for the nation of surviving those ambiguous times only to live in fear of annihilation? To filter such difficult questions through the category of youth allowed the nation to come to a kind of uneasy identification with their recent past and uncertain present that was the only form of confrontation with shame and vulnerability possible.

Faits divers from the popular press had previously inspired novelists like André Gide, whose *Faux-Monnayeurs* also takes up the subject of adolescents playing with politics. But film could bring such journalistic curiosities to a much larger audience.[79] In *Avant le déluge,* a 1954 film based on the J-3 Affair, André Cayatte took on the moral, political, and psychological dimensions of victimization and survival as incarnated in youth that this particular fait divers brought to the surface in the early postwar years.[80] If people had not been aware of the J-3 Affair before, it became impossible to ignore with the wide distribution of Cayatte's film, which quickly gained notoriety both in France and abroad as an urgent message about troubled youth. Profits from an avant-premiere in Paris, for example, went to an organization for abandoned and "morally endangered" children.[81] *Avant le déluge* marked the culmination of the notoriety of the J-3 Affair.

Avant le déluge takes place in 1950 Paris where Cold War paranoia reigns, where adolescent boys fight in the schoolyard over which superpower they side with. In order to fund their escape from the third world war they fear is imminent, a group of high school students plot a robbery, which they bungle, inadvertently killing a night watchman. To cover up the crime, they murder the boy who lent them his car. Generally speaking, all of the characters in *Avant le déluge*, parents and children alike, are caricatures who serve Cayatte's moral purpose: to exonerate the boys, whose acts are portrayed as fully predetermined by the nexus of historical moment, social milieu, and family influence, and blame, on one level, the parents — the Nazi sympathizer, the exploitive businessman, the bitter abandoned wife — as if the parents were not equally products of historical and familial forces beyond their control.

Cayatte's fictionalized film version of the J-3 Affair is literally unbelievable. Paradoxically, it is *too* historical, bringing in connections to the Occupation and the Cold War that were absent from the original fait divers. His J-3s take shape within the major binary divisions that wartime had put into play and were still a delicate subject a decade later: resistance versus collaboration and *engagement* versus apathy. Moreover, Cayatte went beyond the facts and made the primary victim Jewish. Daniel (Roger Coggio) the orphan survivor of his deported family, is a frail, sensitive intellectual who lives in a garret apartment, its walls covered with images of sunsets and palm trees. He spends his days playing island music while taking long hot baths for his nervous condition. The echoes of Marat are not gratuitous — the murder actually takes place in the bathtub.

André Bazin categorized the unbelievability of *Avant le déluge* by terming it, with intentional ambivalence, "un nouveau type de film social."[82] Bazin was referring to the mise en scène itself. The film is ostensibly realist, but it is simultaneously too efficient and too logical, leaving no room for ambiguity. For Bazin, filmic realism required a certain ambiguity, a certain mystery, in the montage and the relationship between image and text in order to provoke a range of sentiments in the viewer. But the needed space for ambiguity in *Avant le déluge* is taken up by clearly stated ideas. Bazin called Cayatte's dependence on ideas to structure his mise en scène "une réalité sans reste,"[83] reality with nothing left over, characters and acts in exact proportion to the concepts they served. An emotional reaction to *Avant le déluge* was impossible for Bazin, who entitled his article "La Cybernétique d'André Cayatte" and concluded by wondering when the robots would revolt. Cayatte's translation of a written fait divers into film effaces the ambiguities of identification and dehumanizes the actors by reducing them to ideas. This is ironic indeed, for the anonymous criminals now have a physical presence, family history, and personal motives.

When youth becomes a reified figure for the ideological conflicts of politics and history, how does gender come into play? In the original fait divers, Nicole, the girl whom both boys wanted to impress, was just a name, a person of little importance. In Joseph Kessel's analysis of the trial, she steals the show. As the ostensible cause of the murder, she was the person who most intrigued the public.[84] While Panconi comes across as a hero, a tortured soul who writes poetry in his cell and is willing to shoulder all the blame, Nicole performs the role of an adolescent femme fatale when she takes the stand. She pronounces Alain Guyader's name without visible emotion, doesn't cry when she tells about the murder, shows remorse solely for having let Alain kiss her, and only demonstrates emotion when she speaks about a girlfriend who refused to see her because of the scandal surrounding the affair. With such a description, Kessel insinuates that Nicole, exonerated by the jury, was in fact the most guilty one of all.

Kessel's insinuation of Nicole's guilt is realized filmically in *Avant le déluge*, in which the character of Liliane (Marina Vlady) becomes a veritable, though protean, actor in the crime. Through her character, a certain ambiguity and trouble do indeed surface in the "cybernetic" mise en scène that Bazin critiqued. In a world of ideological conflict where the choices seem to be limited to either/or, she generates a third position: that of the outsider, the observer. Despite, or possibly because of, her observer position, Liliane can commit baneful action, avoid the politically generated victimization to which her male counterparts tend to fall prey, and elude all verdicts, guilty or innocent, active or passive, a position whose advantage is revealed in her ultimate, and ambiguous, survival.

While Liliane's male friends are overdetermined and essentially victimized by their parents' politics and war memories, Liliane remains impervious within her own family, the most politically committed of all. Her father (Bernard Blier), who happens to be the boys' philosophy teacher (Liliane is even an outsider to this academic configuration), is an antifascist activist; her brother (Paul Bissiglia) is a militant communist old enough to remember the Occupation. The two men are in passionate political opposition. Each is so devoted to his cause that they forget about Liliane, for whom the troubles of adolescence and first love with Richard (Jacques Fayet), the Jewish boy's eventual murderer, are more important than any political rally. The only girl in a group of boys obsessed with the Cold War, the only girl in a family of politicized men, Liliane always remains outside the ideological battleground.

Liliane claims to be scared of a nuclear war because Richard is scared; she takes on his opinions and his fears. But her act is not convincing; she does not *feel* the mal du siècle as he does. Reminiscent of Cocteau's enfant terrible Elisabeth, she theatrically plays the role of the girlfriend. Liliane's character is not in service to any ideas or ideals; she clearly couldn't care less about an imminent World War III. She rejects both sides of the ideological division within her family: her father's antinuclear rallies and her brother's youth group Jeunesses Communistes. Politics and the news are literally just background noise for Liliane. In one long shot, she waits for Richard at an entrance to the métro, a bored look on her face, while newspaper vendors loudly hawk Cold War headlines. While her father reads the humanist newspaper *Combat*, and her brother the Communist *L'Humanité*, Liliane uses newspapers to make her own practical point. She interrupts one of the many ideological spats between her father and her brother when she appears in the kitchen doorway in a "dress" she has scotch-taped together from old issues of *L'Humanité*—her brother's "documentation," as he cries aggrievedly after reading a headline on her derrière—to make the point that she hasn't had a new outfit in ages.

Liliane's preferred reading material consists of novels. She has three books on her night table: two detective novels and Vernon Sullivan's, a.k.a. Boris Vian's, *J'Irai cracher sur vos tombes*. In one scene her father examines their covers at great length while the camera lingers pointedly over his shoulder. *J'Irai cracher sur vos tombes* was itself implicated in a notorious fait divers of 1947. A salesman murdered his female friend in a small hotel in Montparnasse and left Vian's novel open to the scene of the murder next to the corpse. The murder resulted in a trial and a fine of 100,000 francs for Vian, who was charged with offending public morality. The moral message of Cayatte's *mise en abyme* could not have been clearer for the French public in 1954: from reading novels like these, real life plots and murders were only a step away. The long shot of the novels' covers is yet another cog in Cayatte's cybernetic, overdetermined universe and is meant to explain Liliane's eventual behavior. Just as the boys act out the implications of their parents' activities during the Occupation and in the current political climate, fiction determines Liliane's role in the crime. But the parallel is not a clean one. Unlike the salesman of Montparnasse under the influence of Vian, Liliane does not commit the murder; she takes on neither the male role of the criminal nor the female role of the victim from Vian's novel. Conceivably, though, it is fiction that allows her to generate a position for herself from which she can act—for history and politics have not furnished her with that desire.

Liliane's father says to her: "Avec ton frère, le difficile, c'est ses opinions. Avec toi, c'est autre chose" [With your brother, the difficult thing is his opinions. With you, it's something else]. Just what that something else is is never really articulated in the film except for the father's comment that if Liliane's mother were still alive, "le difficile" would somehow miraculously disappear. That is too easy an answer, especially in a film where history and politics are such heavily determinative factors. "Le difficile" does not originate in Liliane's beliefs, since she seems to have none, nor in tensions with her father. Unlike the boys, she has a parent with a good

Fig. 13. *Avant le deluge:* father-daughter complicity
Photo © 1954–Studiocanal Image/Documento Film

heart who wants to have an open relationship, a sort of complicity. It is a complicity, though, where Liliane is always in control.

In one crucial scene, image and text are not in perfect synchrony; Liliane does not act out the implications of parental behavior as her male friends do. It is a scene of verbal seduction—where Liliane's sexuality is the subject—and it is implausible from start to finish. Recalling the lament of François Mauriac and Jacques Laurent that the demure jeune fille who prized her chastity had become an endangered species, Liliane announces matter-of-factly to her father that she is no longer a virgin: "je ne suis plus une petite fille," and his face registers shock and horror (fig. 13). Unshaken, she tells him that she has acquired all her ideas about freedom and love from his home-delivered discourses on philosophy and reminds him that her mother was six months pregnant when they got married. There is a crucial moment of silence before Liliane's father breaks into a proud smile; he puts his hands on her shoulders and says, "Les pères s'imaginent toujours que c'est un fils qui va les continuer. Moi, c'est ma fille" [Fathers always imagine that their sons will carry on their name. In my case, it's my daughter]. The father's unlikely pride in Liliane's ability to argue for the connection between her precocious sexual activity, the abstract concept of freedom, and her deceased mother as a sexually experienced bride is facilitated by the mother's absence, an absence we have previously seen as the catalyst for father-daughter complicity in *Bonjour tristesse* and the Astra margarine advertisement. In all three of these cases, the complicity is nevertheless inscribed within the daughter's need, desire, and disturbingly powerful capacity to please her father.

While Liliane is capable of winning her father over with words, seduction is her explicit role in the attempted robbery. Once again she is implausible in a role too sophisticated for her gawky age. Dressed for the part of the temptress, she lures the man the boys want to rob away from his home to a nightclub in Saint-Germain-des-Prés. Liliane was not at the scene of the crime. From this position of "innocence," she is free to set her own plot into motion, not for any ideological cause, but to save Richard. In order to blame the night watchman's murder on the freshly murdered Daniel, she has the idea of making Daniel's death look like a suicide. Liliane sneaks into his apartment in order to plant the murder weapon there and turn on the gas, while the corpse still lies slumped in the tub.

Here again one is struck by the film's unbelievability, although on a different register from overhistoricization or from the ideological overdetermination of the characters and their actions. While it has been difficult up to now to define Liliane's behavior as either active or passive, her maneuvers in this scene are more evil than the boys' two murders combined. The first of these murders was unpremeditated, the second, as Cayatte wants us to believe, was the logical outcome of Richard's father's anti-Semitic harangues. Liliane, on the other hand, plots her own baneful actions in the knowledge that, as an outsider to the murder, she is above suspicion. When the verdicts are handed down at the trial's end, the boys are each condemned to sentences of varying lengths; Liliane, as we might expect, gets off scot-free.

Cayatte does not intend to make Liliane a likeable character, nor do I. Sweet and disengaged on the surface, calculating and tenacious below, she is more a child of the sensationalistic novels she reads than of her father's tolerant humanism. But even they cannot fully explain her behavior, the vague "autre chose" to which he refers. Rather than choose sides in the ideological battleground of current events, she observes it. When she does act, whether to seduce her father or help out her beau, her actions are manipulative and underhanded. And while not ultimately effective, neither do her actions lead to any sort of punishment, as they do for her male friends. Like Geneviève in *Le Repos du guerrier,* Liliane victimizes boys who have already been traumatized by wartime with nothing but her own happy ending in mind. Geneviève stands at the gates of the clinic as Renaud is led inside; Liliane is left alone in the courthouse as her male accomplices are led away to jail. At a physical remove that translates their emotional detachment from the politically generated angst of young men, Liliane and Geneviève as enfants terribles come to figure in these texts as an exacerbating factor of the 1950s' mal du siècle, its ultimate external cause.

But the endings of these texts also elucidate an angst particular to the young female, now familiar from the antisentimental novels discussed in the previous chapter. More nuanced in the case of Geneviève, who narrates from a position of sexual masochism and conflicted pleasure, the contempt we come to feel for the enfants terribles of Cayatte and Rochefort is worth examining more closely, as an indication of the very nature of the female experience of the contemporary mal du siècle: in a word, turning guilt into narrative. Never fully articulated as such yet well-understood by the reader/viewer, the guilt of Liliane and Geneviève is directly traceable to their sexual misbehavior: precocious, deromanticized, obsessive. Why the elision of guilt and inappropriate female sexuality in fictional texts where the recent memory of the Occupation and the threat of the Cold War lurk? The feminization of political ignorance, of attention to material comfort and "le bonheur personnel," is a vehicle which serves to dismiss as frivolous the urge to close the book on the Occupation and its murky questions. Frivolity, though, is not guilt.

Avant le déluge and *Le Repos du guerrier* play upon the desire to neatly and titillatingly locate a victimizer to contain all that was unspeakable, inassimilable to the ongoing characterization of young men as victims, a cipher for the French nation during World War II. But narratives are only neat for those who desire them to be so. We feel contempt for Liliane and Geneviève at the same time that we are immersed in the narrativization of their guilt; we identify with them uneasily as ambivalent survivors. Cayatte would have Liliane's survival and guilt excised—but male and female characters play their parts together, political and sexual; her narrative is there to be read on the same level as theirs. And in *Le Repos du guerrier,* before Geneviève's unconvincing disavowal of guilt, the reader observes how the roles of victim and victimizer have shifted both socially and sexually in the course of the novel. Such fictional entanglements suggest a way of seeing

France's own entanglement during wartime: both victim and victimizer, a real simultaneity that has long proven painful to grasp as national history.[85] By putting the sexualized young female on parallel trial as the sign of all that was wrong, unnatural, and impure in postwar France, Cayatte imagined a way to repudiate and excise national shame. But in the case of France during the Occupation, the narrative of guilt is so subtly woven into the national experience that the ease with which Cayatte—and the viewer—can ascribe blame speaks largely to the all-too-human desire to find a scapegoat—our own victim—in a history and in stories where complete innocence is hard to find.

Enfants Terribles

4 Technological Society and Its Discontents

As *Avant le déluge* showed, the unpredictable trajectory of the teenage girl as French culture imagined her in the 1950s bears little resemblance to the long-standing prescriptions for the *jeune fille*. With no maternal role model in sight, Liliane finds guidelines for behavior and strategies of self-determination in popular culture—the movie star vamp, the scheming accomplice to murder. But what is always intimated to be bad behavior is also always punished in the end. Even as French culture lamented her disappearance, the jeune fille consistently haunts narratives and images of the sexually knowing teenage girl in the post–World War II period, closing the door abruptly on the vista of freedom and possibility and leaving solitude and guilt in their stead: for Liliane, for Geneviève in *Le Repos du guerrier*, Odile in *La Sensitive*, Cécile in *Bonjour tristesse*.

As the ambiguities of France's wartime role receded in national memory, the cultural context for the discomfort that such punishment for bad behavior translated became, conversely, the nation's awareness of its lurking future. By the mid-1950s, France's sense of national identity was being tested from two directions: Algeria and the United States. How to imagine France without the *département* of Algeria? With the growing influence of American culture and the accompanying encroachment of technology, what would become of the French way of life? This chapter looks at how youth figures in connections, both real and represented, between these two aspects of France's own troubling loss of intactness: the rise of an Americanized technological society and the war for Algerian independence, for which two to three million young men were called up to defend French interests. In the aggregation of these social, economic, and political tensions, the discursive shift from the existentialists and J-3s of the previous chapter entails a depoliticization that is simultaneous to the reality of military conscription, as youth became an economic category: the *copain,* a fun-loving consumer of American-style pop music and its accoutrements. This depoliticized image of youth was overturned by the mid-1960s, through the same channels of the Algerian war and consumer culture, in a repoliticization whose dramatic culmination arrived in May 1968.

As consumers and copains, the line between young men and young women became increasingly diffuse. Youth of both sexes were sharply defined in contrast to their parents by advertisers, manufacturers, and the music industry, all of whom surely saw the economic potential of discourses on the generation gap already in circulation. Wartime victims and survivors were relegated to the annals of history. The accent was now on gender-inclusive "fun"—though many of the same young men hailed as consumers would also be called to military service in the Algerian war. Between 1955 and 1962, censorship of written texts, radio programs, and visual representations that "posed a threat to state security" meant that there could be no direct references to French military tactics or the long duration of the war.[1] However, "the events" could be evoked. Allusions are made to this unsettled political climate in the two films studied in this chapter, Marcel Carné's *Les Tricheurs* and Jacques Rozier's *Adieu Philippine.* But the films are primarily about the lures of Americanized high-tech culture for teenagers of both sexes. While female characters continue to operate in an antisentimental mode, they express their individuality less in precocious sexuality than in the denial or deferral of romance, while other kinds of desire specific to consumer culture come to the fore. I argue that the Algerian war, itself completely off-screen, is what made romance impossible, prematurely cutting off the familiar feminine trajectory whose marks in these films are nevertheless in place: an ambiguous expression of nostalgia for a familiar and certain world.

Technological Society

Albeit to a lesser extent than in the American context, the mid-decade in France marked the beginning of an era where the voices of scientists and technocrats along with their interpreters in popular culture began to be heard, rather than solely those of prophets and ideologues.[2] Following Daniel Bell's *End of Ideology* (1960), we can identify how discourses on technology and its economic promises for France—which alternately evoked the end of the traditional way of life and the coming of a brave new Americanized world—and the glories that advancement conveyed for the nation and its individuals were politicized prophecies in their own right. Along with books such as Jacques Ellul's ominous *La Technique ou l'enjeu du siècle* (1954) and economist Jean Fourastié's excited predictions for advancement in French productivity and quality of life in *Histoire de demain* (1956) and *La Civilisation de 1975* (originally published in 1953 and reprinted every two to four years until 1962), newspaper and magazine articles and films presented technology as the monolith behind various complex processes of social change, a point of view that is called technological determinism.[3] In the spectrum of technological determinism, the "soft" view proposes a dialectic between technology and society and foregrounds human actions and history in their multiple valences, while the "hard" view posits technology as a causal force independent of social constraints. Discourses in mid-1950s France tended toward the latter.

For the present study, the interest of this plethora of analyses of "technology" as a socioeconomic motor for France's future lies in the fact that many commentators positioned youth as the key variable in the transformation of the traditional French way of life. At the end of the decade, the discursive tendency to associate youth with technology in order to make large-scale statements about social change and the nation conjoined with real changes technology introduced on the humbler scale of everyday life. Technological icons such as the scooter, the automobile, the transistor radio, and eventually television dramatically altered the place of the adolescent in the French family and in public life. Teenagers emerged as a new category of consumer whose uncomplicated mission in society, as a popular culture that was now "theirs" told them, was to have fun.

As far as young men were concerned, the underside of such discursive associations of youth with technology, of the emergence of their generation as a new economic category within metropolitan France, was the reality of youth without: the two to three million conscripts (*appelés*) sent to defend French interests in Algeria. In that the period of the Algerian war (1954–62) overlapped precisely with the centrality of youth in popular discourses of technological determinism as well as the eventual emergence of the teenage consumer, it would be an incomplete picture of the images and the realities of youth in this period to consider one without the other. The same popular media culture that formed around the copains, young singers inspired by American pop music, disseminated largely reassuring information about the daily life of conscripts, a concomitance whose oddness, as the following pages will show, does not end in an analytical juxtaposition.

Two world wars had taken their toll on the French economy: the nation would not retrieve the rhythm of its growth curve of 1900–14 until 1965.[4] Economic stagnation along with a widespread nostalgia for life before wartime conspired to maintain the particularly French state of mind known as *immobilisme*. Yet the mass media raised the spectre of the advent of an unrecognizably high-tech society, a brave new world where only the young could find their way. In a France nostalgic for life before wartime and seduced by images of American-style comfort, innovation, and efficiency, the media declared the unfamiliarity of technology to be the cause of a generation gap unlike any previous manifestation.[5] Adults could no longer play their ancestral role of initiating children into society, since they themselves had to be initiated into a world that was equally unfamiliar to them, and certainly stranger: "Nos enfants sont nés dans un monde que nous n'avons su ni leur annoncer ni leur expliquer [Our children were born into a world we knew not how to present or to explain to them], lamented physicist-turned-journalist André Labarthe in a 1955 issue of *La Nef* entitled *Jeunesse qui es-tu?*.[6] Most worrisome was how the distance young people put between themselves and their elders, who could no longer be their guides, echoed the new distribution of power on the global scene. France's youth realized full well, wrote Louis Dalmas in an article from the same issue, that both economically and politically, their nation was no longer a major player:

> Bonne chère et douceur de vivre, tant vantées par les prospectus du tourisme, n'embellissent que des rides: sous le maquillage, la France est vieille. Dans ses veines coule la camomille des retraités; c'est autre chose que le sang des jacobins.[7]

> [The good life and the sweet life, praised so highly in tourist brochures, only embellish wrinkles; underneath the makeup, France is old. In her veins runs the chamomile tea of retired folk; it's not the same thing as the blood of the Jacobins.]

The advent of technological society gave the distinction between Old World and New a troublingly different meaning, decades before Jean Bau-

Enfants Terribles

drillard and Marc Fumaroli would write about the ossification of contemporary France in the nineteenth century. Dalmas may have been referring to the literal fact that the population in France was older in 1955 than it was in 1789, but the tea-drinking retirees he evoked as a demographic metaphor doubled for the quaint desuetude of the French way of life as well as the inconsequentiality of French politics. For all the articles in this issue of *La Nef* posited the eagerness with which youth welcomed technology, and not their technological pessimism, as the logical partner of political apathy. Why would young people care about contemporary politics when they perceived that their nation, once the seat of revolution, had become little more than a tourist venue? "France is old," wrote Dalmas simply and dramatically: revolution was now elsewhere — specifically, as many of these articles posited, in the technological transformation of everyday life most apparent in America.

Writings about youth and technological society made the claim that it was the lure of America that brought with it a newly dismissive attitude toward a France mired in the glories of its past. Openness to the advances of science and technology doubled as a kind of pessimism for the viability of Old-World ways and values. The headline of a 1960 *Le Figaro* survey of twenty-year-old students in the sciences quoted a young engineer who expressed this sentiment in darkly manichean terms: "Quand la terre entière se transforme, rester en arrière c'est mourir"[8] [When the whole world is being transformed, to remain behind is to die]. As one eloquent young man said, old ways were dead, and the rising generation felt there was nothing to learn from them:

A quelles valeurs voulez-vous que nous nous accrochions quand sous nos yeux tout se transforme, se désagrège ou se décompose? Nous sommes neufs dans un monde neuf . . . Nous remarquons très souvent que nos aînés en savent moins que nous sur des problèmes aujourd'hui essentiels.[9]

[What values do you want us to uphold when right before our eyes everything is being transformed, coming apart, or decomposing? We are what's brand new in a brand new world . . . We notice quite often that our elders know less than we do about the essential problems of today.]

Most striking in this dismissal of Old-World values and knowledge is the disproportionate drama of its tone. To speak of transformation, breakdown, and decomposition at the age of twenty in 1960 was to go beyond the lure of technological society that America was seen to incarnate, beyond the contrast between New World and Old. Twenty was precisely the age of conscription for military service in Algeria. An ocean separated France's colonial war from discourses and debates on the nation's vexed relationship to technology. Yet technology came to play a decisive role for conscripts. Though they were at a physical remove from metropolitan France, they remained connected to what was going on at home—musically, that is. Equipped with transistors, young soldiers could listen to the same music as their peers in France did, and until the putsch of 1961, the radio largely served the purpose of linking them to the world of fun they had left behind.

Copains, Copines

The transistor radio was the icon of technological society best suited to the needs as well as the budget of the majority of young people. Transistors had first been imported to France from the United States at the beginning of the 1950s, with the first French model presented at the Salon de la Radio at the end of 1956. The number of transistors manufactured rose from 260,000 in 1958 to over 2,000,000 in 1961, representing 50 percent of radios sold in France in 1959 and 70 percent a year later. With television in the process of becoming a gathering point in the home, teenagers seeking to claim their own taste and space vis-à-vis the nuclear family found the portability of the transistor particularly appealing (fig. 14). It practically became a bodily appendage in new images of the technologically savvy adolescent: the typical young male's first gesture of the day, reported the scandalized authors of a sociological study entitled *La Jeunesse dans la famille et la société moderne,* was to turn on his bedroom radio, a gesture which also opens a short film by François Truffaut about young love in Paris, *Antoine et Colette* (1962).

Young people and their transistors were everywhere: in parks, cafés, beaches, small towns and cities. In 1962, the Michelin restaurant guide inaugurated a new code: the word "radio" with a line through it, indicating establishments where the transistor was not welcome.[10] The transistor's portability and price also made it the ideal going-away present many parents offered sons called to serve in Algeria—a gift that was, furthermore, recommended by the military hierarchy as a way for the young soldier to fill his empty hours and was available for purchase through the army magazine *Bled.*[11]

Fig. 14. Transistor radios offered privacy for teens
Reprinted with permission from Royal Philips Electronics NV

By the end of the decade, the radio medium began to offer transistor-toting teenagers in France and young conscripts listening in from Algeria programs appealing especially to them. Nineteen fifty-nine saw the introduction of a daily program on the station Europe 1 that explicitly targeted the youth sector by featuring American pop music, "Salut les copains."[12] The program was not an immediate widespread success.[13] In 1959 young people were still largely listening to jazz, and jazz was still the musical form associated with them, as the soundtracks of *Les Tricheurs* and *A Bout de souffle* attest. The association conjured intensity, seriousness, nuclear fatalism, and the smoky clubs of Saint-Germain-des-Prés. As the narrator of a 1956 television documentary entitled "Les Jeunes et le jazz" rhetorically queried of the young men and women who unsmilingly shared the dance floor, "n'est-ce pas parce que la jeunesse est anxieuse, inquiète, qu'elle aime le jazz?" [Isn't it because youth is anxious and worried that they like jazz?]

Rather than radio, television was the first medium to offer an alternative to the predominant image of generational ennui that jazz ostensibly expressed so well. Teenagers may have disdained the family-oriented television programming of the early sixties, but TV also orchestrated the breakthrough of the first French rock star, Johnny Hallyday. His songs written to the tunes of American hits were initially unpopular on the radio, for the Hallyday experience was above all a visual one. When Johnny first appeared on the TV show "L'Ecole des vedettes" in 1960 at the age of seventeen, clad in tight black leather pants, to sing "T'Aimer Follement," his French version of Elvis Presley's "Makin' Love," he became notorious overnight. Public opinion was divided, and the division ran clearly along the lines of generation. Parents were horrified; teenagers were thrilled.[14] The record, which had only sold twelve thousand copies before the show, sold over one hundred thousand in the following weeks.

With Johnny's voice now attached to a physical presence, the radio assumed the pivotal role in diffusing his music and that of singers like him. These singers were called copains (buddies) or *yé-yés*, in reference to the typical American-style refrain of their songs ("yeah, yeah"). Stations initiated a "mouvement de 17h," marking the hour when students returned from school.[15] In recognition of the phenomenal popularity of "Salut les copains," Europe 1 moved the show out of its original Thursday slot and broadcast it daily for several years. In another sign of the times, Radio Luxembourg replaced "Passe-temps des dames et des demoiselles," a show for housewives and ladies of leisure, with a program by and for youth and their music: "Balzac 10 10," (pronounced "dix deux fois," ten twice) followed by the opening of a club of the same name on Paris's rue Balzac. Johnny Hallyday's first concert at Paris's Palais des Sports in 1961 was an event that for Jean-René Huguenin, one of the new spokesmen for youth, signaled a sea change in his generation. Previously appraised as hostile, passive, and sluggish with ennui, they seemed to have awakened from their state of semi-consciousness. From Huguenin's point of view, the mad scene at the concert meant that youthful revolt was finally at hand. This generation needed to breathe, he wrote, to rediscover its primitive side, and Hallyday's fans found just that in the "bruit et sang," the blood and noise, of rock n' roll.[16]

Blood and noise perhaps, but there was money to be made. Teens who tuned in to "Salut les copains" could buy postcards, key chains, cups, and bowls featuring the show's mascot, Chouchou, a figure clad in jeans and a T-shirt and sporting a Beatles haircut. The alliance of music and consumer products targeting youth was unabashed. When record producers descended upon the Golf Drouot club in search of the next Johnny Hallyday, they found Eddy Mitchell (his real name was Claude Moine), a sixteen-year-old Americanophile who wore his hair long and played his guitar hooked up to a big amplifiers, eccentricities in France at the time.[17] Mitchell and his friends, some of whom barely knew how to play their instruments, signed a three-year contract with Disques Barclay. Barclay discreetly negotiated with the head of Lainière de Roubaix, a wool company, in order to associate the group's name with a brand of their socks, Chaussettes Stemm. The group was renamed Les Chaussettes Noires [The Black Socks]. With the purchase of three pair of Stemm socks (black, of course), one received a free ticket to the Chaussettes' first concert. A similar alliance was the endorsement of a group called Les Pirates by the milk industry. As soon as the agreement was signed, posters of the group shot up all over Paris. One of their songs, an adaptation of the Jerry Lee Lewis song "Let's Talk About Us," was altered beyond recognition to fit the profile of their sponsors: "Je bois du lait" [I drink milk]. As for free tickets, one only needed to present milk bottlecaps at the ticket window (VF, 77).

Female singers were equally subject to industry fabrication. While it was Julliard's unexpected success with Bonjour tristesse that led to the publishing industry's interest in finding the next Françoise Sagan, there was no one young female singer who set the stage, so to speak, for others like her. Instead, the music industry set about the deliberate construction of a parallel "copine" phenomenon. Sometimes the parallel between the two industries was overt, as in the case of Arielle, a fourteen-year-old christened "la Minou Drouet du twist" (VF, 99). The music industry placed a high value on links with America, in the relentless marketing of the bilingual Nicole Croisille and Cleveland native Nancy Hollaway. Many of the copines, generally ranging in age from fifteen to nineteen, were given stage names that were just first names: Audrey, Sophie, Evy, adding further to their appearance of youthfulness. The singer Sheila presents a case in point. "Sheila" began as an American song reinterpreted with great success by the French singer Lucky Blondo. Producer Claude Carrère decided to find a teenage girl to launch as an automatic star by giving her the name of the hit song. And so the sixteen year-old Annie Chancel, whom Carrère heard at the Golf Drouot, became Sheila (*VF*, 122–24). Carrère came up with her trademark look: demure plaid skirts, white blouses, immaculately curled hair: the incarnation of the *vraie jeune fille* — albeit prefabricated for its economic potential. In keeping with the virginal image, Sheila appeared on television for the first time in polka-dot pajamas and sang while reclining on a couch holding a stuffed animal. She quickly became a fixture on radio and television and in music magazines. As *Le Monde* saw it, Sheila wasn't particularly beautiful, but she was typical, "comme mille et mille jeunes filles" (*VF*, 122). Her stardom was the result of her reassuring familiarity. Indeed, with wholesome hit songs like "L'Ecole est finie" [School's over] and "Ma Première surprise-partie" [My first party], whose lyrics were by and large confined to the title, Sheila had strong family appeal. She was just as appropriate for living room viewing as she was for the bedroom transistor or record player. But Sheila proved to be savvier than she looked; she opened a Boutique Sheila in Paris's fourteenth arrondissement, capitalizing for herself on her commercial value.

One of the best-known copines was Françoise Hardy, whose musical style lies somewhere between the poetic tradition of the French *chanson* and the yé-yés. Hardy was hailed as the new Juliette Gréco because of the similarity of their physiques and the cerebralism of their lyrics, but her connection to the first young Françoise to capture public attention, Françoise Sagan, is practically uncanny, as this write-up in *Disco Revue* shows: "Avec son premier disque, elle retient l'attention. Ses paroles apportent quelque chose de neuf dans la chanson française. En somme, ce sont ses propres problèmes amoureux qu'elle nous expose" (*VF*, 118) [With her first record, she captures our attention. Her lyrics bring something new to French song. In sum, she exposes her own romantic woes to us].

Along with a similar insistence on the autobiographical component, the transition from Françoise to Françoise, from the marketing of young women writers to young women singers, illustrates well the transformation of the mass media in the postwar period and the increasing visibility of the teenage girl. With concerts, album covers, features in teen magazines, and television appearances augmenting radio and jukebox play, the faces, bodies, style of dress, and voices of the copines became intimate fixtures in French life. In its second issue, the teen magazine *Age tendre et tête de bois* could declare 1963 "L'Année Françoise Hardy," and not exaggerate. Such ubiquity made the publishing industry's book signings, cocktail parties, and concerts at the Salle Pleyel seem rarified and quaint. While the print media's marketing techniques may have been old-fashioned in comparison with those of the music industry, increased visibility and audibility entailed necessary restrictions for the actual content of the copines' songs. Singers like Françoise Hardy never shocked the public the way young writers like Françoise Sagan had. Their lyrics did not, and indeed could not, demonstrate an equivalent sexual frankness—making them along with equally desexualized copains, ideal vehicles for marketing products to their fans.

In the early 1960s, manufacturers had only to associate a product with the words "copain" or "jeune" to signify its desirability. An advertisement for the chewing gum brand May, for example, had no need for visual cues when it could claim quite simply to be "le chewing gum des copains" (fig. 15). A grape juice ad pronounced the drink to be "[le] délice énergétique favori des jeunes." Advertisements for transistor radios described them as "jeunes," and the battery-operated Philips record player was touted as the perfect Christmas gift for the under-twenty set (fig. 16).

An advertisement for a brand of blue jeans sold at Caddy, a boutique in Paris's tenth arrondissement, which claimed to be "le créateur en France de la mode «Rock et Twist»," best captures the tone of the market for fun-loving consumerism (fig. 17): "The copains Alain and Claude, stars of Vogue records, prefer, like everyone, Lewis-France jeans, the stars of blue-jeans," the ad reads. The straightforward equivalences this advertisement makes and its overt eagerness to reach the youth market can only disarm the contemporary postmodern sensibility. Alain and Claude—identified by first name alone as befits the casual world of copains—are stars of Vogue Records, just as Lewis-France is a star in the world of blue jeans. Caddy promised the presence of both to potential store customers: "Vous rencontrerez toutes les vedettes du «Rock»" [You will meet all the stars of "Rock"]. Caddy carried not only fashions, but all the latest records. It offered youth who were both musically and fashionably hip the novelty of one-stop shopping in a country where supermarkets were still rare. As if this weren't enough, the ad also contained a coupon giving a 10 percent reduction to all readers of the magazine *Salut les copains*. Everyone stood to profit from the Caddy advertisement: Caddy, Lewis-France, Vogue records, Alain and Claude, and *Salut les copains.*

Teen music magazines were the ideal reinforcement for this commercially driven and naïve youth culture. Producers had originally dubbed young Americanophile singers *"idoles";* following the preference of the singers themselves, however, magazines used the term "copains," or buddies, and for girls "copines," an identification that blurred the distinction between the stars and their fans. In September 1961, with Johnny Hallyday on the cover, *Disco Revue* appeared on the newsstands; it was joined a year later by two other publications, *Salut les* copains and *Age tendre et tête de bois.* All of these were the brainchild of young people (*VF,* 90). *Age tendre* was graced with name recognition from an earlier incarnation as a song title; *Salut les copains* took its name from a radio show. The public response to the novelty of commercial magazines targeting teenagers was enormous: a year after *Salut les copains* first appeared, it was selling one million copies per issue.[18] *Age tendre*'s success led to both radio and television shows by the same name.

Salut les copains featured female singers who could be the copines of any reader, just as their male counterparts were copains. Sylvie Vartan, in *Salut les copains'* first issue, described how she wore her brother's pants, used her father's razor to style her hair, and bought her clothing at Prisunic, the French equivalent of Woolworth's. The September issue asked seven copines what they would do if they weren't stars and photographed them costumed as their responses: teacher, florist, model, artist, homemaker, photographer, and, à la Jean Seberg in Godard's *A Bout de souffle,* vendor of the International Herald Tribune.[19] The October 1963 issue was dedicated to the wave of young female singers, and in December, the magazine *Bonjour les amis* announced its search for a new copine, declaring in a headline, "La Lutte Continue" [The Struggle Continues].

Any reader might give it a try; any girl next door could become a star, or at least look like one. If the majority of female adolescents had not definitively entered the public sphere to find fame and fortune, at least their image had. In the real and fantasized spaces of buying and owning that were stores and advertisements, in the pages of music magazines, and on radio and television shows, youth no longer only meant male. It was just as economically viable to show girls how they could identify with other girls who sang, played the guitar, rode scooters, wore jeans, used Clearasil, and drank grape juice. The consumer culture that grew out of yé-yé

Fig. 15. Chewing gum for savvy youth
Salut les copains, October 1962

Fig. 16. A personal record player for the teenager's musical tastes
Reprinted with permission from Royal Philips Electronics NV

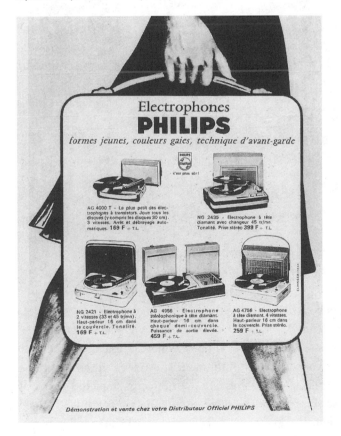

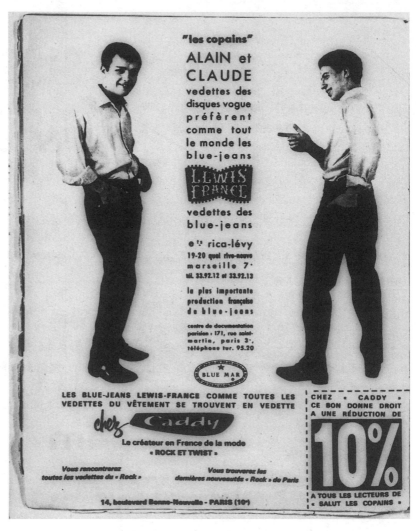

Fig. 17. The many facets of the teenage consumer
Salut les copains, July/August 1962

music was the first to have girls take equal part in the category of generation previously defined as male. This was a marketing phenomenon whose effects were less nefarious than ambiguous. Following real but unspectacular advances for young women of the middle classes and the experience of individual writers and actresses, whom the media depicted as characters no different from those they incarnated in fiction and film, the latest incarnation of female adolescence turned young womanhood into a mass phenomenon. It promoted the fantasy of egalitarian consumption, ostensibly unhindered by traditional definitions of femininity and regardless of actual purchasing power, social class, or educational level (figs. 18 and 19). Equality in consumer society was a dubious empowerment, since above the stage where carefree fun and easy gender relations were on display, record companies and producers, radio stations, manufacturers, and advertisers held the strings.

A War Without a Name

During the same period that saw the development of a consumer and media culture equally oriented toward youth of both sexes, two to three million twenty-year-old males had to absent themselves from this culture for twenty-seven months of military service in Algeria. Of more dramatic consequence than the indifference to politics of their peers back at home, the conscripts have been inscribed in the national memory of the Algerian war as remaining for the most part apathetic. Why the absence of political passions in the very midst of the fray? Novels, films, and first-person accounts have explored why conscription was not the unifying experience it was during the two world wars but rather one of a "multitude of solitudes." [20] Even sympathetic portraits note the tendency of the troops to remain passive, obedient, uninformed, and uninterested in trying to understand a confusing situation in which the enemy remained invisible. [21]

Political passions were everywhere, but the conscripts remained untouched: the book-length *bande dessinée* [comic] *Une Education algérienne* (1982) plays upon the Flaubertian paradigm through the character of a young *appelé* in the days preceding independence, absorbed in the seduction of the wife and daughter of his commanding officer while OAS and FLN attacks provide background scenery. [22] The same disengagement is, instead, framed as a philosophical impasse in Alain Manevy's 1960 account *L'Algerie à vingt ans:* "Rester spectateur: lâcheté; intervenir sans savoir: bêtise; le dire: faire la politique des autres; ne rien dire: lâcheté" [23] [Remain a spectator: cowardice; intervene without knowledge: stupidity; say so: engage in other people's politics; say nothing: cowardice]. The reference here is Sartre rather than Flaubert, but neither of these texts suggested why the conscripts chose to keep their distance from the ideological fray. *Le Déserteur* (1960), the account of a Communist *"refus"* (the official term: one can only desert if war is declared), provided a possible answer.

Figs. 18 and 19.
Marketing youth
as unisex

The pseudonymous author Maurienne (the valley in the Cévennes next to Vercors, the latter the site of a 1944 Resistance battle) recounts a conversation in the barracks between himself and several other young men. One reflects that the primary victims of the war were the conscripts themselves, engaged in a struggle on another continent that had nothing to do with life in France. Another complains of losing his place in history, by which he means finishing payments on a scooter he cannot even enjoy and missing his chances with girls. The narrator tries to get his peers to see how the indifference to the stakes of the war that accompanies their frustration at having to serve are the logical result of the position imposed on them by consumer society:

On commence par l'obnubiler avec des vitrines de «Vespa», de télés, de disques, de «Dauphine». On t'offre un but immédiat à atteindre. Et tu te laisses acheter. Avec le crédit, tu fais ta première acquisition, tu penses à la suivante, etc. C'est comme ça qu'on endort politiquement la majorité du prolétariat! Et dans cette atmosphère de course à confort, toi, tu te désintéresses du reste.[24]

[It begins with Vespa scooters in store windows, televisions, records, and Dauphines clouding your mind. You're offered an immediate goal. And you let yourself be bought. On an installment plan, you make your first acquisition, you think of the next one, etc. That's how the majority of the proletariat is lulled to sleep politically! And in this atmosphere of the race for comfort, you lose interest in everything else.]

Maurienne's analytical appraisal of the political apathy that, in his view, went hand in hand with the seductive promises of a society structured by the acts and desires of buying and selling was not shared by most of his conscript peers. Indeed, only about a hundred young men would refuse to fight in Algeria, unlike the ten thousand Americans who refused to fight in the Vietnam war. The difference can partially be attributed to the phenomenon signaled above: the novelty of the promises of consumer society as a carefree paradise for French youth, particularly welcome after the material hardships that long outlived the war as well as the persistent image of a generation of victims and survivors. As one young man wrote in to *Paris-Match* in response to criticism of a Johnny Hallyday concert, "mieux vaut le rock que la neurasthénie!" [rock n' roll is better than neurasthenia!][25] The conscripts were eager to return to France and to fun. In the meantime, they remained as close to it as they could. In the barracks and the infirmaries, everyone's ear was constantly pressed to his own personal transistor, each tuned in to his own favorite station—music and never news.[26]

Just as in France, the first gesture of the day for young men serving in Algeria was to turn on the radio to hear the latest hit songs.[27] Only on 22 April 1961, soon before the projected negotiations between the OAS and FLN, what greeted them was the news bulletin of the putsch by four generals (Challe, Salan, Zeller, and Jouhaud) who had been removed from their functions for their outlaw attempt to keep Algeria in French hands. Because a successful putsch would mean the continuation of the war, the news functioned as a jolt to the sluggish collective system of the conscripts. Rather than tune in to pop music, they listened for information on the putsch from as many sources as possible, French and Algerian. The conscripts debated and discussed the news bulletins amongst themselves and, in an unusual breakdown in the hierarchy of military communication, even with commanding officers to ascertain their intentions.[28]

On the evening of 23 April, French television and radio broadcast a message from De Gaulle urging the troops not to follow orders from what he called "un quarteron de généraux en retraite"[29] [a handful of generals in retreat]. De Gaulle's direct address rallied conscripts around loyalist officers and legitimated numerous acts of disobedience to orders given by the four generals' supporters. When the putsch was put to an end four days after its inception, even the government recognized the crucial role of the radio. As minister Robert Buran commented most memorably, "c'est la victoire des transistors."[30] Through the intermediary of the transistor radio, icon of depoliticized individualism among French youth, the "multitude of solitudes" who were young men in Algeria came to consciousness, realizing their potential to act together and to affect the course of events, even if it was first and foremost out of self-interest.

Le Petit Ecran

One icon of high-tech everyday life that did not generally appeal to young people in the late 1950s and early 1960s was television. TV's enormous impact in the promotion of Johnny Hallyday was an exception: only one out of four French households owned a set in the fall of 1962—the situation in the U.S. a full decade earlier—and programming was limited.[31] In Truffaut's *Antoine et Colette*, the packed auditorium of teenagers in the Paris concert hall where the two eponymous characters first meet is evidence that many in this age group, at least in Paris, preferred the classical concerts and lecture series of Jeunesses Musicales as entertainment. When Antoine (Jean-Pierre Léaud) visits Colette (Marie-France Pfiser) at home and encounters her parents for the first time, they are ensconced in front of an unusually large television set as signifiers of the generic adult, categorically devoid of interest. At the end of the film, after a dashing and somewhat older young man comes to pick up Colette while Antoine is over for dinner, the humiliated Antoine dispiritedly decides to forego his usual evening out at the concert hall and watch it on TV with Colette's parents instead. Television here, as seen by the cinephile Truffaut, is just about the most depressing way for a young person to spend an evening.

Partisans of high culture were not the only ones to deem television to be a medium "for parents," as one popular music magazine's disdainful claim read in 1963.[32] It was certainly no reliable source of information about what awaited young men called for military service in Algeria. The gap between television reportages and reality was immense: as the medium was state-controlled, the nightly news presented little more than military parades and scenes of young men in uniform performing charitable works for the local people.[33] Journalists had to have authorization before speaking to soldiers or officers.[34] In the goal of rallying the public around Gaullist policy, the enemy was rendered invisible; no violence was shown, and some events were not referred to or depicted at all. For technical reasons as well, reportages were limited: camera equipment was heavy and there were insufficient funds for travel abroad, so producers had to resort to the cheaper option of buying footage from agencies like United Press or France-Vidéo.[35] The net effect was that the *journal télévisé* did little more than put the face of the newscaster on the impersonal voice-over that Pathé newsreels had provided to the movie-going public since 1908.[36]

The Algerian war was the first to enter French homes on the TV screen, but the studied neutrality of these images meant that they were a source of neither news nor opinion. In 1956, Prime Minister Guy Mollet himself picked up the phone to complain to a program director about a newscaster's description of a governmental war communiqué as "vague and general": self-censorship in the interest of keeping one's job necessarily accompanied television's subordination to the official line.[37] In his presidential capacity, Charles de Gaulle increasingly used TV as a medium to communicate policy: twice in 1959, five times in 1960, seven in 1961, eleven in 1962.[38] As a twist on a familiar formula for Leninism, *Express* founder

Jean-Jacques Servan-Schreiber succinctly defined Gaullism as "le pouvoir personnel, plus le monopole de la télévision." [39]

The first step beyond the obfuscation enforced by De Gaulle's Ministry of Information was taken by the monthly news program *Cinq colonnes à la une,* much lauded for one broadcast devoted to the everyday life of a young sergeant performing his military duties in the djebel. "A gift from *Cinq colonnes* to the families of France," what looked like a real link-up had in fact been theatrically prepared on both ends: the sector patrolled by the sergeant cleared of Algerians, the home of his parents providing a "live" frame for their emotional reactions to images of their son filmed twenty-four hours earlier. In 1991, Sergeant Charlie Robert would tersely put a dent into the legend of *Cinq colonnes'* audacity: "C'est du cinéma" [that's all make-believe].[40] Ironic commentary about a medium whose claim was to provide the public with access to an immediacy unavailable in the movies.

The jarring and eventually explosive conjuncture of youth as fun-oriented consumers and the reality of the Algerian war was one that the mass media of the late 1950s and early 1960s could only imply. Most of the first-person accounts, films, and novels directly treating the conscripts' experience appeared after the war, and the better-known avant-garde was more interested in communicating the soldiers' traumatized silence once they returned home (Alain Resnais's *Muriel,* 1963) or ironizing the bipolar political options of *engagement:* FLN or OAS (Jean-Luc Godard's *Le Petit soldat,* released 1963).

The two films discussed in the following pages, Jacques Rozier's *Adieu Philippine* (1962) and Marcel Carné's *Les Tricheurs* (1958) take a different tack. Both comment on the variation that appears in the set of literal and figurative signs of the loss of feminine intactness with the encroachment of an increasingly youth-driven consumerism. In contrast to the imperfect freedom accorded the antisentimental author and her defiant protagonist and their eventual reinscription within received ideas about femininity, consumer culture took girls and their desires out of their familiar inscription in romance and domesticity in the service of market parity only to reinscribe them there, a process that Carné and Rozier reproduce and explore in the context of the Algerian war, to greatly different metaphorical ends.

Jacques Rozier's film *Adieu Philippine* (1962) is a send-up of the promises and artifices of television: a bright new world that stands alone, removed from the traditional French way of life as well as from a war in which the young men who operate high-tech equipment will eventually be called to serve. The Algerian war is the incongruous, invisible, but unassailably real background of *Adieu Philippine*. In the weeks before he leaves for military service, a young low-level TV cameraman, Michel (Jean-Claude Aimini), meets Liliane and Juliette (Yveline Cery and Stefania Sabatini), two girls who come to the studio in the hope of acting in commercials. When he is fired, Michel tries to convince a middle-aged producer to let him direct commercials ("films publicitaires") featuring the two girls; at the same time, the girls try to get Michel out of military service by playing up to a businessman who seems to have political connections. With the cheerfully rambling mise-en-scène and unscripted dialogue that are Rozier's trademark, the camera follows the girls and Michel, together and separately, from the television studio to department stores to their homes, leading up to what the film terms to be Michel's "last vacation" at Club Med in Corsica.

Michel's imminent departure hovers over chatty scenes of ordinariness and comic moments alike. He likes both Liliane and Juliette and vice-versa, but because of the twenty-seven months that await him in Algeria, no triangular intrigue ensues. "Je choisirai celle qui m'aura attendu" [I'll choose the one who will have waited for me], Michel promises; deferral of romance comes to signify the uncertainty of what awaits Michel in Algeria, the uncertainty of the outcome of a war without a name. In a romantic and political situation marked by an absence of clarity, the two girls necessarily remain indistinct. The film's title serves as apt commentary: "Philippine" in French is a nut formed from two kernels, and considered to be a lucky charm. Who will it be? What does the future have in store, romantically and politically? The trope of the woman waiting for her man's return from battle is literally fragmented in Rozier's scenario. Intactness is conversely maintained in a new formulation: the complicity between Liliane and Juliette. The attraction between each girl and Michel comes and goes, but their primary alliance to each other remains (fig. 20). With heterosexual coupling-off deferred by wartime, Liliane and Juliette's complicity is unfamiliar, yet not threatening. Sexuality is completely absent from all aspects of the triangulation. The intactness formed by female complicity instead signifies innocence, a world untouched by wartime, whose most natural context is the childish decor of Liliane's bedroom. Liliane and Juliette may be waiting for Michel together, but they are still familiarly enough jeunes filles.

For ideological and technical reasons, television—despite its promises

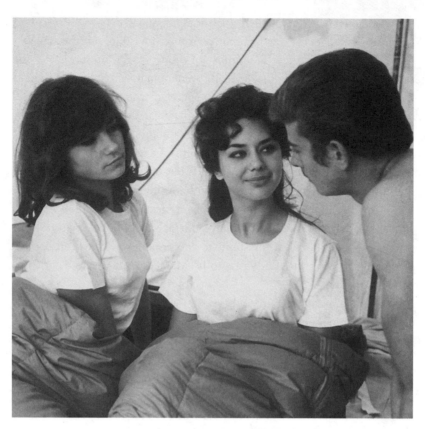

Fig. 20. The complicity of jeunes filles
Copyright Raymond Cauchetier–Paris

of reality and immediacy—could not deliver a true sense of the grimness of this colonial war, its long duration and atrocities. Rozier, who had himself worked in the television industry, did not explicitly critique the programming that was uniformly subject to the scrutiny of the Ministry of Information, but the scenes where Liliane and Juliette realize their dream of appearing in commercials stand as telling commentary on the means of production, intentions, and overall artificiality of the medium. Incongruously, producers always cast these frivolous, giggly girls as housewives in ads for domestic products. In one surrealistic commercial for floor wax, Liliane and Juliette are clad in matching plaid housecoats, accessorized with pumps and hose. They recite the product jingle and ineffectually push mops around in a ring formed by bottles of floor wax. A diapered infant, added as another sign of female domesticity, sits positioned on the floor in front of them. Both the girls' movements and their words are just slightly out of sync. Moreover, Liliane and Juliette have obviously never waxed a floor in their lives; the middle-aged male producer has to come on the set to show them how to use a mop (fig. 21).

New female fantasies made possible by technology come up against the limits of the familiar here—but in a comic mode. Rozier pokes fun at the

Fig. 21. *Adieu Philippine:* the floor wax girls
Copyright Raymond Cauchetier–Paris

desire to appear on TV, to simply "be seen" and not as the effect of any act or idea in the world. This was the culmination of the postwar expansion of the mass media and with it the increased visibility of young women. To make it into the headlines as part of the "reign of the *adolescente*" that *Elle* magazine had proclaimed in 1956 required either an engagement with the world of acts and ideas or the fabrication of a recognizable public image: novelist Françoise Sagan, "existentialist" Juliette Gréco, Brigitte Bardot as "B.B." To appear in television advertising, on the other hand, is to submit to a kind of unnaming, since the product itself assumes the central place of the star. By merging with a product, Liliane and Juliette are granted access to living rooms across the nation, becoming stars of a different kind: the floor wax girls.

As anonymous signifiers of a rejuvenated domesticity, Liliane and Juliette represent a high-tech variation of Astra margarine's cartoon teen Arlette that is also intentionally less subtle. In the transition from print media to the televisual, the father's titillation has become the economics of production—exposed by Rozier to highlight the impossibility of a seamless reinscription of youthfulness into female domesticity. By making television the medium for the tenacious message identifying femininity with domesticity, no matter what the age or kitchen experience, *Adieu Philippine* points to the artifice of both. Commercials for cleaning products are more artificial than even state-controlled television news, with the construction of femininity rather than that of current events primarily at stake. Nevertheless, with Rozier's unabashed satire of commercials, there is an implicit reference to the news: femininity and women's role in the home are staged for living room TV viewers, just like the activities of the French army in Algeria. This is not as far-fetched a comparison as it might sound. *Adieu Philippine* assigns separate spaces to gender from the opening scene on: Liliane and Juliette stand outside the glass doors of the TV studio looking longingly in at the young men absorbed in handling the equipment; after the encounter that follows, they have fun with Michel in Paris, but he will go off to war in Algeria. Michel and his male friends are entranced with the used car they have bought together; Liliane and Juliette giggle and chatter about Michel in Liliane's still girlish bedroom. Technology and the experience of war are male: young women remain at the periphery of masculine experiences, which are marked by their greater social importance.

Yet the abundance of detail in the film belongs to the female experience, to the characters of Liliane and Juliette. This abundant detail is striking in its implied contrast to the eerie presence of the Algerian war, on screen only through suggestion. Jacques Demy's better-known film *Les Parapluies de Cherbourg* (1962) places the conscript's twenty-seven-month service off-screen to similar effect. The originality of Rozier, however, was to take on the question of the representation of the war in Algeria in the context of the promises of television and the reality of information control. In the elaborate commercial scene, Liliane and Juliette "stand in" as references for the appelés, whose activities as represented on TV were also orchestrated, determined by Gaullist rather than patriarchal ideology. Young men work the equipment, but the separation of spheres in relationship to technology in *Adieu Philippine* gives way to an overarching truth: neither war nor domesticity, masculinity or femininity, escapes the mediating effects of representation, even in the cadre of a small screen promising reality and immediacy.

Speed

Wise to the artifices of television, Michel has no interest in tuning in at home. What interests him rather is the newly acquired car. When Michel screeches up to the house, late for the traditional midday meal, his father expresses disapproval: life is too easy for young folk now, he declares in reference to the vehicle. Once again we witness the contrast between Old-World values and New, but as a commonplace, lacking informational value. In Marcel Carné's film *Les Tricheurs* (1958), teenagers and cars come together much more dramatically in an ideologically loaded formula where gender is the key.

Carné's explicit purpose was to document how French youth flagrantly broke with their parents' values. As he announced, "je voudrais que ce film soit vu comme le témoignage d'une époque"[41] [I would like this film to be seen as the testimony of an era], and the media did indeed take *Les Tricheurs* as such (fig. 22).[42] With its release, the press once again began to speak of a "mal de la jeunesse," albeit with different factors in the equation. The narrative is recounted after the fact, framed by the bitterness of a young man. Accompanied by a voice-over reminiscent of the wistfulness with which *Bonjour tristesse* begins and ends — "sur ce sentiment inconnu dont l'ennui, la douceur m'obsèdent, j'hésite à apposer le nom, le beau nom grave de tristesse . . ."[43] –[This unfamiliar sentiment whose sweet listlessness fills me, to which I hesitate to give the grave and beautiful name of

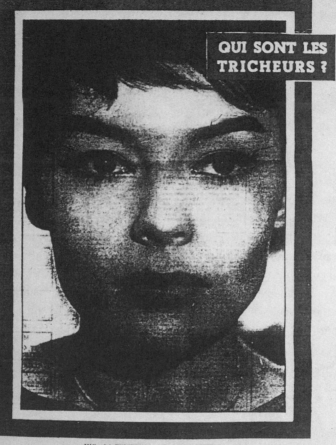

Fig. 22. *Les Tricheurs:* a media event
Reprinted with permission from *L'Express,* 16 October 1958

sorrow] — Bob sips his drink at a café table and observes couples excitedly make evening plans, "heureux comme j'aurais pu l'être" [happy the way I could have been], setting the stage for his own unhappy ending to unfold.

Clean-cut Bob (Jacques Charrier) witnesses a sinisterly good-looking young man steal a record from a store on the Champs Elysées. Bob approaches the thief on the street and is intrigued when Alain (Laurent Terzieff), a lapsed *normalien,* tells him that the act of stealing was purely gratuitous. Bob soon becomes part of Alain's *bande,* a group of young people who are not exactly friends but who share certain tastes and values: easy money, wild parties, jazz, and free love in Saint-Germain-des-Prés. Bob and one of the girls, Mic (Pascale Petit) meet at a party after having sex with other people, and soon fall in love. As love is scorned by their cohort, they deny their sentiments to themselves and each other. Discomfited above all by Alain's sardonic knowing gaze, Mic sleeps with Alain to prove the truth of her slogan: "moi, jamais rien ne m'engage" [I'm never committed to anything, nothing ever holds my interest], but when Bob walks in on Mic's enfant terrible version of an *acte gratuit,* Alain continues to detect her false indifference. Bad faith culminates with a truth-or-dare party game and Mic and Bob's declarations — his after witnessing hers — that each meant nothing to the other. Mic speeds off in her Jaguar and commits suicide by veering into an oncoming truck.

What has changed in the image of Left Bank youth since its association with young "existentialists" of the immediate postwar years is the central place now accorded to high-tech material culture. The stylish "making do" of the late 1940s — roller skates as a mode of transport, Juliette Gréco sporting her one pair of black slacks — has evolved, in Carné's vision, into an insatiable desire for the icons of technological society: records and record players, scooters, and especially cars. Having luxury within easy reach, lacking the political *engagement* of their elders, tricheurs represented a new kind of victim of a new malaise: materialism and, with it, the necessary decline of morality. In a more troubling formulation than Alain's nihilism, the generational limit case is incarnated in Mic. She refuses to live with her widowed mother, reasoning with what Carné presents as the logic of her generation that it would be "too reassuring." She is ready to do anything — to steal from the cash register in her mother's modest lamp store, to blackmail a high society woman — in order to keep a "room of her own" and acquire the used Jaguar of her dreams. Bourgeois Bob, on the other hand, is content with his Vespa scooter. Mic's brother Roger (Roland Lesaffre),

Fig. 23. *Les Tricheurs:* James Dean *au féminin*
Photo © 1958–Studiocanal Image

an auto mechanic, is perplexed: "dans ma jeunesse c'était les robes qui in-téressaient les filles" [when I was young, girls were interested in dresses]. Forecasting her own end, Mic muses that she wouldn't mind dying like James Dean, "jeune, et en pleine vitesse" [young and at top speed]. She is the French, and female, version of a rebel without a cause (fig. 23).

Carné pairs Mic's rejection of her daughterly role and her unladylike love of speed with her antisentimentality. Bob is new to the gang and its codes and takes his cues from Mic, whose reluctance to yield to her true affections comes across as incomprehensible adhesion to peer pressure. To marry Bob would be a conventional and perfectly acceptable means of gaining access to material comfort, if not the excessive luxury she so ardently desires. Mic ostentatiously rejects the possibility of forming a couple, though on several occasions—for example, during an ironic ex-change on a country club dance floor where the ostensibly fake romantic fantasies she pronounces and he echoes are in fact true—her expression betrays the inner battle against familiar sentimentality. And in the truth-or-dare party game, Mic's false declarations of contempt for Bob are only surpassed by his own for her. He could love "une fille propre" [a clean girl], but since girls are all the same, "toutes les filles se valent," he has agreed to marry the aristocratic Chloë, who has announced to him that she is pregnant with the child of an unknown father. At this moment the familiar face of femininity resurfaces on two counts. Abortion (illegal in France until 1967) is never mentioned in this milieu, but incongruously enough, "religious scruples" are. Chloë's only thought is to save herself in more ways than one through a class-appropriate marriage. As for Mic, in self-punishment for turning away from love, she commits a definitive act of self-annihilation. She runs out of the room too fast, jumps into her Jag too fast, and drives too fast for Bob to catch up and pronounce the words that only the viewer can hear: "j'ai triché, Mic!"—[I cheated], meaning he didn't tell the truth and he does love her. In counterpoint to elliptical confession, Mic's swift and wordless escape from the stifling world of her peers conjures up the ghost of the jeune fille. The familiar girlish desires that lurk throughout Mic's trajectory of acts of rebellion and self-determination ultimately and tragically triumph: by rejecting love and mocking purity, she has created an emptiness whose ostensible finality is a sight too terrible to bear.

In the 1954 *Avant le déluge*, adolescent femininity is equivalent to political apathy and sexual deviousness, masculinity to a consuming preoccupation with current events and recent history. Four years later Carné took a similar position. He indicted Mic's unfamiliar antisentimentality, embodied in her passion for Jaguars and speed, by giving her an older brother who is a car mechanic. Roger not only accepts his social place among the working classes, but also has been ethically formed by his adolescence during the Occupation and military service in Indochina, the memories of which remain vivid. One repairs, the other consumes: Carné didactically presents two temporally distinct and gendered experiences of adolescence, the brother engaged in Resistance activities and patriotic duty, the younger sister in the desire for high-tech luxury.

We saw a similar generational subcategorization in *Le Repos du guerrier*'s Renaud and Geneviève. But unlike the nihilistic Renaud, Mic's brother, with his similar situation in recent history, is able to understand his sister's indifference to all but owning a car, her resolute rejection of love. After Mic dies following the car crash that looks like suicide, the doctor asks: "Qu'est-ce qu'ils ont donc dans la peau, ces jeunes gens?" [What do these young people have under their skin?] Her brother's answer takes on the history of the twentieth century: "Un univers qui se débine . . . Cin-

quante ans de pagaille derrière eux et sans doute cinquante autres devant"
[A universe that's run itself into the ground . . . Fifty years of chaos behind
them and undoubtedly fifty more ahead]. The America of James Dean and
Marlon Brando was one reference for the fast cars and reckless behavior
of young people in French films of the late years of the Fourth Republic
and the beginnings of the Fifth; war memories and nuclear fatalism were
another.

The effects of the war under way, however, could only be implied. The
France-Soir headline prominently displayed in one scene reads, "Tension
accrue dans le monde"—and no more. Benjamin Stora asks provocatively
whether Jean-Luc Godard's A Bout de souffle (1959), a film in which the
contemporary political context is even less present than in Les Tricheurs,
told the story of those who knew that military service in Algeria awaited
them. For Stora, A Bout de souffle was this generation's "film-miroir." [44]
This first film of Godard's also associated wayward youth with automobiles,
but with none of the ponderous morality or tragic tone of Les Tricheurs.
Though it was Godard's extremely mobile camera that earned A Bout de
souffle its place in the canon, just as new was the ironic distance taken in
his representation of youth.

A Bout refrained from the decade's tendency to diagnose generational
malaise; nevertheless, Michel's (Jean-Paul Belmondo) choice—never articulated or judged as such—to live only in the present is not unlike that
of Carné's Mic. The incarnation of this choice in a young female, however,
is more jolting. Carné embeds the wildly improbable image of a teenage
girl of modest means in the late 1950s possessing a luxury car in an elaborate and equally fantastic blackmail scheme. Somewhat less improbable in
A Bout de souffle in that the criminal is a young man, the conjuncture in
these two films of the same elements of youth, automobiles, speed, and
crime makes them very much fantasy texts for the end of the decade. As
fantasies, they take on particular resonance in light of the publications and
real crises of the years 1958 and 1959: the revelation of the French army's
use of torture in Henri Alleg's censored testimony La Question; Pierre
Vidal-Naquet's hypothesis that French paratroopers in Algiers had assassi-
nated mathematician and French Communist Party member Maurice Au-
din; the dissolution of the Fourth Republic in its inability to resolve the
crisis in Algeria. In such a context, the violent endings of Mic and Michel
might come less as a brutal intrusion for the moviegoer of the time than
an inexorable one, symbolic of the only way out of a war even De Gaulle
could not bring to an immediate end.

Enfants Terribles

Whereas *Adieu Philippine* satirized the containment of young women in technological society within traditional definitions of femininity, *Les Tricheurs* punished its female character for displacing romance and sentiment with androgynous desires and fantasies. Each film in its own way used the saturation of detail about the feminine to suggest the unrepresentability of the Algerian war. For Rozier, unrepresentability is the effect of the technical and ideological constraints of the media of television and cinema. In Carné's didactic approach, one line at the end of the film is intended to reconfigure Mic's incomprehensible rejection of femininity, her descent into criminality and dangerous and inappropriate desires, as a palimpsest for the self-destructiveness of the nation. "Cinquante ans de pagaille derrière eux" [Fifty years of chaos behind them]—not only Algeria, but both world wars are rendered on screen in ghostly presence by the loss of feminine intactness, the feminine made unfamiliar, and by Mic's suicide. In contrast to the fiction of defamiliarization and refamiliarization, the tone of first-person accounts and media coverage of the depoliticized conscripts' repoliticization was one of triumph. But these final messages do not annul the trajectories, represented or real, that precede them. "Girls will be girls" and "boys will be boys," but only in counterpoint to the blurring of gendered identities and desires and the accompanying erasure of class difference in the shared quest for fun and pleasure that had become a recognizable mode of representation of youth. The fun-loving teen consumer as the brainchild of consumer society itself would, in turn, be seen in terms of the artifice of its commercial apotheosis: in the movements of May 1968, students used the imposed categorization as a form of self-empowerment, making demands of the culture that created it. Emerging from the crucible of the expression of others' ideologies, youth would finally speak for themselves, creating an image in which a new desire came to the fore, the desire for change. As the graffiti reads, "Cours camarade, le vieux monde est derrière toi": an "old world" of existentialists, J-3s, tricheurs, copains—and enfants terribles.

5 Quantifying Youth

The cast of characters has now come to a critical mass. Through the media of newspapers, magazines, novels, films, advertisements, and popular music, we have seen how young men were aligned with the positivity of the social, young women with the sexual. From individuals both real and fictional we can make the connection to categorical labels as they circulated in French culture: young woman writer, existentialist, *hussard,* J-3, *tricheur, copain.* This is the advantage of hindsight: the category of "youth" as it was ceaselessly created and recreated was not exclusively a function of individual characters, but of nameless others they were deemed to represent. What sort of transformation had to take place in order to create the category called youth, in which the thoughts, feelings, actions, and experiences of real and fictional people could be neatly quantified and infinitely collected? How can human subjects in their multidimensionality and self-contradictions be counted as identical? This chapter studies the discursive form that most literally carries out this transformation: the opinion poll, or survey, and its role in creating the category of youth in France in the postwar period. Belonging to the category "youth" meant nothing more than that: theirs was a discursive alliance that required no self-consciousness, in which membership was gained simultaneously to the enunciative act. The plethora of quantitative findings about youth in the 1950s ultimately say too little by limiting the meaning of (male) adolescence to the nexus of history, memory, and politics.

While surveys as straight population counts can be traced back at least two thousand years, they evolved in the twentieth century into a more complex apparatus to study the social, political, and economic habits and attitudes of large populations in industrialized societies.[1] In its contemporary usage the survey has most broadly served social scientists and political and economic elites whose diverse and protean object has been discursively circumscribed as "the public." The public, in turn, has demonstrated a fascination with how surveys see them, looking to statistical findings, according to Jean Converse's history of the phenomenon, as "a mirror of its own time, of its national political opinions, beliefs, and experiences."[2] The mirror may be too passive a metaphor to describe surveys in their capacity to do cultural work: in surveys of youth, the relationship between real people and the findings that claim to mirror them is less a matter of one-way reflection than it is of dialectical formation. The survey's structure and methods make it, in Pierre Bourdieu's words, an artifact: a man-made instrument whose politicized but effaced effect is to impose the illusion that there exists something out there identifiable as "public opinion," a simple sum of its parts. For Bourdieu, public opinion is a complex system that has to be understood in terms of the status of different social groups at a given time, some of which have more weight than others. Opinions are vector-like forces, writes Bourdieu, and there exists nothing more inadequate to express them than percentages.[3]

"Public opinion does not exist," Bourdieu can thus aver; but for those of us who study culture, surveys are no less interesting for it. As discursive instruments with social and political repercussions, as artifacts, surveys have the power to say that categories of people exist in the world: in philosopher Ian Hacking's term, the power to "make up people."[4] What comes first, discursive category or real people? Hacking sidesteps the endlessly debatable question by arguing that they emerge simultaneously. What is at stake, though, is not the establishment of an origin, but the concealed power belonging uniquely to a discourse that effaces its authorial dimension and presents itself as objective.

Boys versus Girls

At the base of the survey's claim to social truth-value is its axiom that individuals can be counted and labeled as identical: residents of Marseilles, workers at Renault, or in the present case, youth. From 1951 on, the onslaught of surveys of youth served to confirm and legitimate the existence of the category and put "youth" into discursive circulation as a structural element of the national human landscape. Many of them acknowledged as the pioneer in the field Agathon's 1910 survey on the state of France's future leaders for the newspaper *L'Opinion*. Agathon was a pseudonym for the collaborative efforts of French Academy member Henri Massis and journalist Alfred de Tarde, the latter a son of sociologist Gabriel de Tarde, who has recently been rediscovered by contemporary conservatives in France. In his book *Lois de l'Imitation* (1890), Gabriel de Tarde challenged the dominant Durkheimian view by arguing that social facts were not collective but individual phenomena, transmitted from person to person. Alfred de Tarde put his father's theory into practice in collaboration with Massis, and the result was one of the first efforts to identify and describe a particular social group.[5] In 1913, Massis and De Tarde's findings were published in book form under the title *Les Jeunes gens d'aujourd'hui*.

This study appeared at a time when a social divide was becoming increasingly apparent within the biological category of "jeunes gens." An effect of the Third Republic's policy of expanding secondary education was the social separation of students and apprentices: two very different class-based experiences of being young. The bourgeois student in his extended period of academic study, removed from the cares of learning a trade and wage earnings, increasingly came to define the category of youth situated vaguely between childhood and adulthood.[6] The *Opinion* survey aptly illustrates how privileged young men were the de facto equivalent of "young people of today" at the turn of the twentieth century. Students at the best schools in Paris, "la jeunesse cultivée et élite," they were also exclusively male. This was less a blind spot than an intentional focus: on the eve of World War I, Massis and Tarde sought out France's future political leaders. In conversations with young men and their teachers, they found a dramatic contrast between the attitudes of this generation and the fatalistic pessimism and antipatriotism of the generation of 1885. Unlike their elders, these young men were capable of balancing practicality, intellect, patriotism, and spirituality.

Objectivity was not the goal of the *Opinion* survey. Participating in the Third Republic consensus that youth should be the bearers of the nation's ideals and that the place to learn those ideals was the army, Massis and De Tarde imbued their findings with an ideological purpose that was clear: to reassure the nation that it was in the good, strong, and patriotic hands of elite young men. At the same time, Massis and De Tarde were aware of the power of a laudatory description of the rising generation when presented as "findings," and its potential to do cultural work. By communicating the ideas and attitudes of the elite, their survey, they asserted, had the potential to mobilize the rest of French youth:

> Il n'est pas interdit, au surplus, de croire que l'influence d'une telle enquête importe autant que son exactitude historique. Elle est elle-même un acte . . . En définissant les ardentes suggestions de beaucoup d'entre eux, elle aide les plus hésitants à les distinguer en eux-mêmes, elle accroît leur foi et double leur énergie.[7]

> [Moreover, it is not prohibited to believe that the influence of such a study is just as important as its historical accuracy. It is itself an act . . . In defining the ardent suggestions of many of them (young men), it helps the most hesitant to articulate such ardency in themselves, it increases their faith and doubles their energy.]

Crucially timed, *Les Jeunes gens* was an instrument of political action that imposed an unequivocal enthusiastic patriotism as the collective identity of France's elite male youth in order to encourage the patriotic ideal in others. The Agathon survey was the first to make youth "the crucible for the expression of ideologies," in this instance the expression of a nationalist imperative whose central literary reference was *Les Déracinés,* Maurice Barrès's "roman de l'énergie nationale."[8] Surveys that put the category of youth to similar use would become ubiquitous in the post–World War II period.

Why do categorizations of youth rather than any other group give rise to the expression of ideologies? Most banally, they are tomorrow's adults. To attempt to define youth as a category of identity is thus to enter into the realm of the hopes and fears for the future, whether those of a culture, a religion, a nation, or the world. More complex was the practice, in the overwhelming majority of surveys in the 1950s, of seeking out a sample that is male. Surveys of youth from this period tell just as much about a long-standing ideology of equating the masculine with universality as they do about a projected future. Again and again, "youth," who are in fact young men, are called upon to speak in the name of their generation about politics, the economy, technology, and science. The unarticulated limit of the category of youth in masculinity facilitates their singular conjuncture with "the positivity of the social": the symbolic order, language, and culture.[9]

It does not necessarily require a late-twentieth-century mode of thought to recognize this slippage between youth, masculinity, and the symbolic order. There was an immediate response to *Les Jeunes gens* and its masculine specificity. It was also a social-science-inspired survey first published in *L'Opinion* and then in book form: *Les Jeunes filles d'aujourd'hui*. The author, Amélie Gayraud, was a lycée teacher whose sample consisted of the female counterparts to Agathon's elite young men: students, artists, and "bourgeoises," between the ages of eighteen and twenty-five. With methods even less objective than those of Massis and Tarde, Gayraud questioned only girls she knew personally. The shadow of war is absent from this survey, whose questions are somewhat more limited in scope but not at all limited to the private sphere. They covered three major areas: love and marriage; patriotism, politics, and religion; work and sport.

Gayraud's goals were just as overtly ideological as those of Massis and Tarde, albeit in a different register. The book's epigraph answered the question, "what are girls like in this day and age?" with a resounding exclamation: "Il y a un point qui dès l'abord se dégage nettement: nous sommes. Nous sommes des personnes, nous existons par nous-mêmes" [There is one point that is immediately clear: we are. We are people, we exist by ourselves]. Gayraud's was clearly a feminist project. In a commentary on the epigraph, she explained that the generation of adolescent girls of 1914 did not adhere to the meek and innocuous image of what at the time was considered to be traditional femininity: "Cette génération est celle de la discipline" [This is a generation of discipline], she emphasized, whose education had formed them to prefer the reason, sense, and order of a philosopher like Auguste Comte to the dreamy poetry of Anna de Noailles.[10]

Although the study hailed an intellectual rigor not usually associated with girls, the tone *Les Jeunes filles* adopted was ultimately a conciliatory one. While the modern girls of 1914 were intellectually rigorous, Gayraud noted that it was still less important for them to have an intellectual doctrine than it was to have a sentimental ideal. The girls of her acquaintance were reflective, but "elles sont moins originales, moins affirmatives dans le domaine purement intellectuel que dans le domaine sentimental qui leur appartient en propre, où elles ont un rôle *spécial* à jouer" [11] [they are less original, less affirmative in the purely intellectual domain than they are in the sentimental domain, which belongs exclusively to them, where they have a *special* role to play]. Gayraud attributed the disproportionate energy her students put into securing love and marriage and starting a family to the tension between girls' own evolving sense of themselves as individuals and the long-standing social norms that dictated that they should live relationally: that female success should be defined as finding a husband, and that female patriotism should take the form of giving birth to future soldiers. There was, however, one sign of resistance that Gayraud detected to the dictates of custom: unlike their male counterparts, these girls exhibited a noticeable decline in religious faith.

Despite its ultimate conservatism and methodological naïveté, Gayraud's survey is remarkable; there is no comparable recognition of, or response to, the absence of young women in post–World War II surveys of youth until 1957. One of Gayraud's own observations provides an important clue. What inspired her to conduct the survey was the difference she perceived between Massis and De Tarde's boys, and girls of her acquaintance: "On peut parler d'une âme collective de l'adolescence virile. L'adolescence féminine est beaucoup plus multiple" [We can speak of a collective spirit of male adolescence. Female adolescence is much more multiple]. Gayraud's definition of "multiple" was a socioeconomic one: she saw girls identifying more strongly than boys did with their social class and allying with each other along those lines, creating divisions rather than community. But her difficulty in establishing a category, an "âme collective," for female adolescence doubles as a recognition of the discursive phenomenon at work, bringing us to the consistent categorization of youth as a social and historical experience that was implicitly male—and the definition of adolescent masculinity in terms that were exclusively sociohistorical.

The New Empiricism

The Agathon and Gayraud surveys stood alone in their time, but in the post–World War II period, there was a constant impulse to quantify and define youth, their goals, desires, world view, cultural and political preferences. Testimony to the intellectual legitimation of the social sciences during these years, the beginnings of a sociology of youth nevertheless remained strongly psychological, as in the work of its foremost practitioner of the time, Maurice Debesse (*Comment étudier les adolescents*, 1948).[12] Journalistic surveys of youth often demonstrate an awkward combination of popularized sociological methods and psychological descriptions. Nineteen fifty-one, 1953, 1957, 1960, and 1961 were especially bountiful years for surveys of youth: 1957 alone saw three major surveys conducted for prominent weeklies. While social statisticians were not usually involved in collecting and analyzing samples prior to the landmark *Nouvelle Vague* poll of 1957, surveys of youth in the 1950s solemnly presented themselves as partisans of what might be called a new empiricism, claiming that the young interviewees, be they a group of twenty or two thousand, represented "French youth," and claiming as well the survey's objective status as a limpid mirror. The interviewer, they averred, was only a scribe.

The new empiricism was not a harkening back to Condorcet's revolutionary "social mathematics" or Comte's positivism, but the importation of the very latest methods and techniques from the United States.[13] The emissary of quantitative methods was Jean Stoetzel, director of the Centre d'Etudes Sociologiques (CES) and creator of the Institut Français d'Opinion Publique (IFOP), a French version of the Gallup Institute. Stoetzel had trained at Gallup and was a friend and student of one of the influential founders of market research, Paul F. Lazarsfeld. Under Stoetzel's influence, sociological research in France became fieldwork as well as intellectual work. Sociologists in the 1950s and into the 1960s considered themselves to be "real" professionals, as opposed to "salon sociologists," meaning philosophers and university professors, who had never gone to see people and written down what they said.[14]

American-style empiricism was welcome in the social research institutes that had originally been founded by the Vichy government and given new life in the Fourth Republic under new names: the Fondation Alexis Carrel Pour l'Etude de l'Homme became the Institut National d'Etudes Démographiques (INED); the Institut National d'Hygiène became the Institut National de la Santé et de la Recherche Médicale (INSERM); the Statistique Générale de la France became the extremely influential Institut National de la Statistique et des Etudes Economiques (INSEE), the national clearinghouse for data. The CES, independent of prior Vichy initiatives, was founded in 1946. Along with the unlikely pairing of Americanization and the recycling of Vichy's institutes, the increasing availability of automobiles also facilitated the establishment of empirical sociology. An interviewer in a car could reach populations outside major cities with an ease and efficiency train travel could never provide.

Along with applied social research, academia was also opening up to the social sciences in this period. In order to combat what Kristin Ross terms the "structuralist conquest of the humanities," dominated in the early postwar years by the politicized Marxist philosophy of Jean-Paul Sartre and Henri Lefebvre, historians of the *Annales* school, with their focus on long duration and the cyclical nature of historical time, began to welcome the social sciences and structuralism into a new alliance, though one in which history would retain its dominance.[15] Nineteen fifty saw the founding of the PUF series Bibliothèque de sociologie contemporaine, directed by Georges Gurvitch, and the publication of his *La Vocation actuelle de la sociologie* as well as Maurice Halbwach's *La Mémoire collective* and Marcel Mauss's *Sociologie et anthropologie.* In that same year, the first statistical study of a French city was published: Charles Bettelheim and S. Frère's monograph *Une ville française moyenne. Auxerre en 1950: étude de structure sociale et urbaine,* with a preface by *Annales* historian Lucien Febvre. Such an eminent assemblage was instrumental in sociology's intellectual legitimation. This had its institutional culmination in 1958, when with the advocacy of Raymond Aron, the *normalien* founder of the Centre Européen de Sociologie and an early advocate of the discipline, the undergraduate degree *(licence)* and *doctorat de troisième cycle* in sociology were established.

American-style empiricism in the social sciences took hold in France under the auspices and with the funds of a sort of intellectual Marshall Plan.[16] The Eisenhower administration took interest in French cultural life because of the perceived dual threat of Communism and anti-Americanism. As a State Department memorandum of 1946 dramatically stated, "The world drama of Russian expansion is being played in miniature on the stage of France."[17] The American response, beginning in 1948 and peaking in 1952, took the form of a cultural and informational campaign to promote the American national image in the French mass media: press releases, radio programs, documentaries, libraries, and glossy magazines presented in glowing terms the "American way of life" and American achievements in science and the arts.[18] The U.S. State Department saw the social sciences as the best point of access to combat the influence of Communism in French intellectual life. The new journal *Preuves,* for example, received subsidies from the United States Information and Education Agency in France. And it was American money from the Rockefeller and Ford Foundations that helped establish the social sciences at the Ecole pratique des hautes études and the Maison des sciences de l'homme.[19] The new empiricism did present a strong challenge to the intellectual mood of philosophical inquiry and politicized *engagement* that had dominated the early postwar years, but more in dialogue than as replacement: even in their quantitative data, French sociologists consistently situated themselves in relation to Marxism and focused their studies in the early 1950s on the working classes and industry.[20]

Politicizing Malaise

One of the American-style sociologists' principal guarantees of scientific rigor was the opinion poll. It was readily taken up as a means of access to France's population of youth. A significant early attempt to survey the post–World War II generation was conducted by Robert Kanters and Gilbert Sigaux for the journal *Hommes et mondes* in 1951. Kanters and Sigaux stated that their objective was to look beyond the stereotypes of postwar youth, beyond the seedy chic milieu of the Latin Quarter, and at the rest of the nation. They limited themselves to the age group of seventeen to twenty-five, with the goal of portraying a generation "telle qu'elle est, et telle qu'elle parle, au plus près" [as it is, as it speaks, as closely as possible]. They aimed to find out what this group thought about love, society, culture, and the fate of the earth.[21] The surveys were later published in book form under the title *Vingt ans en 1951*. Why 1951? According to the authors, it was a moment of respite between the Occupation and the future conflicts that augured in North Africa and elsewhere. In 1951, young people had not yet been remobilized or repolarized by the next great cause or conflict.[22] But the Cold War was at hand, exacerbating an already existing polarization in French culture. In January of that year, the French Communist Party mobilized what turned out to be a fiery protest against Eisenhower's visit to Paris, resulting in over three thousand arrests; in April, the Rosenbergs received the death penalty, triggering an international campaign for their pardon; Sartre railed against the rabidity of McCarthyism in *Les Temps modernes;* in June, the French Communist Party lost half a million votes in the legislative elections; the French translation of Orwell's *1984,* was published as was Camus's equally anti-totalitarian *Homme révolté,* to outright criticism from the Left and praise from the Right.[23] In such an ideologically heated climate, the only place to talk about a difficult recent past that did not fit the Right-Left divide—the memory of the Occupation—was in diagnoses of youth. Surveys quantified the persistence of the Occupation's irresolutions in a one-to-one equivalence with the psychology of adolescence, and made the formulation into a social fact.

In *Vingt ans en 1951*, it is the J-3 affair that continually crops up as the key reference to a generation's simultaneous trauma and coming of age. Towards the end of the book version of the survey, the authors wondered how many teenagers, although they might not have gone as far as murdering one of their friends, had been exposed to the same moral contamination, "les germes des mêmes maladies morales" as the Melun youth, simply because they too were twenty years old in 1951. In a tone worthy of the Cayatte film, they set the stage of early adolescence during the Occupation:

[L]eurs parents avaient menti et fraudé pour se procurer le nécessaire pour leur repas de première communion; leurs premières cigarettes étaient doublement clandestines, parce qu'elles étaient achetées au «noir»; ils ont peut être perdu leur pucelage dans les bras d'une fille qui venait de se vendre à un soldat ennemi; leur conscience s'est éveillée dans le black-out, tandis que la ville était sans lumière . . . Ce sont des enfants de la nuit, certes; les larves d'une certaine nuit de la conscience.[24]

[Their parents had cheated and lied to get what they needed for their first communion dinner; their first cigarettes were twice clandestine, because they were bought on the black market; they lost their virginity, perhaps, in the arms of a girl who had just sold herself to an enemy soldier; their conscience was awakened in the blackout period, while the city was without light . . . These are children of the night, it is certain; the larvae of a certain night of conscience.]

The rare reference here to male adolescent sexuality is striking, but loss of intactness, along with other coming-of-age rites, is completely circumscribed by the sociopolitical context of the Occupation: the black market, curfew, and Nazi soldiers, overlaying each of the differently formative moments of communion, sexual initiation, and first cigarettes with a uniform sense of abjection. One has to be a teenage boy for this overlay to function. The solely masculine attribution of the invariable third person plural adjective and pronoun repeated in the series of clauses, *leur* and *ils*, makes itself understood with the evocation of the first sexual encounter. The girl who is their willing partner, who has "just sold herself to an enemy soldier," is implicated in the chain of signifiers of abjection, but she herself lacks subjectivity in the reductive superposition of psychosocial development with the political. Not until Marguerite Duras's *Hiroshima mon amour* (1959) would the female experience of first love with a German soldier be imagined in the true ambiguity of the situation: illicitness and innocence, pleasure and danger, loss and plenitude and shame. In the picture of coming-of-age and the Occupation presented in *Vingt ans en 1951,* on the contrary, war memories are given an easily assimilable psychic place, that of corrupter of the morality of the nation's young men, for whom the lying, cheating, and betrayal they had observed in adults had become a matter of course. Ultimately, it was far easier to speak about corrupted youth than about either the realities or ambiguities of individuals' wartime dealings with the Germans.

Whereas the masculine bias of *Vingt ans en 1951* went unarticulated and unexamined, the authors did remark, to their credit, the middle-class nature of the malaise. But they give no further analysis and, in view of the title, made middle-class teenage boys as a group speak for all twenty year-olds in France. Quantitative analysis was not the objective of *Vingt ans en 1951*. Kanters and Sigaux were very much authors of their survey, which in effect is a work of melodrama. Lyrical passages imagining what life must be like young men abound; individual responses to survey questions are interpreted with literary references. Inflated language establishes the tone. The truth-value of this melodrama, though, required both the framing presence of history and politics and the legitimation of the survey as the outwardly quantitative discursive form at its base.

The moral chaos of the Occupation along with the sense of imminent death and destruction that characterized the Cold War mentality were certainly not the realm of young men alone. To portray them as such was a convenient means to reduce and categorize a disaffection whose causes were multiple and diffuse and not only historical, to neatly explain a desire for immediate pleasure, the disregard for any moment but the present, as a coping mechanism unique to adolescents in 1951. By "politicizing" male adolescent malaise, Kanters and Sigaux contained it within the conceptual limits of current events.

The New Wave

Lyricism, melodrama, and historicopolitical objectifications of adolescence did not last, however. In a world increasingly dominated by scientific invention and technological advances, it was not long before the methods used to survey youth became more "scientific," and the resulting concepts of the subjects devoid of the references to global politics and wartime trauma that had dominated earlier inquiries. In 1957, the news magazine *L'Express* conducted extensive surveys of French youth between the ages of eighteen and thirty, and named them—several years before the filmmakers associated with the *Cahiers du cinéma* took the label as their own—*la Nouvelle Vague,* or the New Wave. As a designation for youth, the term *Nouvelle Vague* held sway for several years. In her solicitation for the survey, editor Françoise Giroud wrote that this would be the first truly exhaustive look at France's youth, "de tous les milieux, toutes les classes sociales, destinée à faire apparaître, pour la première fois, ce qu'est en profondeur la nouvelle génération des Français"[25] [from all milieus, all social classes, destined to show, for the first time, in depth, what the new generation of French are like]. To assure the desired diversity, the questionnaire appeared in newspapers that targeted readerships other than the somewhat Left, somewhat young, and somewhat intellectual bourgeoisie of *L'Express:* the populist *France-Soir, Paris-Presse* on the Right, and *La Terre Nouvelle,* read in agricultural milieus. What was quite new about the *Express* survey was the size of the sample—fifteen thousand responses collected—and the fact that it was the first to be conducted and analyzed by the Institut Français d'Opinion Publique (IFOP) using quantitative methods.

The questions in the Nouvelle Vague survey ranged from the personal, to the national, to the global: for example, do you think your generation will be different from the previous generation, and how?; do you feel lucky to be living at this time, and why?; what is the best job for a young man of twenty?; what is the best direction for a young woman? Workers, students, young professionals, farmers, housewives, secretaries, and employees, responded; *L'Express* printed a selection of their letters during the months of October and November. When compared with other images of youth that were in circulation at the time, the statistics on the Nouvelle Vague generation are startling. There were eight million people between the ages of eighteen and thirty in France in 1957. Of the males, most (44 percent) were workers, and fewer than 10 percent were students. Of the females, 46 percent were "sans profession," a catchall category generally meaning housewives; the next largest category was workers (19 percent). Students and "others" accounted for only 9 percent. Seventy-six percent of the youth surveyed said they were no different from their parents' generation; 69 percent of the men said that the best orientation for a woman was to devote herself to her home. In the responses quoted from this supposedly apolitical generation, there were strong opinions on all sides regarding the war with Algeria. The Right was largely represented for its racist shock value with quotations in bold, such as "les Juifs au four crématoire!"

Despite the findings, the reality of the *Nouvelle Vague* generation—conservative, working class, politicized—quickly evaporated from the popular imagination; only the catchy label remained. The term became even more of a tag after 1958 when Gallimard published a volume that compiled the results of the study along with an analysis and commentary by Françoise Giroud.[26] The media did not hesitate to christen as *Nouvelle Vague* the singular young stars who were most nonrepresentative of their eight million peers: writer Françoise Sagan; filmmaker Roger Vadim; actress Brigitte Bardot.

Before the Giroud volume appeared, *L'Express* printed the reactions of Alfred Sauvy, director of the Institut National d'Etudes Démographiques, and Marxist sociologist Henri Lefebvre to the results of the Nouvelle Vague survey. While Sauvy, like many others at the time, focused on how technology had transformed the lives of young people, Lefebvre was more interested in the discursive phenomenon of the survey, its capacity to do cultural work. He began with the observation that the decision to focus on this particular age group was itself more revealing than what young people actually had to say: "On les a traités en groupe particulier, non intégré à la réalité sociale actuelle . . . N'expriment-ils pas, dans ce sentiment de non-intégration, l'exigence d'une transformation sociale beaucoup mieux que dans leurs opinions politiques?"[27] [They have been treated as a particular group, nonintegrated into today's social reality . . . Do they not thus express the exigency of a social transformation much better in this sentiment of nonintegration than they do in their political opinions?]

Young people, wrote Lefebvre, like women, peasants, and workers, were becoming one of the "nonintegrated" groups that made up French society—an effect of representation ("they have been treated") rather than a sentiment shared by real people. Paradoxically, most of those surveyed felt completely integrated. Seventy-six percent claimed that their world was no different from that of their parents, that generations were all the same, "les générations se valent," a nonchalant position bearing little resemblance to the melancholy of the Romantics, Agathon's fervent Catholics on the eve of World War I, or the dispiritedness of the young "existentialists" and the J-3s.

Lefebvre brilliantly turned such unsensational commentaries into the survey's most significant findings. According to him, young people's averred traditionalism and sense of continuity pointed to a lack of audacity and confidence to affirm their own newness. To deny their difference from any other generation was self-delusional: there were real, political issues particular to youth in the 1950s, signaled by the ineffectual attempts of Fourth Republic institutions to address them. Youth's paradoxical sense of continuity in the face of governmental concern about them was the most historically meaningful finding for Lefebvre. He hypothesized rejection of dramatic theories about the particularity of the postwar generation to be the unconscious translation of the two great social and political failures of modern times: the Popular Front and the Liberation. By the overwhelming proportion of young people who identified themselves, most banally, as "assez houroux" [happy enough], youth in 1957 captured for him the economic, social, and political stagnation of *immobilisme*.

On the other hand, by affirming that they were "happy enough," the *Nouvelle Vague* generation accepted—or, says Lefebvre, believed they accepted—the state of things in the late 1950s. Such indifference translated the adamant refusal to come off as poorly adapted to the fast pace of contemporary life and its new technology. Desperately, they wanted to appear integrated with the world around them: "Le sentiment juvénile de révolte, puissant autrefois, s'estompe, s'il n'a pas disparu" [The youthful sentiment of revolt, powerful in the past, is effaced, if it hasn't completely disappeared]. For Lefebvre, all the evidence pointed to the fact that youth was becoming a new sector of the bourgeoisie. Yet at the same time, he could not dismiss them: the Nouvelle Vague generation was highly aware of the world around them, of social injustice and inequality. A decade before May 1968, Lefebvre wondered whether a "silent revolution" was not occurring within the ranks of the generation of the Nouvelle Vague—silent, for they certainly lacked the theatricality of their predecessors.

Lefebvre nuanced the findings of the *Express* survey with observations about profound yet undramatic social change, fitting for a Marxist theorist of everyday life. Furthermore, he addressed the question of representation, offering cogent commentary on the kind of cultural and ideological work the survey performed: putting the category of youth into circulation, making it exist for others to perceive, transforming a diverse assortment of people into a new and cohesive social group. What was left out were all the paradoxes of which human experience was woven.

In the same year as the Nouvelle Vague survey, other highly reputed weeklies focused on the group who was most nonrepresentative of youth: students. Most reminiscent of Agathon was Henri Perruchot's "Jeunesse d'aujourd'hui France de demain" [Youth of Today France of Tomorrow], an ambitious survey conducted and printed over a period of nine months for *Les Nouvelles Littéraires* and also published a year later in book form.[28] Perruchot made the astute observation that the Nouvelle Vague survey tended to quote only intelligent respondents from the "extreme Left." His goal was to restore the equivalence between youth and patriotism, selecting a sample he dubbed the "new aristocrats." Unlike the nihilistic youth of the postwar years who reveled in the bitter pleasure of denying all values, unlike the *tricheurs* one read about in the papers and saw on screen, these young men, Perruchot found, were partisans of order and idealism to an extent greater than any previous generation. Another, much less congratulatory 1957 survey focusing on students was conducted by Jean-René Huguenin and René Matignon for *Arts*. Their prescient goal was to make readers aware of the unfolding crisis in the nation's educational system. France had a higher percentage of students than any other country in Europe, but material conditions were poor, teachers scarce, and scholarships hard to find. Each installment of the *Arts* survey was devoted to a different academic field: literature, political science, art, the sciences. The authors took care to address differences in social class, everyday life, taste in the arts, and moral values.

In one year, three surveys claimed to present the true significance of French youth, and they all came to very different conclusions. Besides their contradictions, what remains is the sense that youth mattered: a meaningfulness deriving primarily from young men.

Imagining Empiricism

Following the survey-turned-media-event that was the Nouvelle Vague, young filmmakers began to make films about youth as an observable category. They took pains to distinguish their approach from that of the older generation of filmmakers, what came to be known as the "cinéma de papa" of directors like Cayatte and Carné. Rather than proffer yet another historically overdetermined diagnosis of the malaise or adjustment of youth, they took on, as Lefebvre did, the question of diagnosis and categorization itself. Some did this indirectly: Eric Rohmer's *La Carrière de Suzanne*, Jean-Luc Godard's *A Bout de souffle* and *Tous les garçons s'appellent Pat-*

rick, Roger Vadim's *Et Dieu créa la femme* all focus on the youthfulness of their protagonists without moralizing or explaining their behavior through current events. In a more explicit vein, two films take on the actual methods and form of the ubiquitous social-science-inspired surveys of youth: Bertrand Blier's *Hitler . . . connais pas!* [Hitler . . . don't know the guy!] (1963) and Jean-Luc Godard's *Masculin/Féminin* (1965). Blier and Godard both imagine empiricism, narrating and visualizing an encounter that is ordinarily reduced to "findings," a written text. They ultimately make a statement about the superiority of cinema as a medium where youth are observed rather than defined—a bid for the highest truth-value, which, as we shall see, can be just as troubling.

Hitler . . . connais pas! is composed of interviews of eleven nameless twenty-year-olds, edited and spliced together as a kaleidoscope of responses to never-pronounced questions. The camera jumps abruptly from one person to the next and back again, with no apparent logic. It communicates the all-powerful position of the interviewer to fit the overwhelming diversity of real people into a singular unifying category. By making power visual, Blier raised provocative questions about the subjectivism hidden in empiricism. He did so while eschewing the humorlessness that characterizes the myriad written surveys and exposés of the 1950s. For *Hitler . . . connais pas!* is steeped in irony from the title on. Blier plays upon what had come to be the French public's preconceived notion of the apolitical nature of the nation's youth, who were nevertheless molded by the experience of wartime. Not once do any of the interviewees in Blier's film mention Hitler's name—or indeed, anything having to do with current politics or recent history (fig. 24).

The film opens "behind the scenes," with slow pans over the studio where the interviews will take place. Lights, cameras, technicians, all the inner workings used to create a sense of naturalness in cinema are placed on screen. The lights descend with exaggerated slowness toward the first girl to be interviewed, as if she were an exotic species under a monstrous microscope. We never see the interviewer or hear a voice. The camera is the sole testimony of the interviewer's presence, playing coyly and sometimes cruelly with its specimens, noticing a leg crossed and uncrossed, catching an expression of disdain, quickly coming in for a closeup from several different angles, coming in yet closer and lingering on a particularly unhappy moment of revelation (fig. 25). It dwells on the aimless boy living in one room with his entire family, the unwanted pregnancy of a fac-

Fig. 24. A sensationalistic juxtaposition: Hitler and French youth
Reprinted with permission from Claude Schwartz, photographer

tory worker, the uptight student's fixation on his mother, the wealthy girl spending days on end alone in her parents' vast apartment.

The only parts of the interviews we see, after the violent editing and cutting obvious to any viewer, are the shocking ones: from both sexes, emotionless admissions of disregard for parents and teachers; from the middle-class girls, a calculatingly cold relationship to romance and sexuality. As one says dispassionately of her first lover, who stole from her to go out with other girls, "Ça a été Philippe. Ça aurait pu être n'importe qui" [It was Philippe. It could've been anyone]. As another tells it, the worst part of breaking up with her boyfriend was that she had to spend more time with her parents. What do these antisentimental girls dream of? Money. Expensive cars. Married life, on the other hand, "la vie bourgeoise," is a prospect they all hold in horror. The boys want just that: love, romance, stability, someone to spend quiet evenings with at home. The "real" girls Blier interviews go beyond all the fictional machinations of *enfants terribles*. "Les jeunes filles sont devenues des jeunes gens"—and vice-versa.

While *Hitler . . . connais pas!* exposes the subjectivity inherent to a form that pretends to objectivity, its content is familiar, and it would seem

that Blier intended it as such. Diagnosed and exposed, hackneyed and de-
pleted, "youth" in 1963 held no surprises. Even as he reveals the used-up
content of diagnoses of youth and the relations of power inherent to the
survey, Blier deploys both. His film thus remains within the discourse he
simultaneously critiques. *Masculin/Féminin*, on the other hand, explores
the subversive possibilities of character development alongside the quasi-
empiricism of the pollster's methods, undermining content as well as form.
Within and without the five "interviews" that punctuate the film, Godard
exposes the binary division of the title, not as a neat coupling, but as two
spheres that may be incompatible. Who knows Madeleine more intimately:
Paul, her boyfriend who happens to be a pollster, or her roommate Elisabeth? *Masculin/Féminin* is loosely based on a Guy de Maupassant short
story, "L'amie de Paul," where the protagonist commits suicide when he
discovers that the girl he loves is a lesbian. "Lesbian" is never pronounced
in Godard's version, where female complicity nevertheless goes beyond
the innocence of Rozier's *jeunes filles*, expressing itself outside of definitions and categories, questions and answers. It is rather the insistent gazes,

Fig. 25. Youth "behind the scenes"
Reprinted with permission from Claude Schwartz, photographer

innuendo, and knowing silence between Madeleine and Elisabeth that prove most exasperating and exclusionary for Paul, interrupting his sense of complacency as "Madeleine's boyfriend" when he least expects it: on the dance floor, in the movie theatre, over lunch.

Paul (Jean-Pierre Léaud), a vaguely Communist intellectual who has just completed his military service, runs into Madeleine (Chantal Goya), rising star of the *yé-yé* music scene. She gets him a job at the magazine where she and her friends work, *Mademoiselle 19 ans*(based on the magazine *Mademoiselle Age Tendre*) after which he is able to get a position at the IFOP, the national market research institute. Such are the employment possibilities in 1965 for a young man like Paul, who in his free time puts up anti-Gaullist posters, signs petitions against colonial wars even if he knows nothing about them, and scribbles anti-American graffiti on a limousine parked in front of the American embassy. Madeleine, like every other female character encountered thus far, has no such conflict between her convictions and her professional options. She has no interest in current events; she knows and cares little about history. When she and Paul overhear a conversation between a prostitute and a young German about her price that turns to a debate about German guilt, all Madeleine notices is that the woman is a prostitute.

With her disregard for the irresolutions of history and the minefield of current events, Madeleine incarnates instead the discursive link between the worlds of market research and women's magazines; their language is most eerily her own. In the diary entry she reads aloud in voice-over, for example, a description of her winter coat and Elisabeth's suffices to encapsulate November 1965—the same month in which Paul engages in guerilla tactics on the streets of Paris. In one of the film's two "official" interviews, a television reporter approaches Madeleine on the occasion of the release of her second record. Her friend and colleague Catherine (Catherine-Isabelle Duport), stands close by. The reporter is bewildered by Madeleine's averral that her favorite "singers" are the Beatles and Bach, the latter Paul's preferred composer, but he duly takes note of it. He then asks a purposely vague question:

INTERVIEWER: Vous avez des signes particuliers?
MADELEINE: Comme signes particuliers, je me maquille pratiquement jamais, et puis, dans mes habits voyez, je porte . . . des kilts . . .
INTERVIEWER: C'est la tenue jeune fille?
MADELEINE: Voilà.

INTERVIEWER: Vous aimez ça?

MADELEINE: Oui, j'adore ça.

INTERVIEWER: D'autre part j'ai remarqué aux Etats-Unis le long des routes d'énormes panneaux, et sur ces panneaux on voit, "Vous faites partie de la génération Pepsi." Vous en faites partie?

MADELEINE: Ah oui! J'adore le Pepsi-Cola!

INTERVIEWER: C'est vrai?

MADELEINE: Oui oui, c'est vrai.

[INTERVIEWER: Have you any special characteristics?

MADELEINE: Well, as for special characteristics, I almost never use make-up. And then as for, as for clothing, you see I wear . . . I wear flat shoes and then a kilt . . .

INTERVIEWER: The girlish look.

MADELEINE (smiling): That's it.

INTERVIEWER: You like that?

MADELEINE: Yes, I adore it.

INTERVIEWER: On the other hand, I've noticed enormous billboards along the highways in the United States, and on these billboards one sees: "You're in the Pepsi Generation." You're in it?

MADELEINE: Oh yes, I adore Pepsi Cola.

INTERVIEWER: Is that true?

MADELEINE: Yes, yes, it's true.[29]

During the interview, a shot rings out, inexplicably, but no one reacts to it. Instead, Madeleine answers the reporter's search for her essence, her "special characteristics," with details of her wardrobe, which he in turn assimilates to ready-made, appealing discursive categories, "the girlish look," and "the Pepsi generation." Madeleine, thus identified, put into language, is glad to "belong." What does that mean? The reporter probes no further. Madeleine's reductive answers signify the impossibility of expressing anything meaningful when gender and generation have become reified terms, which, for the mass public, speak sufficiently for themselves. Catherine's presence on screen is as enigmatic as Madeleine's responses are programmatic. She looks up at the sky, then straight in front of her, when she hears the reporter's questions. How would she answer them? Madeleine's glibness and Catherine's silence form a complicity that the interview format cannot grasp—but Godard's camera can, and so it is rendered on screen for the viewer.

The would-be empiricism of market research and interviews in women's magazines always undoes itself in *Masculin/Féminin*. In an early scene at the offices of *Mademoiselle 19 ans*, Paul bustles about purposefully while Catherine, in voice-over, pronounces a monologue which clearly could not be printed in the magazine's pages:

> Aujourd'hui. Paris. A quoi rêvent les jeunes filles? Mais quelles jeunes filles? Les vérificatrices de Simca qui n'ont pas le temps de faire l'amour parce qu'elles sont abîmées par le travail? Les petites shampooingueuses et les manucures des Champs Elysées qui font déjà à 18 ans les putes dans les grands hôtels de la Rive Droite? Les écolières du Boulevard Saint-Germain qui connaissent Bergson et Sartre et rien d'autre, parce que leurs parents les bouclent dans leur appartement bourgeois? La Française moyenne n'existe pas.

> [Paris today. What do young women dream of? But which young women? The inspectors at the Simca plant in Nanterre who have no time to make love because they are so overworked? The little hairdressers and manicurists on the Champs Elysées, already, at eighteen, whoring in the big hotels on the Right Bank? The schoolgirls on the Boulevard Saint-Germain who know Bergson and Sartre, but nothing else because their parents keep them locked up in their bourgeois apartments? (a title flashes across the screen: the number 3) The average French girl does not exist.][30]

Catherine's monologue begins with the sort of question we saw in *Elle* and *Mademoiselle* magazines and goes on to expose the purely rhetorical nature of such questions. For rather than quantitative findings, the question can only yield more questions and polemical ones at that, challenging the initial premise by introducing the dimension of social class and putting an abrupt end to ambitious universal inquiry and categorization before it is even undertaken. How can anyone posit the existence of a creature called "the average girl" and presume to enumerate her dreams, when faced with the utter lack of resemblance among experiences in the world of people within an age category? In Godard's Marxist critique, "La Française moyenne n'existe pas."

Surveys throughout the 1950s claimed to expose the face of "average youth," who always happened to be male. In *Masculin/Féminin*, Godard calls our attention to the factor of gender. When the male characters, Paul and his friend Robert (Michel Debord), turn ordinary conversations with Madeleine and Catherine into interviews, the alignment of masculinity with the social and political, of femininity with the sexual and enigmatic are revealed for the viewer as forms of power and powerlessness coded in language. The interview format reveals the vexing nature of gender norms. For the female characters are incapable of what Paul and Robert would call an honest answer.

"What do young women dream of?": Godard visualizes and satirizes the dynamic of interviews that ask the sort of questions that by 1965 could be recognized as unanswerable. We hear the questions, but the camera never directly observes Paul or Robert in the interview scenes. The girls, while dutifully answering questions that immediately take the tone of an interrogation, are present on screen for uninterrupted takes of up to seven minutes before the unflinching eye of the camera. While Blier's camera circles around the interviewees predatorily and vertiginously, zooming in rapidly at different angles and on different body parts, Godard's focuses on the respondent head-on, waist up. And while their responses are strings of clichés, inarticulate mumblings, hesitations, and giggles, the physical presence of the interviewee on screen, the ways in which she signals her discomfort—or her strategies of evasion—are stark reminders of the impossibility of putting real people into language. This is especially noticeable with Madeleine, who is constantly under observation and interrogation. Indeed, what is most memorable about the character (and what I remembered from my first viewing to the second, ten years later) is her tic of constantly touching her already immaculate hair.

In the first of these conversation-interviews, Paul and Madeleine are in the washroom of the offices of *Mademoiselle 19 ans*. Paul wants to know why Madeleine won't go out with him. At first, Paul, unsmiling, is visible only peripherally in the mirror above the sink. We watch Paul watching Madeleine wash her hands, comb her hair, apply makeup, powder her face, put her comb back in her purse, take it out again, look up and down and away. Then Paul is largely off-screen as the camera observes Madeleine giggle and answer his disembodied questions: is he not her type, does she find his nose too big. Madeleine playfully puts Paul in the interviewee position: "Allez, répondez-moi maintenant"—"Now it's your turn"—we see his jaw working, testimony to a discomfort she never manifests. Then Paul reassumes command, and the exchange takes a metaphysical turn:

PAUL: Regardez-moi dans les yeux. A quoi pensez-vous en ce moment quand vous êtes en train de me regarder?

MADELEINE: Mais à rien.

PAUL: Comment rien? Vous êtes bien obligée de penser à quelque chose. On pense toujours à quelque chose. Là quand vous me regardez.

MADELEINE: Ben, je vous regarde.

PAUL: Tout de suite. Mais à quoi vous pensez là, comme ça?

MADELEINE: Ben . . .

PAUL: Oui?

MADELEINE: Qu'est-ce que c'est pour vous le centre du monde?

[PAUL: Look me in the eyes. What are you thinking about right now while you're looking at me?

MADELEINE: Okay. Nothing.

PAUL: What, nothing? You always have to be thinking something. People are always thinking of something: now, when you look at me.

MADELEINE: I am looking at you.

PAUL: Now, but what are you thinking?

MADELEINE: Ah, well . . .

PAUL: Yes?

MADELEINE: What is the center of the universe for you?][31]

By the end of the interview, the tenuousness of Paul's control of the situation becomes loss of control. Even when he is on the offensive, Madeleine does not give him what he wants: quantifiable answers, the meaningful expression in language that one assumes to accompany a direct gaze. When she isn't looking down or away, Madeleine's gaze seems as empty as her smile, as empty as her thoughts when she looks at Paul. Or is it? "Ah, well": whatever she may be thinking she cannot—or does not—articulate as a lucid response to the question "what are you thinking?" What she offers to Paul in its stead is another question, one that turns out to be a canny observation of her own narcissism. For when Paul says without hesitation or reflection that for him the center of the universe is love, Madeleine muses aloud about what her answer would have been: "me." In Godard's version, "market research" comes apart into subversive ellipsis, and the true findings belong to the interviewee.

Godard's choice of always making the interviewer male and the interviewee female places the will to quantify and control human knowledge in the hands of the former, and the impossibility of doing so in those of the latter. This is excruciatingly apparent in the second "real" interview, where Paul interrogates "Elsa"—Elsa Leroy, a real-life teen beauty queen, who was crowned *Mademoiselle Age Tendre* by the eponymous magazine. While Madeleine ultimately slips out of her interviewers' grasp despite a docile appearance, Elsa is mercilessly manipulated by Paul, whose tone is robotically devoid of inflection and whose questions jump abruptly and overtly into the realm of judgement and diagnosis. They are, in the following order: "For you, does socialism still have a chance?" "What is socialism to you?" "What is the American way of life to you?" "Does the word reactionary mean anything to you?" "Do you want to have children?" "What do you know about birth control?" "Do you fall in love often?" "Can you tell me at this moment where there's a war going on in the world?"

Elsa cannot answer these questions; she claims she's confused, she's not qualified to respond. She is only capable of pronouncing clichés. And after her description of the "American way of life," Paul asks her tonelessly, "Does the word 'reactionary' mean anything to you?" Paul's questions do have a logic and order, and they are authorial, testimony to his mounting incredulousness in the face of the person he sees as his apolitical, apathetic, naïve, vacuous interlocutor. Each question is, in fact, his comment on her. Paul's methods may look empirical, but the only element missing from his judgement of Elsa is the prefatory "I think" or "you are."

Towards the end of the film, Paul recalls in voice-over some of the many questions he posed over the preceding three months, while the camera roams over the streets of Paris: in the daytime, at night, in the sun and the rain, over construction sites, crowds of pedestrians, exteriors of cafés, banks, restaurants, boutiques, people descending the stairs of a metro entrance or browsing in a department store. Like the questions he asked Elsa, these shots jump irrationally from subject to subject: "Why are vacuum cleaners selling badly? Do you like cheese in tubes? . . . Poetry, does that interest you? And winter sports? What do you think of short skirts? When you see an accident, what do you do?" He ruminates about his work for the IFOP, the conscious and unconscious roles of the pollster and his object:

Peu à peu, au cours de ces trois mois, je m'aperçus que toutes ces questions souvent, loin de refléter une mentalité collective, la trahissaient et la déformaient. A mon manque d'objectivité, même inconscient, correspondait en effet la plupart du temps un inévitable défaut de sincérité chez ceux que j'interrogeais. Sans le savoir, je les trompais peut-être, et j'étais trompé par eux. Pourquoi? Parce que, sans doute les enquêtes et les sondages oublient vite leur vraie mission qui est l'observation du comportement et partent à la place assidieusement à la recherche d'un jugement de valeur. Je découvris ainsi que toutes les questions que je posais à n'importe quel Français traduisaient en fait une idéologie qui ne correspondait pas aux moeurs actuelles, mais à celles d'hier, du passé.

[Little by little during these three months I've noticed that all these questions, far from reflecting a collective mentality, were frequently betraying and distorting it. My own lack of objectivity, often unconscious, most of the time corresponded to an inevitable lack of sincerity on the part of the people I was questioning. So, without knowing it . . . I was deceiving them and being deceived by them. Why? No doubt because polls and samples soon forget their true purpose, which is the observation of behavior, and insidiously substitute value judgments for research. I discovered that all the questions I was asking conveyed an ideology that didn't correspond to actual customs but to those of yesterday, of the past.] [32]

Masculin/Féminin's critique of the status of surveys as an objective tool of research and analysis is embedded in what is essentially a manifesto for Godardian cinema: the capacity of the camera to observe behavior in the moment, the tendency of people to unintentionally reveal themselves in front of a camera when they are unhindered by scripted dialogue. An iconoclastic film, it could not have been made if there had been no idols to break. By observing all that does not enter into quantitative findings—the tone of voice and physicality of interviewer and interviewee, the order of questions, the moments of inarticulateness—Godard's film takes on the subjective and gendered dimension of the process and exposes it as a game of bad faith. By rendering visible the norms of gender that are inscribed in language and culture, *Masculin/Féminin* self-consciously perpetuates these norms and holds them up for the viewer's critique. Madeleine's poker-faced assent that she is part of the Pepsi generation is a far cry from Amélie Gayraud's spirited "nous sommes!," testifying not only to the depletion of consumerist categorizations of youth but to their nonspectacular gender-inclusiveness as well. No one overtly says "we" in *Masculin/Féminin.* In 1966 no one needed to. Consumer culture had taken over as the ventriloquist for an undifferentiated "youth" of both sexes and all social classes.

Outside of the film's Marxism and oddly reminiscent of Gayraud's privileged girls at the turn of the century is the on-screen complicity between

Fig. 26. Female complicity in *Masculin/Féminin*
Jean-Luc Godard

Madeleine and her roommate Elisabeth, a step away from the solitary machinations of the *enfants terribles* as well as from father-daughter complicities encountered in the previous chapters. In the presence of the two, Paul is noticeably less in control than in a one-on-one interview. This disjointedness is most apparent in scenes that otherwise would conform to the binary heterosexuality of the title. At the movies, Elisabeth initiates a wordless game of musical chairs by putting herself between Madeleine and Paul; Madeleine complies by moving over a seat; Paul reacts by going to the end of the row to sit next to Catherine (fig. 26). Paul goes to the bathroom and opens the door to find two men kissing; when he returns to his seat, Madeleine moves next to him. But when he gets up yet again to complain that the film is being projected with a panoramic lens, we see another hand playing with Madeleine's hair—and the coat sleeve is Elisabeth's.

"Nous ne sommes pas des filles pour vous" [We're not your kind of girl—] says Elisabeth mysteriously to Paul over lunch before Madeleine's arrival. In another scene, the three of them leave the dance floor, and the two girls go off together, leaving Paul to ad-lib a love poem in a public recording booth. Elisabeth's insistent gaze testifies to an entirely different level of communication with Madeleine. Female complicity, its sexual overtones never realized on-screen, brings us back to the Maupassant story of Godard's inspiration and forward to Jean Eustache's film about three members of the post-'68 generation, *La Maman et la Putain* (1973). Alexandre (again Léaud) is a self-defined intellectual without a job who lives with his older girlfriend Marie (Bernadette Lafont). Marie, who owns a small boutique, brings home the paychecks, cooks and cleans, and puts up with Paul for reasons that are less than apparent. At home he either listens to music, reads the same page of Proust, or theorizes extemporaneously; otherwise he prowls the streets and cafés of Paris looking for new romantic conquests and hoping to see his ex-girlfriend Gilberte, whom he used to rough up on occasion. When he picks up Véronika (Françoise Lebrun), a nurse, he finds more than his match: she constantly eludes his romantic and dramatic scenarios and eventually reveals that, for her, sex is a way to fill time. Like Godard's Paul, the equally verbal Alexandre is brought to a halt at several moments by the spectre of his own expulsion from the center of feminine pleasure and absorption. This occurs less in an explicit ménage-à-trois scene than when he unexpectedly finds Marie and Véronika —who ought to be battling for him—in easy conversation.

In both films, female complicity throws the proverbial wrench into the signifying chain, in the form of brief scenes that imagine an alternate narrative course. Unlike the lesbian episodes in *Le Repos du guerrier, Le Rempart des béguines,* and *Histoire d'O,* which are intended to signify abjection, unlike the convoluted plotting in *Avant le déluge* and *Les Tricheurs,* female complicity in *Masculin/Féminin* and *La Maman et la Putain* involves neither guilt nor punishment. It is a less dramatic and yet more threatening way to say "we," one that exists on the same narrative surface as the male-driven plot of female self-determination, always sexual even when it is antisentimental. The unexpected appearance of complicities between young women in *Masculin/Féminin* and *La Maman et la Putain* hints at the possibility of different stories for them within popular texts that, nevertheless, ultimately punish them for bad behavior—Madeleine's pregnancy and Paul's mysterious accidental death at the end of Godard's film, Véronika's unwanted pregnancy and abject confession of her yearning for sex to be an expression of love at the end of Eustache's. Despite the daring moments, there is in these films a nostalgia for the *vraie jeune fille* and the intact cultural space of her integration, a piece of the heritage of the 1950s that is still with us today.

Conclusion: From Object to Subject?

From the "existentialists" to the *copains*, representations of youth in the post–World War II period, no matter what their ideological perspective, ultimately mutate into diagnoses. Godard's ironic flash across the screen in *Masculin/Féminin* identifying the film's characters as "les enfants de Marx et de Coca-Cola," is another link in the chain, a diagnosis of French youth in the mid-1960s as the embodiment of an ideologically inconsistent duality: railing against "capitalist" America whose products they nonetheless consume. *Masculin/Féminin* takes apart the category of "youth" in its gendered components and attributes to each the appropriate aspect of the duality. In the process, Godard's film reveals something new: the alignment of young men with the political and young women with consumer culture as conscious choices rather than innate nature. In Godard's juxtaposition, both the *engagement* of young men and the consumerism of young women have their share of deliberate inanity. By diagnosing male and female youth alongside each other, *Masculin/Féminin* puts forth a categorical gender-inclusiveness that is not a marketing opportunity, but a matter of fact. The identification of French youth as "children of Marx and Coca-Cola" incorporates girls into the familiar sociopolitical base and adds a new factor: desire, in a dual resonance. Knowing a little about Marx, they are automatically dissatisfied with the bourgeois status quo. Simultaneously, they are drawn to American culture and seek out its brand names. Theirs is a Cold War identity crisis. And yet it is more than a historical phenomenon. The yearning for the transcendence of revolution as well as the yearning to belong to the Pepsi generation both exemplify the unresolvable syncopation that is the condition of desire. Godard's youth, masculine and feminine, are always wanting.

With desire factored in, Godard's representation of youth as a category no longer comes with all the answers. But scripted ideological inconsistencies are still a form of reification for others to evaluate. For young people themselves to speak, on the other hand, to take action in the world as the conscripts did in Algeria, is to assert a position as a subject, however fleeting that may be. Another much-documented incident serves as a case in point. On the occasion of the first anniversary of the magazine *Salut les copains* on 22 June 1963, the radio station Europe 1 organized a "Fête de la Nation," a free concert at the Place de la Nation in Paris's twelfth arrondissement to showcase the young singers whose careers it had helped launch: Johnny Hallyday, Les Chaussettes Noires, Sylvie Vartan, Richard Anthony, Les Chats Sauvages, and others. To the organizers' surprise, by early evening the area was so packed with young people who had come from all over the country using any means possible that the performers could not reach the stage. They needed a police escort to make their way through the crowd.[1] Accounts of the Fête de la Nation recall Sartre's standing-room-only lecture on existentialism in 1945, only on a much more spectacular scale. Over two hundred thousand fans attended the concert. The center stage once occupied by the philosopher *engagé* now belonged to rock stars. Attentive and respectful listeners had become delirious fans who shrieked and sobbed at the sight and sound of idols who looked a lot like them. Unlike Sartre's fans, some of the thousands of teenagers at the concert caused damage in the streets bordering the Place de la Nation, a fact which remained the most salient feature of the concert for those who did not like the copains' sound in the first place.

Like Sartre's lecture, the Fête de la Nation was the talk of the entire spectrum of the French press in the days that followed, from *France-Soir* to *La Croix* and *Le Figaro Littéraire*. In an implied comparison to the politicized "modern times" over which Sartre's journal presided in the immediate postwar years, "le bruyant prophète des temps nouveaux" [the noisy prophet of new times], wrote Jean Cau, Sartre's former secretary, was an Americanophile visionary by the name of Johnny Hallyday.[2] In an ambivalent formulation for the new decade, Cau noted that the intellectual's responsibility to be politically engaged in the world had been replaced by youth and noise: a very different kind of act.

Accustomed to crowds formed by political passions, how was adult France to understand the capacity of pop music with its derivativeness and minimal content to unite the nation's teenagers? In a lengthy article on the first page of *Le Monde,* sociologist Edgar Morin made an unprecedented move: rather than sensationalize the Fête de la Nation, he held the concert and its culture up for serious analysis as an event, a "collective phenomenon" in which young people went beyond diagnostic frameworks and took action in the world.[3]

Morin explained for his uninitiated readers the terminology required in order to understand this collective phenomenon. Its members were generally under twenty but could be as old as thirty as long as they had, like the British import Petula Clark, that "je ne sais quoi copain." Record companies had initially dubbed their young singers "idoles," but the key word turned out to be "copain." For Morin, the difference was essential: one worships idols from a respectful distance, while copains and their fans were equals. The shared identity contained both the omnivorous consumerism that spurred youth on to become salarymen and women and the seeds of revolt against such a life path: "C'est qu'en ce yé-yé sont encore indistincts le nihilisme de consumation et le nihilisme de consommation[4] [Within the *yé-yé* the nihilism of dissipation and the nihilism of consumerism are not yet well-defined]. Which would it be for French youth?

As early as 1957, the young members of the avant-garde Situationist International movement had recognized that youthful dissatisfaction as well as pleasure could easily be recuperated as merchandise in an economic system where the act of seeing had been reduced to consuming.[5] The signifiers of youthfulness were for sale to all. For Guy Debord, this was at the very heart of the "société du spectacle," its most patently false opposition, that of youth versus adults:

> Là où s'est installée la consommation abondante, une opposition spectaculaire principale entre la jeunesse et les adultes vient en premier plan des rôles fallacieux: car nulle part il n'existe d'adulte, maître de sa vie, et la jeunesse, le changement de ce qui existe n'est aucunement la propriété de ces hommes qui sont maintenant jeunes, mais celle du système économique, le dynamisme du capitalisme. Ce sont des choses qui règnent et qui sont jeunes; qui se chassent et se remplacent elles-mêmes.[6]
>
> [Where mass consumerism has taken hold, the principal spectacular opposition between youth and adults comes to the forefront of deceptive roles: for

nowhere can there be found the adult who is master of his own existence, and youth, the change in what exists is in no way the property of those who are now young, but that of the economic system, of the dynamism of capitalism. What reigns over us are things: things are what is young; what pursue each other and replace themselves.]

Debord urged readers to recognize that their society's most profound divisions were economic and not generational. Several years before the movements of May, the situationists unveiled the reification of youthfulness as a spectacle, a product to be viewed, bought, and sold in movies, advertisements, the press, and television. Outside of their own avant-garde praxis of appropriating and irreverently recontextualizing these images through what they called *détournement*[7] [literally, a change of direction, with alternative connotations of fraud and seduction], the situationists saw the individual's situation in consumer society as ineluctable. As long as youth were on display *as* youth, whether traumatized or well integrated, politicized or apathetic, the essential question of social class, as Godard noted as well, remained hidden away (fig. 27).

Perhaps for many people at the time it was. But not only was youth on display: equally probable in a nation where in 1957, 44 percent of the population under thirty was working class and only 10 percent were students,[8] was the awareness of simultaneous and more subtle references in the barrage of images proclaiming the pleasures of being young to a type and a milieu that were always middle class. This conjuncture of class and generation were the components of the premier image of pleasure offered to young people whose lives would necessarily bear little resemblance to media images of their peers. Teenagers who worked for low wages did not need to see the *détournement* of advertisements to understand that the disjuncture between reality and fantasy was an economic one. In a culture where such a clear social disjuncture existed in images of youthfulness, young people themselves were neither passively victimized nor triumphantly empowered. More ambiguously, they were recognized: addressed as a coherent category of identity whose needs and desires could be anticipated and created by a market economy.

Grouped together by economic forces around icons and objects that were "jeunes," youth themselves came to recognize and act upon the very forces that had constituted them as a category in the movements of May 1968. Just over a decade after the literary *hussards,* French students and

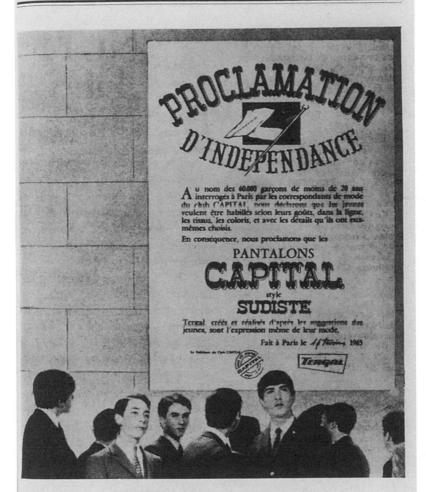

L'INDÉPENDANCE DE LA MARCHANDISE

L'autonomie de la marchandise est à la racine de la dictature de l'apparence ; de la tautologie fondamentale du **spectacle**, où l'importance est toute présupposée et définie par la mise en scène de l'importance. Le pseudo-événement préfabriqué qui y domine et oriente le réel, c'est un événement qui n'est plus visible pour ce qu'il contient, mais qui n'a pas d'autre contenu que d'être visible. Que peuvent exprimer de plus grandiose les pantalons Capital, par exemple, forts de la soumission de leurs milliers de **ressortissants** recensés ; soumission dont, on ne manque pas de l'afficher, ils « ont eux-mêmes choisi » les détails ? Précisément ce que ces fétiches proclament : ils sont « l'expression même de leur mode ». Ce sudisme esclavagiste des marchandises se présente évidemment comme indiscutable devant le bétail humain qu'il a marqué. Rarement une image publicitaire d'une telle débilité d'invention concertée aura si bien su exprimer **inconsciemment** la scission entre les hommes et leur objectivation ; la rébellion insolente de leurs propres actes qui se retournent contre eux comme une puissance étrangère. Tous les désirs de l'époque sont suspendus à notre victoire dans cette **guerre de Sécession**.

Fig. 27. Situationniste *détournement* of the teenage consumer
International Situationniste, February 1965

workers recognized the differences among themselves in order to go beyond them and to say "we," to speak and act with the power of a group identity rather than have that identity imposed through external diagnosis. It is important to note, however, that the assertions and demands of the *soixante-huitards* within the consumer society that had been promised them were less utopian than they were practical. During the course of the 1960s, increasing numbers of students from more diverse socioeconomic backgrounds chose to continue their education at the university level. The children of the baby boom were confident of attaining a better quality of life than that of their parents, but their numbers undermined the dream of success. In the 1950s, it had been easy for workers and university graduates alike to find employment; in 1968 even banks began to hire young people with the *licence* degree for jobs that had previously required only the *bac*. Graduates of the elite *grandes écoles,* who had also become more numerous, held the better-paid positions: the situation was stagnant.

For economic historian Henri Mendras, it was legitimate for the newly massive body of students to reach a point of collective frustration at being robbed of the promise that carefree youth would naturally lead to socioeconomic advancement and to react violently.[9] The revolts of May were less a matter of cause and effect than a dialectic, arising from the situation that had been created for youth in French culture as a result of the social, economic, and discursive processes under way since 1945. Using similar but more mystical terms, Gilles Deleuze and Félix Guattari have called May 1968 "a visionary phenomenon," a coming to consciousness that was above all an act of seeing: "comme si une société voyait tout d'un coup ce qu'elle contenait d'intolérable et voyait aussi la possibilité d'autre chose"[10] [as if suddenly a society saw its intolerable aspects and also saw the possibility of something else]. From a position in which the media and various "experts" diagnosed them as victims, criticized them as apathetic, hailed them as fun-loving, and targeted them as consumers, young people came to see the manipulations and insufficiencies underlying such concern and promises. The gaze they returned took the form of revolt, leading to the paralysis of the nation's services and industries with ten million people on strike, bringing the franc down with them.

Along with reacting against the unkept promises of consumer society, the *soixante-huitards* expressed the desire to change "society," to dismantle hierarchies in the educational system, the family, and relations between

Fig. 28. May 1968: liberation of the teenage girl?
Photograph Gilles Caron. Reprinted with permission from Contact Press Images

the sexes. In the latter realm, utopianism was abetted by the 1967 legalization of the birth control pill, the most practical step toward a sexual liberation that Brigitte Bardot's films and the antisentimental novel could only
ever offer as fantasy. The new discourse of "liberation" and "revolution"
inspired new representations of youthful femininity as well. Through the
early 1960s, sexually experienced *enfants terribles* in fiction and film were
always punished in the end, their unfamiliarity and bad behavior routed by
the spectre of the *jeune fille*. During the movements of May, on the other
hand, the mass media captured real young women on the streets in imagery
that triumphantly communicated their power, their equal capacity to demand social change (fig. 28).[11] By the late 1960s, the nation's loss of intactness as well as that of young women was no longer a threat, but a reality.
The time for conflicted nostalgia for the *jeune fille* was over. Or was it? Recent reevaluations of May 1968 have noted that the movements did little to
improve the real lot of female students and workers. They remained dramatically underrepresented in unions, and the discourse of universalism
proved insufficient for their particular concerns and needs. Disappointments, however, served as fodder for the radicalism of the MLF (Mouve-

ment de Libération des Femmes), for whom 1970 was "l'année zéro de la libération des femmes."[12]

In the years immediately following May 1968 and the founding of the French feminist movement, reaction often accompanied the revolution's effects in texts where free love seems to be only a matter of course. Indeed, the character of the teenage girl was largely stranded where we found her in these five chapters, in the struggle between the familiar and the unfamiliar, playing out her fate on an ideological battleground not so very different from *Elle* magazine's tendency to bring its Modern Woman into a confrontation with the Eternal Feminine where conservativism always won out in the end. Conservative endings are important, for they show that liberation from old models, whether *jeune fille* or Eternal Feminine, is a slow and multifaceted process. Well beyond the 1950s, texts that put forth outward signs of the sexual freedom of teenage girls routed them in ambivalence, expressed or not. A history several decades long of representations of *enfants terribles* in their imperfect freedom is what we find in the interstices of events like the legalization of the birth control pill and the founding of the MLF, and alongside gradual processes of social change like the increasing feminine presence in higher education and the workplace.

Even the sexual revolution could not banish the spectre of the *jeune fille* from the cultural imagination. In one of the key films of the post-1968 era, Jean Eustache's *La Maman et la Putain* (1973), the *enfant terrible* becomes the sign of its failure: young people in Eustache's view do not really want to be sexually liberated—nor do they even know how to be. Antoine is caught between Marie, a capable business owner, and Véronika, a nurse. Marie cannot get out of her mothering mode with Antoine, nor can Antoine give up the passive role of being taken care of by Marie. The thrill of conquest with Véronika quickly fades when Antoine finds out that she is more sexually active and less committed to stability than he has ever been. Antoine is pathetic, but Véronika is abject: in the final scene, the first shot of the miserable dormitory room she lives in, Véronika's lack of affect falls away and she delivers a desperate and unforgettable monologue about the emptiness of sex for pay, of work in order to drink, the loneliness and lovelessness of her life. Longing underlies Véronika's verbal and physical performance of freedom and insouciance, and self-inflicted loss of love haunts her just as it did Cécile in *Bonjour tristesse*. If this is the lot of the young after the revolution, it is a troubling conclusion indeed. The subtlety of Eustache's film lies in its observation that guilt, loss, and "bad behavior" are no longer exclusively the province of the young woman. Young people of both sexes find themselves in an ethical void where they can neither retrieve the purity of singular love nor abandon themselves completely to chaos. Popular culture has not yet tired of commenting on this void, perhaps because it has come to characterize the lives of so many people today, suspended in the deceptive freedoms of adolescence.

Notes

Introduction

1. Much has been written about teenage girls in the United States, for example, Winifred Breines, *Young, White, and Miserable: Growing Up Female in the Fifties* (Boston: Beacon Press, 1992) and Susan J. Douglas, *Where the Girls Are: Growing Up Female with the Mass Media* (New York: Random House, 1994), to name just two. Most influential for the present study has been Lesley Johnson's *The Modern Girl: Girlhood and Growing Up* (Buckingham, Eng.: The Open University Press, 1993), which has an excellent general theoretical and historical section about the relationship between the teenage girl as a category of identity and postwar modernization, before going on to specifically treat the Australian context.

2. Mary Louise Roberts, *Civilization Without Sexes: Reconstructing Gender in Postwar France, 1917–1927* (Chicago: University of Chicago Press, 1994), 216.

3. Yvonne Knibiehler et al., *De la Pucelle à la minette. Les Jeunes filles de l'âge classique à nos jours* (Paris: Messidor, 1983), 91–92. My discussion of female virginity in the eighteenth and nineteenth centuries is greatly indebted to this book, the only one on its subject from a French perspective.

4. Sherry Ortner, "The Virgin and the State," *Feminist Studies* 4 (1978): 19–37. Ortner argues that this cultural imperative is linked to the ideal of hypergamy, or marrying upwards, in state systems. Whereas hunting/gathering societies exclude women, whom they see as dangerous, in patriarchy women are "seen to be in danger, justifying male protection and guardianship. Before they were polluting, and this had to be defended against, but now they are said to be pure, and to need defending," (26). The best-known reflections on female virginity are those of Mary Douglas, *Purity and Danger* (New York: Praeger, 1966), and Sigmund Freud,

"The Taboo of Virginity," *Standard Edition,* vol. 11 (London: Hogarth, 1957), 193–208.

5. Virginity was the ideal, no matter what the real behavior of young women may have been. See Lawrence Stone, *The Family, Sex and Marriage in England* (London: Weidenfeld and Nicolson, 1977). Stone makes the argument that across social classes men and women engaged in premarital sex despite a broad-based cultural disapproval. I am less interested in real behavior as far as the eighteenth and nineteenth centuries are concerned than in the values and ideals on which the contemporary period has built.

6. Knibiehler et al., *De la Pucelle,* 77.

7. Thomas Laqueur, "Orgasm, Generation, and the Politics of Reproductive Biology," in *The Making of the Modern Body,* eds. Thomas Laqueur and Catherine Gallagher (Berkeley: University of California Press, 1987), 35.

8. Jean-Jacques Rousseau, *Emile; or, On Education,* bk. 5, trans. Allan Bloom (New York: Basic Books 1979), 359 and 362n., quoted in Laqueur, "Orgasm, Generation," 19–20.

9. Gabrielle Houbre, *La Discipline de l'amour. L'Education sentimentale des filles et des garçons à l'âge du romantisme* (Paris: Plon, 1997), 162.

10. Ibid., 165–66. In the eyes of the Church and the *Code Civil,* a girl who was seduced was the guilty party rather than the man who seduced her.

11. Ibid., 175.

12. *Trois routes pour jeunes filles* (Paris: Editions Spes, 1937). The origin of the term "vieille fille" can be traced to the growing numbers of female students in the nineteenth century. See Yvonne Knibiehler, "L'Education sexuelle des filles au XXe siècle," *Clio: Histoire, Femmes et Sociétés* 4 (1996): 139–60.

13. Jean Mypont, *Une jeune fille d'aujourd'hui* (Paris: Librairie de l'Arc, 1934), 10–11.

14. *Journal anonyme d'une jeune fille,* Wednesday and Thursday, 8–9 juin 1842, ff. 23 (Bibliothèque Historique de la Ville de Paris, Ms. 1040), quoted in Houbre, *La Discipline,* 167. For a study of girls' diaries in the nineteenth century, see Philippe Lejeune, *Le Moi des demoiselles. Enquête sur le journal de jeune fille* (Paris: Editions du Seuil, 1993).

15. Jann Matlock, *Scenes of Seduction: Prostitution, Hysteria, and Reading Difference in Nineteenth-Century France* (New York: Columbia University Press, 1994), 50–55.

16. I have chosen the word "haunt" carefully. To quote Joan Copjec, "no historical moment can be comprehended in its own terms; the circuit of self-recognition or coincidence with itself which would enable such comprehension is deflected by an investment that cannot be recuperated for self knowledge. This impossibility causes each historical moment to flood with alien, anachronistic figures, spectres from the past and harbingers of the future." Joan Copjec, introduction to *Supposing the Subject* (London: Verso, 1994), ix.

17. Angela Carter, *The Sadeian Woman and the Ideology of Pornography* (New York: Harper Colophon Books, 1978), 79.

18. Luce Irigaray, *Speculum de l'autre femme* (Paris: Editions de Minuit, 1974), 10.

19. Joan Copjec, *Read My Desire: Lacan Against the Historicists* (Cambridge: MIT Press, 1994), 4.

20. Ibid., 2.

21. Irigaray, *Speculum,* 85.

22. Geneviève Dormann, "Les Jeunes filles réduites à rien," *Arts* 758 (18–24 January 1961): 3.

23. Carter, *The Sadeian Woman,* 47.

24. Examples of the former category would be Dr. André Arthus's eight pamphlets collected under the title *Ce que toute jeune fille devrait savoir* (Paris: Editions Jcheber, 1948), in the tellingly named Pureté and Vérité series, or the Abbé André Bragade's pamphlet "Jeune fille, toi qui rêves à l'amour," first published in 1938, then reprinted in 1944 and again in 1951 (Paris: n.p.); examples of the latter would be "Aux jeunes gens et jeunes filles," a voluminous series of pamphlets of the association Pour un foyer chrétien (Paris: Editions Familiales de France, 1945); Cécile Jéglot's pamphlet "L'Adolescente," one of fifteen in a series entitled La Jeune fille (Paris: Editions Spes, 1948); a series of brochures put out by the Association du mariage chretien. An example of the latter is Myriam Dominique, "Quand l'amour s'éveille," (Paris: Editions Ouvrières, 1946).

25. François Mauriac, L' Education des filles," in *Le Romancier et ses personnages* (Paris: Editions Corrêa, 1952), 219.

26. Ibid., 194.

27. Jean Jousselin, *Jeunesse: fait social méconnu* (Paris: PUF, 1959), 164.

28. For statistics on the female presence in French higher education, see Pierre Bourdieu, *Les Héritiers. Les Etudiants et la culture* (Paris: Editions de Minuit, 1964); for the student population, see Claire Laubier, ed., *The Condition of Women in France 1945 to the Present: A Documentary Anthology* (London: Routledge, 1990), 13, 51.

29. From 1954 to 1962, the number of paid female agricultural workers in France dropped by 43 percent; most (one out of one hundred) found factory work, which did not offer them the same training that expanding industries offered young men. Of those remaining on farms, 75 percent were "family workers," usually unpaid. Claire Duchen, *Women's Rights and Women's Lives in France 1945–1968* (London: Routledge, 1994), 132–40; Laubier, *The Condition of Women,* 2.

30. Duchen, *Women's Rights,* 132.

31. Jean Fourastié, *Les Trente glorieuses ou la révolution invisible de 1946 à 1975* (Paris: Fayard, 1979).

32. One group I do not treat are the disaffected youth known as *blousons noirs* for the black leather jackets they tended to wear. In their case, real behavior played

a much more significant role in media representations. See Emile Copfermann, *La Génération des blousons noirs. Problèmes de la jeunesse française* (Paris: François Maspero, 1962).

33. See in particular Pierre Bourdieu's seminal essay "La Jeunesse n'est qu'un mot," in *Questions de sociologie* (Paris: Editions de Minuit, 1984), 143–54.

34. Dick Hebdige, *Subculture: The Meaning of Style* (London: Routledge, 1979), 45, 79.

35. Jean Cocteau, *Les Enfants terribles* (Paris: Editions Grasset, 1929) 64, 89–90.

36. Simone de Beauvoir, "Brigitte Bardot et le syndrome de Lolita," in *Les Ecrits de Simone de Beauvoir. La Vie—l'écriture. Textes inédits ou retrouvés*, eds. Claude Francis and Fernande Gontier (Paris: Editions Gallimard, 1979), 365. (This piece was originally published in *Esquire* [August 1959] 32–38.)

37. Ibid., 363.

38. Luce Irigaray, *Ce sexe qui n'en est pas un* (Paris: Editions de Minuit, 1977), 76.

39. Olivier Galland, *Sociologie de la jeunesse. L'Entrée dans la vie* (Paris: Armand Colin, 1991), 35.

40. *Lettres françaises* 602 (January 1956): quoted in Verena Aebischer et Sonia Dayan-Herzbrun, "Cinéma et Destin des Femmes," *Cahiers internationaux de sociologie* 80 (1986): 154.

41. The French *Mademoiselle* was unrelated to the American *Mademoiselle*, which was founded in the 1930s to address the needs of young working women.

Chapter One. From *Elle* to *Mademoiselle*

1. I am not taking into consideration romance magazines like *Nous deux* or magazines published by religious groups. For examples and analyses of the former category see Evelyne Sullerot, *La Presse féminine* (Paris: Librairie Armand Colin, 1966); Sylvette Giett, "Vingt années d'amour en couverture," *Actes de la recherche en sciences sociales* 60 (1985): 17–22. For the latter category, see Martine Muller et al, *Etre féministe en France. Contribution à l'étude des mouvements de femmes 1944–1967* (Paris: IHTP, 1985). More than half the readership of women's magazines in the 1950s was between the ages of 15 and 35. See L. Brams, "La Presse hebdomadaire féminine," *L'Ecole des parents* (April 1956), quoted in Andrée Michel et Geneviève Texier, *La Condition de la Française d'aujourd'hui*, vol. 1, *Mythes et réalités* (Paris: Editions Gonthier, 1964), 28.

2. René de Livois, *Histoire de la presse française*, vol. 2 (Lausanne: Editions Spès, 1965), 563.

3. For a good overview of feminist goals in the nineteenth century, see Dorothy McBride Stetson, *Women's Rights in France* (New York: Greenwood Press, 1987).

4. The first series of dates are given by McBride Stetson, *Women's Rights,* 177; the second by Michel and Texier, *La Condition de la Française,* 192.

5. For a history of the suffrage movement in France, see Steven C. Hause, "More Minerva than Mars: The French Women's Rights Campaign and the First World War," and Jane Jenson, "The Liberation and New Rights for French Women," in Margaret Randolph Higonnet et al., *Behind the Lines: Gender and the Two World Wars* (New Haven: Yale University Press, 1987), 99–113, 272–84.

6. The latter view is expressed by Michel and Texier, *La Condition de la Fran-çaise,* 178.

7. Claire Duchen, *Women's Rights and Women's Lives in France 1944–1968* (London: Routlege, 1994), 176.

8. Rémi Lenoir, "Transformations du familialisme et reconversions morales," *Actes de la recherche en sciences sociales* 59 (1985): 4. *La Revue de l'Alliance Nationale contre la dépopulation* (1899–1945) was given the catchier title of *Vitalité française* in 1950. Depopulation anxiety in France has outlasted the postwar period; in 1971, *Vitalité française* was still in existence and was renamed *Population et avenir.* It continues publication today.

9. For accounts of the family planning movement in France, which began as a private, non-profit organization under the initiative of a coalition consisting of women doctors, sociologist Evelyne Sullerot, Clara Malraux, and a contingent of activists from the Protestant young women's group Jeunes Femmes, see Muller et al. *Etre féministe,* 25–27; Huguette Bouchardeau, *Pas d'histoire les femmes. 50 ans d'histoire des femmes 1918–1968* (Paris: Editions Syros, 1977), 118–20; Duchen, *Women's Rights,* 170–75.

10. Duchen, *Women's Rights,* 30. The Occupation, when women performed traditionally "male" duties and held "male" jobs, was a hiatus, rather than a step forward, in the long-standing political and cultural view that the female role should be limited to motherhood. This recognition of the "illusory nature of wartime change" for women is a relatively new view. See Margaret R. Higonnet and Patrice L.-R. Higonnet, "The Double Helix," in Higonnet et al., *Behind the Lines,* 31–47.

11. The political vision of women as mother-citizens was not unique to postwar France. Feminist historians have noted the connection made between a woman's responsibilities in her home and to her nation in the nineteenth century as well. Karen Offen, "Liberty, Equality, and Justice for Women: The Theory and Practice of Feminism in Nineteenth-Century Europe," in Renate Bridenthal, Claudia Koonz, and Susan Stuard, eds., *Becoming Visible: Women in European History,* 2d ed. (Boston: Houghton Mifflin Company, 1987), 335–66.

12. Antoine Prost, "L'Evolution de la politique familiale en France de 1938 à 1981," *Le Mouvement social* 129 (October-December 1984): 10.

13. For a history of the *allocations,* see Pierre Laroque, ed., *La Politique fa-miliale en France depuis 1945* (Paris: Documentation Française, 1985), 187–91.

14. Ibid., 191–94.

15. Rémi Lenoir, "Transformations," 23, and "L'Effondrement des bases sociales du familialisme," *Actes de la recherche en sciences sociales* 57–58 (1985): 69.

16. Duchen, *Women's Rights*, 104–5.

17. Ibid., 122–26.

18. "C'est en effet la proportion des femmes exerçant des professions liées à des activités intellectuelles (professorat notamment) mais également administratives (cadres supérieurs) qui s'est accrue le plus, contribuant du même coup à modifier la représentation sociale de la femme dans les classes supérieures, qui valorise désormais la femme «moderne,» «active,» «dynamique,» «indépendante,» «autonome,» et «responsable.»" [It's the proportion of women in professions tied to intellectual activity (notably teaching), but also administrative (executives) that has increased the most, contributing simultaneously to modify the social representation of women in the upper classes, which henceforth valorizes the woman who is "modern," "active," "dynamic," "independent," autonomous," and "responsible."] Rémi Lenoir, "L'Effondrement," 84. See his statistics on the evolution (within the privileged classes) of women's education from 1945 to 1982, and of women's place in the work force during these years. Changes that were significant in the 1950s became even more dramatic in the late 1960s—which is why, according to Lenoir, the 1950s were long neglected as a chapter in women's history.

19. Linda Nicholson, "Gender and Modernity: Reinterpreting the Family, the State, and the Economy," in *Gender and History: The Limits of Social Theory in the Age of the Family* (New York: Columbia University Press, 1986).

20. For the eighteenth century see Nancy Armstrong, introduction to *Desire and Domestic Fiction* (London: Oxford University Press, 1987); for the sixteenth century see Joan Kelly-Gadol, "Did Women Have a Renaissance?," in Bridenthal et al., *Becoming Visible*, 175–201.

21. Jean-Pierre Rioux, *La France de la IVe République*, vol. 2, *L'Expansion et l'impuissance 1952–1958* (Paris: Editions du Seuil, 1983), 212–13.

22. Michel et Texier, *La Condition*, 69. See also my "*Consommatrice* of the 1950s in Elsa Triolet's *Roses à crédit*," *French Cultural Studies* 6 (June 1995): 123–44.

23. Rioux, *La France de la IVe République*, 234–36.

24. *De la 4 CV à la vidéo 1953–1983. Ces trente années qui ont changé notre vie* (Paris: Communica International, 1983), 14. This book commemorates the thirtieth anniversary of the credit organization CETLEM for the financing of home appliances.

25. [She brought over America.] Françoise Giroud, *Si je mens. Conversations avec Claude Glayman* (Paris: Editions Stock, 1972), 118. Giroud was editor-in-chief at *Elle* until 1952. In 1953, she founded *L'Express* with Jean-Jacques Servan-Schreiber. She went on to a political career as Ministre de la Condition Féminine

from 1974 to 1976. Today, she is a columnist for the weekly *Nouvel Observateur*, a member of the Prix Fémina jury, and the author of several books on a variety of subjects.

26. Sullerot, *La Presse féminine*, 59, 61.

27. For a biography of the founder of *Elle*, see Denise Dubois-Jallais, *La Tzarine: Hélène Lazareff et l'aventure d'«Elle»* (Paris: Editions Robert Laffont, 1984).

28. Ibid., 136. Hélène Gordon was the first French magazine editor to use color photographs. Giroud, *Si je mens*, 123.

29. Giroud, *Si je mens*, 119–20.

30. Nicole Benoît, Edgar Morin, and Bernard Paillard, *La Femme majeure* (Paris: Editions du Seuil, 1983), 43.

31. *Elle*, 1 April 1948.

32. "Salopettes et 'Slacks'," *Elle*, 28 November 1945, 10.

33. Dubois-Jallais, *La Tzarine*, 138.

34. As the January 1948 cover reads.

35. According to Henri Amouroux, actor Georges Milton starred in a film entitled *Le Roi des débrouillards*. Henri Amouroux, *Les Français sous l'Occupation* (France Inter: Cassettes Radio France, 1984), "La Vie quotidienne pendant l'Occupation." I thank Alice Kaplan for calling my attention to this film.

36. Bread rations ended in 1948. In 1949, the end of all rationing was declared. Non-alimentary rations for building materials and school supplies continued to be issued through the 1950s.

37. *Elle*, 19 November 1951, 14.

38. "1 million recompense 15 ans d'expérience de la ménagère idéale," *Elle*, 17 March 1952, 14. "«Je préfère la vaisselle au reprisage», a dit Mme d'Harlaborde, ménagère idéale 1952. Mais ce n'est ni le lavage de la vaisselle ni le reprisage des chaussettes qui lui ont valu ce titre. C'est la façon à la fois spirituelle et technique dont elle a répondu aux quatres pages du questionnaire adressé à vingt sept mille cinq cents concurrentes . . ." ["I prefer washing dishes to mending," said Mme d'Harlaborde, ideal housewife 1952. But it isn't washing dishes or mending socks that earned her this title. It's the clever and technical way she answered the four pages of the questionnaire addressed to 27,500 contestants.]

39. Like Harlequin romances, *Elle* probably had many more readers than the statistics indicate; magazines are also passed around among friends and family.

40. Françoise Giroud, "Puissance USA no. 1: Les Femmes," *Elle*, 12 January 1953, 14.

41. Giroud, *Si je mens*, 128.

42. Ibid., 130–31.

43. Roland Barthes, "Cuisine ornementale," in *Mythologies* (Paris: Editions du Seuil, 1953), 128–30. And Annette Lanvers, trans., *Mythologies* (New York: Hill and Wang, 1972), 78–80 (trans. amended).

44. See chapter 5 for a discussion of the new appeal of quantitative methods in the social sciences in 1950s France.

45. Louis Pauwels, "Lettre inutile à «Elle»," *Arts,* 368 (17–23 July 1952), 1.

46. Colette Audry, "Elle," *Les Temps modernes* 78 (April 1952): 1788–94.

47. Deirdre Bair discusses the political differences between Audry and Beauvoir in *Simone de Beauvoir* (New York: Simon and Schuster, 1990), 182–83.

48. Audry, "Elle," 1790.

49. Ibid., 1791.

50. "In the context of women, she [Simone de Beauvoir] felt that the vast majority of them found themselves trapped in situations like rats and were thus forced into a state of 'mauvaise foi,' i.e. a game of duplicity or complicity with men. Hence the idea of 'situation' as found in *Le Deuxième sexe* is an entirely Beauvoirian one." Claire Laubier, ed., *The Condition of Women in France from 1945 to the Present* (London: Routledge, 1990), 19.

51. A popular women's magazine from 1833 to 1922. Sullerot, *La Presse féminine,* 10.

52. "Juliette Gréco: la mariée du 25 juin," *Elle,* 6 July 1953, 17–19.

53. Françoise Giroud, "Où en est la haute couture française?" *Elle,* 26 November 1951, 22–23.

54. Aujourd'hui, la mode n'a qu'un âge: le vôtre," *Elle,* 23 March 1953, 20–21.

55. "*Elle* vous révèle les secrets de la secrétaire — personnage-clé du XXe siècle" *Elle,* 7 February 1955, 24–31.

56. *Elle,* 5 January 1953, 10–11.

57. A feminist position today as well, in our nuclear age. Sara Ruddick suggests that peacemakers can learn from maternal nonviolence, for while not all mothers are peaceful, "peace is their business": "Nonviolent action, like maternal practice at its best, requires resilient cheerfulness, a grasping of truth that is caring, and a tolerance of ambiguity and ambivalence. For mothers, issues of proper trust, permissable force, and the possibility and value of control are alive and complex in daily work as they are in any nonviolent action." Sara Ruddick, *Maternal Thinking: Toward a Politics of Peace* (Boston: Beacon Press, 1989), 220.

58. I found one short story by one of the young woman writers discussed in the following chapter, Françoise Mallet-Joris: "Charmante nature," *Elle,* 17 January 1955, 52–54.

59. Colette, "Souvenirs inédits," *Elle,* 21 November 1945, 8–9. Continues in following issues.

60. *Elle,* 22 November 1954.

61. Roland Barthes, "Romans et enfants," in *Mythologies,* 56–57; Lanvers, *Mythologies,* 50 (trans. amended).

62. *Elle,* 18 February 1952, 45–46. Colette had a respectable showing (8/15). Most women surveyed (seventeen in the under-thirty group, nineteen in the over-forty-five) claimed, interestingly, they wouldn't want to be anyone but themselves.

63. "En 1954 les Français font 5 rêves," *Elle,* 22 March 1954. What follows the number one desire for a house, in ranking order, are: a trip to Italy; a car; a library; self-employment.

64. "Un personnage mystérieux, un esprit lucide, une femme simple, un écrivain violent: Simone de Beauvoir Prix Goncourt 1954," *Elle,* 3 January 1955, 22.

65. For a discussion of Simone de Beauvoir and domesticity in the context of the Occupation, see Elizabeth Houlding, "Between the Lines: Women Writing the Occupation of France" (Ph.D. diss., Columbia University, 1991), 226–56.

66. *Elle,* 17 February 1948.

67. "Etes-vous pour ou contre?," *Elle,* 16 March 1953, 23.

68. "La France record du monde de députées," *Elle,* 21 November 1945, 3.

69. Françoise Giroud, "Apprenez la politique," *Elle,* 2 May 1955, 28.

70. "Les Françaises ont conquis le droit de vote, elles ont le devoir de voter," *Elle,* 2 January 1956, 10.

71. Despite the fact that participation in the election was strong (1,500,000 people voted in the last hour or so that the polls were open) there was no clear winner. One of the reasons for the confusion was the success of Pierre Poujade, a right-wing extremist and xenophobe who was able to mobilize small-town artisans and store owners for his "République des petits": one out of ten people voted for him. The situation was resolved on 26 January by René Coty who appointed Guy Mollet as Prime Minister. His first mission: to put an end to the conflict in Algeria.

72. Rioux, *La France de la IVe République,* 92.

73. Ibid., 88–90.

74. "Et trois ministres promettent aux femmes . . . ," *Elle,* 3 January 1955, 14–15.

75. Françoise Giroud, "Apprenez la politique," *Elle,* 2 May 1955, 28.

76. Ibid., 29.

77. According to Evelyne Sullerot, "De Gaulle était l'élu des femmes." [De Gaulle was elected by women's vote.] "La Démographie en France," in Georges Santoni, ed., *Société et culture de la France contemporaine* (Albany: State University of New York Press, 1981), 121.

78. Giroud, "Apprenez la politique," 14.

79. There were similar tensions between the ideology of domesticity and increased opportunities in the public sphere for American women in the 1950s. As in France, educated women were working in prestigious jobs more than ever before. The unintended consequence, according to historian William H. Chafe, was the slow erosion of the belief that women's place was in the home. William H. Chafe, *The Paradox of Change: American Women in the Twentieth Century* (New York: Oxford University Press, 1991), 188–93.

80. The Inspecteur général de l'education nationale Paul Crouzet advocated a specifically female program of studies that would have *enseignement ménager* as one of its components. Paul Crouzet, *Bachelières ou jeunes filles?* (Paris: Privat-Didier, 1949), 9.

81. "La jeune fille qui veut arriver," *Elle,* 27 February 1956, 36.

82. Ibid., 36.

83. One can study to become an art historian or curator at the école du Louvre, or just take courses for the pleasure of it.

84. "Les adolescentes qui les prirent pour modèle . . . passaient de la simple opposition au monde des adultes à une mise en question de la définition tradition-nelle des rôles sexuels" [The teenage girls who took these idols for role models . . . went from a simple opposition to the adult world to questioning the traditional definition of sex roles]. Verena Aebischer et Sonia Dayan-Herzbrun, "Cinéma et destin des femmes," *Cahiers internationaux de sociologie* 80 (1986): 158.

85. *Mademoiselle* 1 (February 1962).

86. *Mademoiselle* 3 (1963): 23. I take up the subject of the "yéyé" scene and stars like Johnny Hallyday at the end of chapter 4.

87. Raymonde Carroll observes that while adolescence in America is a time of intense parental surveillance and childhood a time of freedom, it is the other way around in France. See her *Evidences invisibles* (Paris: Editions du Seuil, 1987) translated by Carol Volk as *Cultural Misunderstandings* (Chicago: University of Chicago Press, 1988), chapter 3.

88. *Mademoiselle* 3 (1963): 1.

Chapter Two. Fictions of Female Adolescence

1. "Françoise Sagan vous parle," interview by Madeleine Chapsal, *L'Express,* 13 September 1957, 15–16.

2. Television in France, notably *Apostrophes* in the 1980s and *Bouillon de Culture* in the 1990s, has been instrumental in promoting book sales. For details on the postwar press, see Claude Bellanger et al., *Histoire générale de la presse française* (Paris: Presses Universitaires de France, 1975), vol. 4, especially part 4, "La Presse française de la IVe République."

3. Anne-Marie de Vilaine, interview with author, Paris, 12 October 1990. See her *Des Raisons d'aimer* (Paris: Editions Julliard, 1959).

4. Christine Planté, *La Petite soeur de Balzac. Essai sur la femme auteur* (Paris: Editions du Seuil, 1989), 13.

5. "René Julliard, grand aventurier de l'édition," *Le Soir Illustré,* 12 juillet 1962, Julliard archives.

6. *Elle,* 11 mai 1953.

7. I thank Nicholas Hewitt for calling this fact to my attention. See his *Literature and the Right in Postwar France: The Story of the "Hussards"* (Oxford: Berg, 1996).

8. Jacques Laurent, a member of *Action française* before the war, supporter of Pétain and civil servant in his Ministère de l'Information, strategically joined the FFI (Forces Françaises de l'Intérieur) in 1944, and thus was spared in the post-

war purges. He took a leave of absence from politics, and under the pseudonym of Cécil Saint-Laurent penned the best-selling novel *Caroline chérie* (1947). Laurent returned to politics, this time cultural politics, by joining the anti-Sartrian literary and cultural review *La Table ronde.* Laurent became known as the leading figure of the reactionary literary group known as the *hussards.* In 1953 Laurent founded his own journal, *La Parisienne;* in 1954, he purchased *Arts* and made himself its director. See Hewitt as well as Michel Winock, *Le siècle des intellectuels* (Paris: Editions du Seuil, 1997) 476–78.

9. "Le Livre de la Semaine: *La Vie de palace* de Claude Martine," *Arts,* 29 June–5 July 1955, 6. *Arts* was a newspaper that reported on the Parisian arts scene and literary and cultural trends, and was edited by members of the anti-Sartrian "Hussard" group discussed in the following chapter. Like *Le Figaro Littéraire,* it happened to have a primarily female readership, according to Evelyne Sullerot. See her *La Presse féminine* (Paris: Librairie Armand Colin, 1966), 70.

10. Pierre Assouline, *Gaston Gallimard. Un demi-siècle d'édition française* (Paris: Editions Balland, 1984); Jean Bothorel, *Bernard Grasset. Vie et passions d'un éditeur* (Paris: Editions Grasset, 1989).

11. "Avec René Julliard, l'édition perd un de ses capitaines les plus entreprenants," *Libération,* 2 July 1962, Julliard archives.

12. Françoise Giroud, "L'Autre René Julliard," in *En souvenir de René Julliard* (Paris: Editions Julliard, 1963), 54.

13. Jean-Claude Lamy, *René Julliard* (Paris: Editions Julliard, 1992).

14. *Les Temps modernes* was associated at its inception with the Editions Gallimard. As Françoise D'Eaubonne recounts the incident which led to the change of publisher, "Malraux était venu faire des menaces précises à Gallimard; le Sauveur était très mécontent des attaques décochées contre lui par cette impertinente gazette; on rappelait à Gallimard que certains autres éditeurs comme Grasset avaient pu avoir des ennuis politiques . . . Gallimard refila l'affaire à son jeune et ambitieux concurrent." *Les Monstres d'été. Mémoires précoces,* vol. 2 (Paris: Editions Julliard, 1966), 152. [Malraux had come to Gallimard with precise threats; the Savior was very displeased with the attacks fired at him by this impertinent gazette; Gallimard was reminded that certain other editors like Grasset had been able to have political difficulties . . . Gallimard passed on the affair to his young and ambitious competitor.] The "ennuis politiques" she refers to are accusations of collaboration. D'Eaubonne dates the incident from 1946. Simone de Beauvoir tells a slightly different version in *La Force des choses:* Malraux threatened to leave Gallimard if he continued to publish *Les Temps modernes,* which had insulted him in one of its issues, and Gallimard chose Malraux over the existentialists. I thank Toril Moi for calling Beauvoir's version to my attention.

15. André Parinaud, "René Julliard: Sur 417 de mes auteurs, 22 ont été «payants,»" *Arts,* 24–30 October 1956, 1.

16. "René Julliard intime," *Le Phare dimanche,* 15 July 1962, Julliard archives.

17. Although they have soft covers, the books put out by the major French publishing houses in the 1950s (and now as well)—Gallimard, Julliard, and Seuil—are not considered "livres de poche." Pocket books are smaller, printed on cheaper paper, and are bound more cheaply. For a history of the innovations of the postwar publishing industry, see Henri-Jean Martin, Roger Chartier, Jean-Pierre Vivet, *Histoire de l'édition française* (Paris: Promodis, 1986), vol. 4.

18. [Mister Young Authors] "René Julliard," obituary in *Point de vue*, 6 July 1962, 23.

19. Christian Bourgois, who got his start in publishing at the Editions Julliard in the late 1950s, is the publisher of Editions Christian Bourgois. As Bourgois sees it, Julliard's success in this period prior to television's domination lay in his ability to take advantage of social and media connections, both through his socialite wife, and their friends Hélène and Pierre Lazareff (she was the founder of *Elle* magazine, he was the publisher of *Paris-Soir* and *L'Express*). Interview with author, Paris, 6 June 1991.

20. Victoria Thérame, *Journal d'une dragueuse* (Paris: Editions Ramsay, 1990), 241–45.

21. She calls writers "young colts" because the press in the 1950s referred to the ensemble of writers vis-à-vis their publishing houses as "l'écurie Gallimard," or "l'écurie Julliard" [the Gallimard stable, the Julliard stable].

22. "La Devanture du libraire," *Le Figaro littéraire*, 26 May 1951.

23. "Romancière à 19 ans, Françoise Mallet voit son oeuvre traduit en 13 langues," *Le Soir illustré* (Brussels), 18 August 1955. Mallet was Mallet-Joris's first pseudonym. She wrote under a pseudonym, most probably, because she was the daughter of Suzanne Lilar, a well-known lawyer, writer, and member of the Académie de Belgique. After the publication of *Le Rempart*, she added on Joris, a Flemish surname, to avoid any confusions with the novelist Robert Mallet.

24. "Françoise Mallet-Joris romancière," *Le Phare* (Brussels), 4 November 1956.

25. *Le Figaro littéraire*, 16 June 1951, Julliard archives.

26. R. D. Fournier, "Un phénomène de l'écurie Julliard: Françoise Mallet-Joris," *Dernières nouvelles d'Alsace*, 12 September 1956, 22.

27. Jacques Laurent, "Les malheurs de Minou," *Arts*, 21–27 December 1955, 1.

28. *Le Figaro Littéraire, Elle, L'Express*, to name a few. The Minou Drouet story even warranted Roland Barthes' interest. He wrote about her in one of his columns for *Les Lettres nouvelles* in the 1950s—self-advertising for Julliard, since this was a journal he published. See "La Littérature selon Minou Drouet," in *Mythologies* (Paris: Editions du Seuil, 1953), 153–60.

29. Laurent, "Les Malheurs," 7.

30. Bourgois, interview.

31. Jean-Claude Lamy, *Sagan* (Paris: Mercure de France, 1988), 12.

32. According to Françoise D'Eaubonne, she herself brought Rochefort's manuscript of *Le Repos du guerrier* to Julliard. The chief literary editor and D'Eaubonne's personal supporter, François Legrix, read it then returned it to Rochefort and said, "C'est très bien, mais le public ne vous suivra pas!" [That's very nice, but the public won't follow you!] D'Eaubonne, *Les monstres*, 407.

33. Lamy, *Sagan*, 18.

34. "René Julliard intime."

35. Bourgois, interview.

36. *Le Figaro*, 1 June 1954, 1.

37. (Paris: Editions Julliard, 1962).

38. Although *Bonjour tristesse* was the novel that first brought the packaged product of the young female author into the public eye, it was not responsible for any kind of onslaught of publications of novels by women. In selections from publishers' catalogues at the Bibliothèque Nationale from 1950 to 1959, which list new books and reprints, the years 1950 (Julliard) and 1951 (Plon) are marked by an extremely strong presence of women writers: fifteen with Julliard, twenty-five with Plon, and many of them have more than one title to their name.

39. While this anglicism first appeared in French in the mid-1930s, it was not until after World War II, in 1948, that it became associated specifically with books. The *Dictionnaire des anglicismes* quotes from Simone de Beauvoir's *La Force de l'âge* and *L'Amérique au jour le jour* to define the best-seller in reference to American writing. For more details, see Pierre Nora, "L'évolution des best-sellers," *Lire* 181 (October 1990): 76.

40. Jean-Jacques Servan-Schreiber and Françoise Giroud created *L'Express* in 1953 as a vehicle for the ideas of Pierre Mendès-France. They were spurred to create this alternative news forum after hearing Mendès-France give an impassioned speech on the budget and Indochina in the Chambre des Députés in 1951, which none of the next day's papers reported. According to Giroud, *L'Express* was the first of the nonspecialized French press to report on business and the effects of business on politics in a language that was accessible to all. Françoise Giroud, *Si je mens . . . Conversations avec Claude Glayman* (Paris: Editions Stock, 1972), 134, 171.

41. Jacques Laurent, "Sagan et les vieillards," *Arts*, 11–17 April, 1.

42. The distinction I make here is primarily between the attentions of the popular audience and the "professionals"—meaning literary critics, most of whom happened to be male.

43. Dominique Aubier, "Cette année un roman sur trois est écrit par une femme," *Arts*, 8–14 October 1958, 3.

44. *La Table ronde* 99 (March 1956).

45. Jacques Chardonne, review of *Bonjour tristesse*, by Françoise Sagan, *Arts*, 23–29 June 1954, 1.

46. Pierre Nora, "Entrées et clés," *Le Débat* 50 (May-August 1988): 192–93.

47. According to Jane Tompkins, the chief characteristic of the sentimental novel is that it is written "by, for, and about women." The critical dismissal of American sentimental fiction has prevented both students of literature and feminist critics from appreciating what Tompkins calls "a powerful and specifically female novelistic tradition . . . a monumental effort to reorganize culture from the woman's point of view." Tompkins, "Sentimental Power: *Uncle Tom's Cabin* and the Politics of Literary History," in Elaine Showalter, ed., *The New Feminist Criticism: Essays on Women, Literature, and Theory,* (New York: Pantheon Books, 1985)82–83. To describe the well-intentioned feminist critics of the sentimental novel, Tompkins adds in a note: "The most typical move is to apologize for the poor literary quality of the novels in a concessive clause — 'melodramatic and simplistic though the plots may be, wooden and stereotyped as the characters may appear' — and then to assert that these texts are valuable on historical grounds." Tompkins, 101, note 2. Also see her *Sensational Designs: The Cultural Work of American Fiction 1790–1860* (New York: Oxford University Press, 1985).

48. Jean-Claude Ibert, "La Jeune littérature féminine en France," 30 September 1957, Julliard archives.

49. Ibid.

50. Matthieu Galey, "Six ouvrages de dames à ne pas conseiller aux jeunes filles," *Arts,* 22–29 September 1960, 7.

51. Nicole Louvier, *Qui qu'en grogne* (Paris: La Table Ronde, 1954), 162–63.

52. Lucette Finas, *Les Chaînes éclatées* (Paris: Mercure de France, 1955). Finas (born 1921), now a literary critic, continues to write novels today.

53. Suzanne Allen, *La Mauvaise conscience* (Paris: Editions Gallimard, 1955). I was unable to find any information about this writer. Interestingly, Gallimard reissued this novel in 1968. What was deemed to be shocking and in poor taste in 1955 became material for serious reading with the growing feminist consciousness of the late 1960s.

54. *La Bâtarde* (1964) was nominated for all the major literary prizes but rejected at the last moment from competition for the Goncourt because it was ostensibly an autobiography and not a novel. Following the success of this book, Gallimard published the prologue to *Ravages* (1955) under the title of *Thérèse et Isabelle* (1966). For details on Leduc's life and work, see Isabelle de Courtivron, *Violette Leduc* (Boston: Twayne, 1985).

55. "Vous savez . . . je suis encore plus Renaud Sarti que Rafaële." [You know . . . I'm a lot more like Renaud Sarti than Rafaële.] D'Eaubonne, *Les Monstres*, 407.

56. Claudine Chonez, "Hier, aujourd'hui, demain," *La Table ronde* 99 (March 1956): 62.

57. Dominique Aubier, "Les Femmes envahissent la littérature," *Arts,* 8–14 October 1958, 3.

58. Elisabeth Trévol, *Mon amour* (Paris: Editions Julliard, 1954), 37.

59. I thank Linda Orr for an astute observation she made in 1993 about narrators being "killed off" in this corpus of novels—an observation that is now central to the present study.

60. Mallet-Joris, *Le Rempart des béguines* (Paris: Editions Julliard, 1951), 55. Translated by Herma Briffault, under the title *The Illusionist* (New York: Farrar, Strauss and Young, 1952), 58.

61. As per remarks made in fifty-five interviews with women who were teenagers in the 1950s. Verena Aebischer and Sonia Dayan-Herzbrun, "Cinéma et destins des femmes," *Cahiers internationaux de sociologie* 80 (1986): 147–59.

62. Mallet-Joris, *Le Rempart,*196; *The Illusionist,* 226–27.

63. Mallet-Joris, *Le Rempart,* 214; *The Illusionist,* 249–50.

64. Christiane Rochefort, *Le Repos du guerrier* (Paris: Editions Grasset, 1958), 121. Translated by Lowell Bair under the title *Warrior's Rest* (New York: David McKay Company, 1959), 89.

65. Rochefort, *Le Repos,* 283; *Warrior's Rest* 211.

66. Rochefort, *Le Repos,* 285; *Warrior's Rest* 212.

67. Rochefort, *Le Repos,* 286; *Warrior's Rest* 214.

68. Roger Faligot et Rémi Kauffer, *Porno business* (Paris: Librairie Arthème Fayard, 1987), 28–31; 110–12.

69. For a fascinating reading of *Histoire d'O*, see Kaja Silverman, "*Histoire d'O*: The Construction of a Female Subject," in Carole S. Vance, ed., *Pleasure and Danger: Exploring Female Sexuality* (Boston: Routledge and Kegan Paul, 1984), 320–49.

70. Pauline Réage, *Histoire d'O* (Paris: Editions Jean-Jacques Pauvert, 1989), 265.

71. Ibid., 309.

72. Anne Marie de Vilaine, *Des Raisons d'aimer* (Editions Julliard, 1959), 56–57.

73. Alfred Appel, Jr., ed., *The Annotated Lolita* (New York: Vintage Books, 1991), 49, 148.

74. Ibid., 48.

75. Michèle Perrein, *La Sensitive, ou l'innocence coupable* (Paris: Editions Julliard, 1956), 192.

76. Ibid., 209.

77. Michèle Perrein, *La Sensitive, ou l'innocence coupable* (Paris: Editions Grasset, 1986), 10.

78. Madeleine Chapsal, *Vérités sur les jeunes filles* (Paris: Editions Grasset, 1960), 49–51.

79. For information on Deharme, see *Times Literary Supplement* 2504 (27 January 1950): 53; Jean Chalon, "Lise Deharme: Je suis la dame au gant de Nadja,"

Figaro littéraire 1070 (20 October 1966): 2; "Mystère de Paris," *Les Lettres françaises* 1258 (20–26 November 1968):15; Gilles Lapouge, "Entretien avec Lise Deharme," *Quinzaine littéraire* 87 (16–31 January 1970): 10.

80. Lise Deharme, *Laissez-moi tranquille* (Paris: Editions Julliard, 1959), 139.

81. Ibid., 132.

82. Edgar Morin, *Les Stars* (Paris: Editions du Seuil, 1957), 50.

83. Simone de Beauvoir, "Brigitte Bardot et le syndrome de Lolita," in Claude Francis et Fernande Gontier, eds., *Les Ecrits de Simone de Beauvoir: La vie — l'écriture* (Paris: Editions Gallimard, 1979), 363–76.

84. Ibid., 365.

85. Ibid., 366.

86. Writers I spoke with, Christiane Rochefort, Christine de Rivoyre, Anne Marie De Vilaine, Françoise D'Eaubonne, were adamant in their opinion that *Le Deuxième sexe* went unnoticed until the late 1960s. They agreed with Betty Friedan, who called the fifties "a lost decade for women" in *The Feminine Mystique* (New York: Norton, 1963). One has to wonder if these French writers gained their perspective on Beauvoir's seminal work through Friedan's assessment of the decade, until recently acknowledged as definitive.

87. Claude Francis and Fernande Gontier, *Simone de Beauvoir: A Life . . . A Love Story,* trans. Lisa Nesselson (New York: St. Martin's Press, 1987), 255.

88. Deirdre Bair, *Simone de Beauvoir* (New York: Simon and Schuster, 1990), 408.

89. Francis and Gontier, *Simone de Beauvoir,* 251–52.

90. Simone de Beauvoir, *La Force des choses* (Paris: Editions Gallimard, 1963), 206.

91. Bair, *Simone de Beauvoir,* 408.

92. *Paris-Match,* 30 octobre 1954, Gallimard archives.

93. Robert Poulet, "Les livres et la vie," *Rivarol,* 5 November 1954, Gallimard archives.

94. *L'Express,* 11 May 1954, Gallimard archives.

Chapter Three. The *Mal du Siècle:* Politics and Sexuality

1. André Parinaud, "La Génération des J-3 à la conquête de Paris," *Arts* 657 (12–18 February 1958), 1.

2. Robert Garric, "Les Problèmes familiaux de l'adolescence," *L'Adolescence de l'après-guerre et ses problèmes* (Paris: Editions Sociales Françaises, 1948), 15. The common perception at the time was that the problems unique to the adolescent crossed national boundaries; indeed, this volume constitutes the proceedings of the first meeting of the Congrès International des Ecoles de Service Social. While my study focuses on the French case, French journalists and sociologists

drew many comparisons throughout the period in question between the French *mal de la jeunesse* and its equivalent in Poland, England, Italy, and the United States.

3. Ibid., 23.

4. Juvenile courts were first established in France in 1912.

5. Claude Roy, preface to *La Confession d'un enfant du siècle* by Alfred de Musset (Paris: Editions Gallimard, 1973), 7.

6. Musset, *Confession,* 25.

7. Ibid., 25.

8. Ibid., 33.

9. Jacques Lebar, "Petit manuel du mal du siècle," *La Nef,* 77–78 (June-July 1951): 7–15.

10. Waller argues that in early nineteenth century Romantic novels "while it is the heroine's task to interest the reader as an object, it is the hero's function to elicit the reader's sympathetic identification with him as a subject." Margaret Waller, *The Male Malady: Fictions of Impotence in the French Romantic Novel* (New Brunswick, N.J.: Rutgers University Press, 1993), 104.

11. For an in-depth discussion of *Lélia* see Waller, *The Male Malady;* Naomi Schor, "The Scandal of Realism," in *A New History of French Literature* (Cambridge: Harvard University Press, 1989), 656–61.

12. George Sand, *Lélia* (Paris: Editions Garnier, 1960), 170.

13. Which comes from reading too much, according to Chateaubriand: "On est détrompé, sans avoir joui; il reste encore des désirs et on n'a plus d'illusions. L'imagination est riche, abondante et merveilleuse, l'existence pauvre, sèche et désenchantée. On habite, avec un coeur plein, un monde vide . . ." [One is disabused, without having taken pleasure; desires still remain and one has no more illusions. Imagination is rich, abundant, and marvelous, existence impoverished, dry, and disenchanted. One lives with a full heart in an empty world]. *Le Génie du christianisme,* quoted in Sand, *Lélia,* note 2, 166.

14. Bernard Franck, "Grognards et hussards," *Les Temps modernes* 86 (December 1952): 1005–18. A hussar is a member of a uniformed European unit of light cavalry, originally a horseman in fifteenth-century Hungary.

15. Nicholas Hewitt, *Literature and the Right in Postwar France: The Story of the "Hussards."* Oxford: Berg, 1996), 120.

16. Ibid., 44.

17. Ibid., 81.

18. Raoul Girardet, quoted in Michel Winock, *Le Siècle des intellectuels* (Paris: Editions du Seuil, 1997), 479. Also see Girardet's article "L'Héritage de «L'Action française»," *Revue française de science politique* 7, no. 4 (October-December 1957): 765–92.

19. Hewitt, *Literature and the Right,* 120.

20. Ibid., 61.

21. Ibid., 92–94.

22. As Marc Dambre describes the intellectual climate at the time, "dominée par *La Peste* d'Albert Camus et par l'exposé de la théorie sartrienne de l'engagement, l'année littéraire 1947 n'est pas tournée vers l'écriture du moi et du plaisir" [dominated by Albert Camus's *La Peste* and by the exposé of the Sartrian theory of *engagement,* the literary year 1947 is not turned toward the writing of the self and pleasure]. See his *Roger Nimier. Hussard du demi-siècle* (Paris: Editions Flammarion, 1989), 201.

23. Winock, *Le Siècle,* 477–80.

24. Louis Pauwels, "Une génération," *Paris-Presse,* 17 January 1956, 1.

25. Jacques Laurent, "Plat du jour," *La Table ronde* 20–21 (August-September 1949): 1259.

26. Pauwels, "Une génération," 1.

27. Dambre sees Nimier's admiration for Maurras, hostile to both the Resistance, the Nazis, and the Communists, as comprehensible: "Pour l'engagé volontaire de dix-neuf ans, l'héritage maurrassien valide une opposition à ce qui menace la France: l'impérialisme américain et la bonne conscience démocratique à l'Ouest, l'Armée rouge et le communisme soviétique à l'Est, autre matérialisme ascendant" [For the nineteen-year-old enlistee, the Maurassian heritage validates an opposition to what menaces France: American imperialism and democratic self-satisfaction in the West, the Red army and Soviet Communism in the East, that other ascending materialism]. Dambre, *Roger Nimier,* 10, 163, 288, 480.

28. Ibid., 198–99.

29. Roger Nimier, "Vingt ans en 1945," *La Table ronde* (August-September 1949): 1265. Reprinted in *Le Grand d'Espagne* (Paris: Editions Gallimard, 1950), a collection of seven essays written as letters to Georges Bernanos.

30. Nimier, *Le Grand d'Espagne,* 177.

31. Roger Nimier, *Le Hussard bleu* (Paris: Editions Gallimard, 1950), 8.

32. Michel Déon, *Les Gens de la nuit* (Paris: La Table Ronde, 1958).

33. Stephen Hecquet, "Trois personnages en quête de génération," in *La Tête dans le plat* (Paris: La Table Ronde 1989), 161.

34. Ibid., 160.

35. For example, Bernard Franck, *Le Dernier des Mohicans* (Paris: Fasquelle, 1956); Paul Sérant, *Gardez-vous à gauche* (Paris: Fasquelle, 1956); François Nourissier, *Les Chiens à fouetter* (Paris: Editions Julliard, 1956); Jean-François Bourbon, *A nos pères, deux mots!* (Paris: La Table Ronde, 1956). Also see Simone de Beauvoir, "La pensée de droite aujourd'hui," in *Les Temps modernes* 112–13 (May 1955): 1539–75 and vols. 114–15 (June-July 1955): 2219–61; reprinted in *Faut-il brûler Sade?* (Paris: Editions Gallimard, 1955), 83–184.

36. Nimier, *Le Hussard bleu,* 7.

37. Opportunities to prove one's virility did exist. See John Talbott, "The Myth and Reality of the Paratrooper in the Algerian War," *Armed Forces and Society* 3 (Fall 1976): 69–70.

38. The former in a parodic tract sent to Antoine Blondin; the latter in a review of De Gaulle's *Mémoires de guerre* Nimier wrote for *Arts*. Both are quoted in Dambre, *Roger Nimier,* 468.

39. (La Table Ronde, 1952).

40. Paul Van Den Bosch, *Les Enfants de l'absurde* (Paris: La Table Ronde, 1956), 11. To be a child of the absurd in the United States at the same time was more a function of the encroaching technological society, as attested by a similar title: Paul Goodman, *Growing Up Absurd: The Problems of Youth in the Organized Society* (New York: Random House, 1956).

41. Van Den Bosch, *Les Enfants,* 11.

42. Ibid., 60.

43. Ibid., 15.

44. Michel Déon, *Lettre à un jeune Rastignac* (Paris: Fasquelle Editeurs, 1956).

45. Ibid., 9.

46. Ibid., 18–19.

47. Ibid., 59.

48. Stephen Hecquet, *Les Garçons* (Paris: Fasquelle Editeurs, 1956).

49. Ibid., 23.

50. Coincidentally, they happen to be the as-yet-unknown Roger Vadim and Juliette Gréco.

51. Simone de Beauvoir, *La Force des choses* (Paris: Editions Gallimard, 1963), 51.

52. Anna Boschetti, *The Intellectual Enterprise: Sartre and Les Temps Modernes,* trans. Richard C. McCleary (Evanston, Ill.: Northwestern University Press, 1988), 108–9.

53. "Too Many Attend Sartre Lecture. Heat, Fainting Spells, Police. Lawrence of Arabia an Existentialist," was the title of Maurice Nadeau's article in *Combat.* Nadeau and a good number of the other reviewers delighted in describing the panic and excesses of the crowd. They spoke of "elbow fights," a "nonexistential angst," and the fear of "dying of suffocation," They spoke of the boos and screams— "a *No Exit* situation"—and the heat that dissolved make-up, clothes, bodies. Each newspaper had something to say on the crowd that was "a mob rather than an audience," the "fifteen fainting spells," the "thirty broken chairs," and the "victory" of the lecturer. The lecture itself was perceived by everybody as "a university course," "too scholarly," and the lecturer was unanimously praised for his "cool," his "courage," his "grit," his "personal magnetism," and the "impact of his mere presence." Annie Cohen-Solal, *Sartre: A Life,* trans. Anna Paola Cancogni (New York: Pantheon Books, 1987), 251–52.

54. Ibid., 255–56.

55. *Samedi-Soir,* 3 November 1945.

56. Cohen-Solal, *Sartre,* 261. "*Samedi-Soir's* tireless haranguing of Sartre ranged from ridiculous anecdotes to more serious accusations, such as the claim that existentialists control the theatre, the press, and the publishing houses, and that 'Sartre wants to impose his doctrine and his rule over the entire world,'" Cohen-Solal, 262.

57. Déon, *Les Gens de la nuit,* 184.

58. Claudie Lessalier, "Aspects de l'expérience lesbienne en France 1930–68." (Thesis for the DEA in sociology, Université de Paris 8, November 1987).

59. See, for example, C. Jéglot, *La Jeune fille et le redressement national* (1942); Jacques Aubrun, "De la captivité à l'enseignement ménager," in *Enseignement secondaire et technique,* 25 May 1945, quoted in Paul Crouzet, *Bachelières ou jeunes filles?* (Paris: Privat-Didier, 1949), 105.

60. Quoted in Guillaume Hanoteau, *L'Age d'Or de Saint-Germain-des-Prés* (Paris: Editions Denoël, 1965), 76.

61. Ibid., 79. In her autobiography, Anne-Marie Cazalis writes that it was all a pack of lies: "Les gens étaient assis bien sagement. Parfois ils dansaient [People were seated, well-behaved. Sometimes they danced]. "*Mémoires d'une Anne* (Paris: Editions Stock, 1976), 53.

62. Hanoteau, *L'Age d'or,* 82.

63. Cazalis, *Mémoires,* 90. Jean Cau, Sartre's secretary in those years, describes this generation—his own—with a combination of pity and disdain in a novel entitled *Les Paroissiens* (Paris: Editions Gallimard, 1958). In their early twenties during the Occupation, they became the first wave of postwar intellectuals: journalists at respected papers, filmmakers, readers at publishing houses, and café philosophers. According to Cau, his was a tortured, bitter generation, willful outsiders, who by 1950 were idle, poor, and unmarried, who persisted in their allegiance to Stalin and the Communist Party despite their awareness of human rights violations in Soviet labor camps. Quoted in Maurice Nadeau, "Une génération perdue?," *Lettres nouvelles* 6 (June 1958): 948. Cau's sentiments were echoed quite recently in Tony Judt's *Past Imperfect: French Intellectuals, 1944–1956* (Berkeley: University of California Press, 1992).

64. Cazalis, *Mémoires,* 82.

65. Deirdre Bair, *Simone de Beauvoir: A Biography* (New York: Simon and Schuster, 1990), 402.

66. Georges Amado, "Les Jeunes gens inadaptés de Saint-Germain-des-Prés et du Quartier Latin," *La Nef* 77–78 (June-July 1951): 31.

67. All of these landmark studies are mentioned and annotated in Anne Simonin et Hélène Clastres, *Les Idées en France 1945–1988. Une chronologie* (Paris: Editions Gallimard, 1989).

68. Amado, "Les Jeunes gens," 32.

69. Cohen-Solal, *Sartre*, 264.

70. Cazalis, *Mémoires*, 105.

71. "Pour vous, les jeunes, l'existentialisme est-il déjà du passé?" *Elle* 24 March 1952, 28–29.

72. *Marie-Claire*, 4 (January 1955): 14.

73. Michèle Perrot, "Fait divers et histoire au XIXe siècle," *Annales. Economies, sociétés, civilisations* 38, no. 4 (July-August 1983): 911–19.

74. Joseph Kessel, *Le Procès des enfants perdus* (Paris: Editions Julliard, 1951), 15. The book also contains a transcript of the trial.

75. *Le Figaro* 22 May 1951; 4 May 1951; *Arts* 377 (19 September 1952): 10.

76. Maurice Descotes, "Le Mal du siècle n'est pas seulement littérature," *La Nef* 77–78 (June-July 1951): 25–26.

77. Maurice Descotes, *L'Eprouvo* (Paris: Editions Julliard, 1951).

78. Descotes, "Le Mal," 29.

79. Marc Ferro, "Présentation," *Annales. Economies, sociétés, civilisations* 38, no. 4 (July-August 1983): 824.

80. Despite the disclaimer at the beginning of the film, the J-3 affair was clearly Cayatte's inspiration. In 1952, Michelangelo Antonioni began production on a film he never finished based on three crimes committed by adolescents in 1951, in England, Italy, and the J-3 affair in France, to be entitled *Sans amour*.

81. "Le vagabondage des mineures," *Rééducation. Revue française de l'enfance délinquante, déficiente, et en danger moral* (March-April 1954).

82. André Bazin, *Le Cinéma français de la Libération à la Nouvelle Vague (1945–1958)* (Paris: Editions de l'Etoile, 1983), 79.

83. Ibid., 83.

84. Kessel, *Le Procès*, 90.

85. This is the thesis advanced in Daniel Schneidermann's *L'Etrange procès* (Paris: Editions Fayard, 1998).

Chapter Four. Technological Society and Its Discontents

1. Benjamin Stora, *La Gangrène et l'oubli. La Mémoire et la guerre d'Algérie* (Paris: Editions la Découverte, 1991), 25–26.

12. Robert Bonnaud, *Les Tournants du XXe siècle* (Paris: L'Harmattan, 1992), 149, 152.

3. Merritt Roe Smith and Leo Marx, eds., *Does Technology Drive History?: The Dilemma of Technological Determinism* (Cambridge: MIT Press, 1994).

4. "Il a donc fallu vingt ans pour réparer les pertes et les manques à gagner de trente années de guerres et de crises économiques, et se retrouver au point où l'on aurait été si sa croissance s'était poursuivie calmement sur la pente du début du

siècle" [Twenty years had to pass in order to repair the losses and shortages earned from thirty years of war and economic crises, and for the nation to find itself at the point it would have been if growth had proceeded calmly on the curve of the beginning of the century]. Henri Mendras, *La Seconde Révolution française 1965-1984* (Paris: Editions Gallimard, 1994) 14.

5. Leo Marx, "The Idea of 'Technology' and Postmodern Pessimism," in Smith and Marx, *Does Technology Drive History?*, 237-58.

6. Jean Jousselin, "Actualité d'une politique de la jeunesse," *La Nef* 12, no. 8 (March 1955): 151; André Labarthe, "Préparons des Français pour l'an 2000," *La Nef* 12, no. 8 (March 1955): 7-8.

7. Louis Dalmas, "Ainsi vieillit notre jeunesse," *La Nef* 12, no. 8 (March 1955): 172.

8. Pierre Macaigne, "Ils ont vingt ans," *Le Figaro* 21-22 May 1960, 9.

9. Ibid.

10. Jean-François Remonté et Simone Depoux, *Les Années radio* (Paris: Editions Gallimard, 1989), 54.

11. Marc Martin, "La Radio dans les crises politiques contemporaines," in Jérôme Bourdon et Cécile Méadal, eds., *Techniques et politiques de l'information. Actes du séminaire Histoire des politiques de la communication* (Paris: CNRS, 1987), 177. And Maurice Vaisse, *1961, Alger, le putsch* (Brussels: Editions Complexe, 1983).

12. The title comes from an extremely successful song written by Gilbert Bécaud. François Jouffa et Jacques Bensamian, *Vinyl fraise. Les années 60* (Paris: Editions Michel Lafon, 1993), 16.

13. Editorial, *Salut les copains* 1 (July-August 1962): 1.

14. Jouffa et Bensamian, *Vinyl fraise,* 35, 42.

15. Remonté et Depoux, *Les Années radio,* 72.

16. Jean-Paul Huguenin, *Une autre jeunesse* (Paris: Editions du Seuil, 1965), 117.

17. Jouffa et Bensamian, *Vinyl fraise,* 43-46. All subsequent references are cited in the text with the abbreviation VF.

18. Paul Yonnet, *Jeux, modes et masses. La Société française et le moderne* (Paris: Editions Gallimard, 1985), 146.

19. "Si les twisteuses ne twistaient pas," *Salut les copains,* 2 (September 1962): 44-53.

20. Philippe Labro, *Des feux mal éteints* (Paris: Editions Gallimard, 1967) quoted in Philip Dine, *Images of the Algerian War: French Fiction and Film, 1954-1992* (New York: Oxford University Press, 1994), 117-18. Dine has done the invaluable work of constituting this corpus and identifying its tropes; more extensive textual analysis has yet to be done.

21. Jean-Pierre Vittori, *Nous les appelés d'Algérie* (Paris: Messidor, 1983), 52.

22. Guy Vidal et Alain Bignon, *Une Education algérienne* (Paris: Dargaud Editeur, 1982).

23. Alain Manevy, *L'Algérie à vingt ans* (Paris: Editions Grasset, 1960), 53.

24. Maurienne, *Le Déserteur* (Editions Manya, 1991), 27. The book was seized soon after its initial 1960 publication.

25. *Paris-Match* 667 (January 1962): n.pag.

26. Vittori, *Nous les appelés,* 55.

27. Ibid., 121.

28. Ibid., 126.

29. "Au nom de la France, j'ordonne que tous les moyens, je dis tous les moyens, soient employés pour barrer la route à ces hommes-là, en attendant de les réduire. J'interdis à tous Français, et d'abord à tout soldat, d'exécuter aucun de leurs ordres" [In the name of France, I order that all means, I repeat, all means, be employed to obstruct those men while waiting to defeat them. I forbid every Frenchman and, foremost, every soldier to execute any of their orders]. Quoted in Martin, "La Radio," 176.

30. Remonté et Depoux, *Les Années radio,* 54.

31. René Rémond et Claude Neuschwander, "Télévision et comportement politique," *Revue française de sciences politiques* 13, no. 2 (June 1963): 337.

32. "Leurs rubriques de jeunes, nous n'en pensons rien puisque nous ne les lisons pas," *Age tendre et tête de bois* 11 (November 1963): 50–53.

33. Benjamin Stora, *La Gangrène,* 42.

34. Hélène Bousser-Eck, "Cinq colonnes et l'Algérie," in Jean-Noël Jeanneney et Monique Sauvage, eds., *Télévision, nouvelle mémoire. Les Magazines de grand reportage 1959–1968* (Paris: Editions du Seuil et l'Institut National de l'Audiovisuel, 1982), 95.

35. Monique Sauvage and Denis Maréchal, "Les Racines d'un succès," in *Télévision, nouvelle mémoire,* 40.

36. Ibid.

37. Jérôme Bourdon, "La Guerre d'Algérie à la télévision," in Laurent Gervereau, Jean-Pierre Rioux, Benjamin Stora, eds., *La France en Guerre d'Algérie* (Paris: BDIC, 1992), 242–44.

38. Rémond et Neuschwander, "Télévision," 325.

39. Ibid., 325, 327.

40. Bourdon, "La Guerre d'Algérie," 243.

41. Raoul Girardet, lecture on *Les Tricheurs,* Vidéothèque de la Ville de Paris, May 1988.

42. The special issue of *L'Express* on *Les Tricheurs,* with an unsmiling Pascale Petit on the cover, featured an article by Françoise Giroud about the reception of the film; an investigative story by Jean Cau on "real-life" *tricheurs* who frequented Paris cafés; an interview with Marcel Carné; articles about youth cultures, all with

their own labels, in England (teddy boys), Italy (*vitteloni*), Poland (hooligans), and the United States (beats). Reminiscent of Jacques Robert's piece on the existentialists for *Samedi-Soir*, captioned stills from the film took the reader on a diagnostic tour of *tricheur* territory: "L'amour: une affaire technique"; "Le café: le centre d'un univers qui se débine"; "La «surboum»: dans l'alcool, dans la danse, la fuite." [Love: a technical affair; The café: the center of a universe in decay; The party: in alcohol, in dance, escape.] *L'Express*, 16 October 1958.

43. Françoise Sagan, *Bonjour tristesse* (Paris: Editions Julliard, 1954), 11.

44. Stora, *La Gangrène*, 40.

Chapter Five. Quantifying Youth

1. Jean M. Converse, *Survey Research in the United States: Roots and Emergence (1890–1960)* (Berkeley: University of California Press, 1987), 1.

2. Ibid.

3. Pierre Bourdieu, "L'Opinion publique n'existe pas," in *Questions de sociologie* (Paris: Editions de Minuit, 1984), 224, 231.

4. Ian Hacking, "Making Up People," in *Reconstructing Individualism: Autonomy, Individuality, and the Self in Western Thought*, ed. Thomas C. Heller et al. (Stanford: Stanford University Press, 1986).

5. Olivier Galland, *Sociologie de la jeunesse. L'Entrée dans la vie* (Paris: Armand Colin, 1991), 33.

6. Ibid., 39. Also see Pierre Bourdieu, "La «Jeunesse» n'est qu'un mot," in *Questions de sociologie*, 145.

7. Agathon, *Les Jeunes gens d'aujourd'hui* (Paris: Plon, 1913), v.

8. Galland, *Sociologie*, 33–35.

9. Joan Copjec, *Read My Desire: Lacan Against the Historicists* (Cambridge: MIT Press, 1994), 4.

10. Amélie Gayraud, *Les Jeunes filles d'aujourd'hui* (Paris: G. Oudin, 1914), 36, 39.

11. Ibid., 62.

12. Galland, *Sociologie*, 44.

13. Michael Pollak, "La Planification des sciences sociales," *Actes de la recherche en sciences sociales* 2–3 (1976): 108.

14. Ibid.

15. "The main tactic employed by the group of historians that came to be known as the Annales school against the threat of structuralism was that of cannibalism: encompass and absorb the enemies as a means of controlling them. Immediately after the war the official journal of the Annales school underwent a significant name change: from *Annales d'histoire économique et sociale* to *Annales: économies, sociétés, civilisations* . . . [T]he disappearance of the word 'history' from

the revised title showed a new degree of willingness to embrace the other social sciences, particularly those of demography and economics. Behind the gesture of self-effacement, however, lurked a continuing will to prevail as absent or invisible master." Kristin Ross, *Fast Cars, Clean Bodies: Decolonization and the Reordering of French Culture* (Cambridge: MIT Press, 1995), 187–88.

16. Michael Pollak, "Paul F. Lazarsfeld, fondateur d'une multinationale scientifique," *Actes de la recherche en sciences sociales* 25 (1979): 56.

17. Quoted in Richard Kuisel, *Seducing the French: The Drama of Americanization* (Berkeley: University of California Press, 1993), 24.

18. Ibid., 25.

19. Ross, *Fast Cars,* 187.

20. Pollak, "La planification," 110; and François Bourricaud, *Le Bricolage idéologique. Essai sur les intellectuels et les passions démocratiques* (Paris: PUF, 1980), 116.

21. Robert Kanters et Gilbert Sigaux, *Vingt ans en 1951* (Paris: Editions Julliard, 1951), 12, 77.

22. Ibid., 10.

23. Anne Simonin et Hélène Clastres, *Les Idées en France 1945–1988. Une chronologie* (Paris: Editions Gallimard, 1989), 102.

24. Kanters et Sigaux, *Vingt ans,* 163–64.

25. *L'Express* 3 October 1957.

26. Françoise Giroud, *La Nouvelle vague. Portraits de la jeunesse* (Paris: Editions Gallimard, 1958).

27. Henri Lefebvre, "La Jeunesse aurait-elle découvert le bonheur?," *L'Express* 19 December 1957, 10.

28. *Les Nouvelles littéraires* 3 January-19 September 1957; Henri Perruchot, *La France et sa jeunesse* (Paris: Hachette, 1958).

29. *Masculin/Féminin: A Film by Jean-Luc Godard* (New York: Grove Press, 1969), 169. All transcriptions from the original French of the film are my own.

30. Ibid., 26–27.

31. Ibid., 41–42.

32. Ibid., 174–75.

Conclusion. From Object to Subject?

1. François Jouffa et Jacques Barsamian, *Vinyl fraise. Les Années 60* (Paris: Editions Michel Lafon, 1993), 142.

2. Ibid., 160.

3. Edgar Morin, "«Salut les copains» I: Une nouvelle classe d'âge," *Le Monde,* 6 July 1963, 1. And Morin, *Les Stars* (1957; reprint Paris: Editions Galilée, 1984), 42–46.

4. Morin, "«Salut les copains» II: Le "yé-yé," *Le Monde*, 7–8 July 1963, 12.

5. Guy Debord, *La Société du spectacle* (Paris: Editions Champ Libre, 1983), 15, 37.

6. Ibid., 39.

7. Elizabeth Sussman, introduction to *On the passage of a few people through a rather brief moment in time: The Situationist international, 1957–1972* (Cambridge: MIT Press, 1989), 4–8.

8. Françoise Giroud, *La Nouvelle vague. Portraits de la jeunesse* (Paris: Editions Gallimard, 1958), 23.

9. Henri Mendras, *La Seconde révolution française 1965–1984* (Paris: Editions Gallimard, 1994), 328–30.

10. Gilles Deleuze et Félix Guattari, "Mai 68 n'a pas eu lieu," *Les Nouvelles,* 3–9 May 1984: 75–76.

11. Hervé Lebras's documentary "Reprise" (1993) traces his recent attempt to discover what became of a factory worker photographed during the strikes of 1968 when she was in her early twenties. The film returns periodically to the photograph. The rage of her expression and the violent physicality of her resistance to the men in the crowd who attempt to force her back inside the factory justify a search that dead-ends at every turn: whatever can become of such an unfamiliar, indeed "unfeminine" rage?

12. Sylvie Chaperon, "La Radicalisation des mouvements féminins français de 1960 à 1970," *Vingtième siècle* 48 (October-December 1995): 61, 67–70. Also see Christine Delphy, "Les origines du MLF en France," *Nouvelles questions féministes* 16, 17, 18 (1991); Danièle Voldman, "Mai 68 ou la féministe refusée," *Nouvelle revue socialiste,* August-September 1985: 41–48.

Bibliography

L'Adolescence de l'après-guerre et ses problèmes. Paris: Editions Sociales Françaises, 1948.

Aebischer, Verena and Sonia Dayan-Herzbrun. "Cinéma et destins des femmes," *Cahiers internationaux de sociologie* 80 (1986): 147–59.

Agathon. *Les Jeunes gens d'aujourd'hui*. Paris: Plon, 1913.

Allen, Suzanne. *La Mauvaise conscience*. Paris: Editions Gallimard, 1955.

Amado, Georges. "Les Jeunes gens inadaptés de Saint-Germain-des-Prés et du Quartier Latin," *La Nef* 77–78 (June–July 1951): 31–38.

Amouroux, Henri. *Les Français sous l'Occupation*. Paris: Cassettes Radio France, 1984.

Armstrong, Nancy. *Desire and Domestic Fiction*. London and New York: Oxford University Press, 1987.

Arthus, Dr. André. *Ce que toute jeune fille devrait savoir*. Paris: Editions Jeheber, 1948.

Assouline, Pierre. *Gaston Gallimard. Un Demi-siècle d'édition française*. Paris: Editions Balland, 1984.

Attias-Donfut, Claudine. *Sociologie des générations. L'Empreinte du temps*. Paris: PUF, 1988.

Audry, Colette. "Elle." *Les Temps modernes* 78 (April 1952): 1788–94.

Bair, Deirdre. *Simone de Beauvoir: A Biography*. New York: Simon and Schuster, 1990.

Barthes, Roland. *Mythologies*. Paris: Editions du Seuil, 1953. Translated by Anne Lanvers as *Mythologies* (New York: Hill and Wang, 1972).

Bazin, André. "La Cybernétique d'André Cayatte." In *Le Cinéma français de la*

Libération à la Nouvelle Vague (1945–1958), 79–83. Paris: Editions de l'Etoile, 1983.

Beauvoir, Simone de. "Brigitte Bardot et le syndrome de Lolita." In Francis and Gontier: 363–77. Originally published in *Esquire,* August 1959: 32–38.

———. *Le Deuxième sexe.* Paris: Editions Gallimard, 1949.

———. *Faut-il brûler Sade?* Paris: Editions Gallimard, 1955.

———. *La Force des choses.* Paris: Editions Gallimard, 1963.

———. *Les Mandarins.* Paris: Editions Gallimard, 1954.

———. *Mémoires d'une jeune fille rangée.* Paris: Editions Gallimard: 1958.

———. "La Pensée de droite aujourd'hui." *Les Temps Modernes* 112–13 (May 1955): 1539–75; 114–15 (June–July 1955): 2219–61.

Bell, Daniel. *The Coming of Postindustrial Society: A Venture in Social Forecasting.* New York: Basic Books, 1976.

———. *The End of Ideology: On the Exhaustion of Political Ideas in the Fifties.* 1960. Reprint, Cambridge: Harvard University Press, 1988.

Bellanger, Claude et al. *Histoire générale de la presse française.* Vol. 4. Paris: Presses Universitaires de France, 1975.

Benoît, Nicole, Edgar Morin, and Bernard Paillard. *La Femme majeure.* Paris: Editions du Seuil, 1983.

Bonnaud, Robert. *Les Tournants du XXe siècle.* Paris: L'Harmattan, 1992.

Boschetti, Anna. *The Intellectual Enterprise: Sartre and Les Temps Modernes.* Translated by Richard C. McCleary. Evanston: Northwestern University Press, 1988.

Bothorel, Jean. *Bernard Grasset. Vie et passions d'un éditeur.* Paris: Editions Grasset, 1989.

Bouchardeau, Huguette. *Pas d'histoire les femmes. 50 ans d'histoire des femmes 1918–1968.* Paris: Editions Syros, 1977.

Bourbon, Jean-François. *A nos pères, deux mots!* Paris: La Table Ronde, 1956.

Bourdet, Denise. *Visages d'aujourd'hui.* Paris: Plon, 1960.

Bourdieu, Pierre. *Les Héritiers. Les Etudiants et la culture.* Paris: Editions de Minuit, 1964.

———. *Questions de sociologie.* Paris: Editions de Minuit, 1984.

Bourdon, Jérôme. "La Guerre d'Algérie à la télévision." In *La France en Guerre d'Algérie,* edited by Laurent Gervereau, Jean-Pierre Rioux, Benjamin Stora, 242–46. Paris: BDIC, 1992.

Bourricaud, François. *Le Bricolage idéologique. Essai sur les intellectuels et les passions démocratiques.* Paris: PUF, 1980.

———. Introduction to *Vers la société postindustrielle,* by Daniel Bell. Paris: Editions Laffont, 1976.

Breines, Winifred. *Young, White, and Miserable: Growing Up Female in the Fifties.* Boston: Beacon Press, 1992.

Bridenthal, Renate, Claudia Koonz, and Susan Stuard, eds. *Becoming Visible: Women in European History.* 2d ed. Boston: Houghton Mifflin Company, 1987.

Burniaux, Jeanne. *L'Education des filles. Problèmes de l'adolescence.* Paris: Editions Universitaires, 1965.

Butler, Judith. *Gender Trouble: Feminism and the Subversion of Identity.* London and New York: Routledge, 1990.

Camus, Albert. "Ni victimes ni bourreaux." In *Actuelles. Chroniques 1944–1948.* Paris: Editions Gallimard, 1950.

Carroll, Raymonde. *Evidences invisibles.* Paris: Editions du Seuil, 1987.

Angela Carter. *The Sadeian Woman and the Ideology of Pornography.* New York: Harper Colophon Books, 1978.

Cau, Jean. *Les Paroissiens.* Paris: Editions Gallimard, 1958.

Cazalis, Anne-Marie. *Mémoires d'une Anne.* Paris: Editions Stock, 1976.

Chafe, William H. *The Paradox of Change: American Women in the Twentieth Century.* Rev. ed. New York: Oxford University Press, 1991.

Chaperon, Sylvie. "La Radicalisation des mouvements féminins français de 1960 à 1970." *Vingtième siècle* 48 (October–December 1995): 61–74.

Chapsal, Madeleine. *Vérités sur les jeunes filles.* Paris: Editions Grasset, 1960.

Clark, Linda L. *Schooling the Daughters of Marianne: Textbooks and the Socialization of Girls in Modern French Primary Schools.* Albany: SUNY Press, 1984.

Cocteau, Jean. *Les Enfants terribles.* Paris: Editions Grasset, 1929.

Cohen-Solal, Annie. *Sartre: A Life.* Translated by Anna Paola Cancogni. New York: Pantheon Books, 1987.

Converse, Jean M. *Survey Research in the United States: Roots and Emergence (1890–1960).* Berkeley: University of California Press, 1987.

Copfermann, Emile. *La Génération des blousons noirs. Problèmes de la jeunesse française.* Paris: François Maspero, 1962.

Copjec, Joan. *Read My Desire: Lacan Against the Historicists.* Cambridge: MIT Press, 1994.

———. *Supposing the Subject.* London: Verso, 1994.

Courtivron, Isabelle de. *Violette Leduc.* Boston: Twayne, 1985.

Crouzet, Paul. *Bachelières ou jeunes filles?* Paris: Privat-Didier, 1949.

Dalmas, Louis. "Ainsi vieillit notre jeunesse." *La Nef* 12, no. 8 (March 1955): 163–202.

Dalsimer, Katherine. *Female Adolescence: Psychoanalytic Reflections on Works of Literature.* New Haven: Yale University Press, 1986.

Dambre, Marc. *Roger Nimier. Hussard du demi-siècle.* Paris: Editions Flammarion, 1989.

De la 4 CV à la vidéo. 1953–1983, ces trente années qui ont changé notre vie. Paris: Communica International, 1983.

D'Eaubonne, Françoise. *Les Monstres d'été. Mémoires précoces.* Vol. 2. Paris: Editions Julliard, 1966.

Debesse, Maurice. *La Crise d'originalité juvénile.* Paris: PUF, 1947.

Debord, Guy. *La Société du spectacle.* 1967. Reprint, Paris: Editions Champ Libre, 1983.

Deharme, Lise. *Carole ou ce qui plaît aux filles.* Paris: Editions Julliard, 1961.

———. *Laissez-moi tranquille.* Paris: Editions Julliard, 1959.

De Lauretis, Teresa. *Alice Doesn't: Feminism, semiotics, cinema.* Bloomington: Indiana University Press, 1984.

Delbourg-Delphis, Marylène. *Le Chic et le look: Histoire de la mode féminine de 1850 à nos jours.* Paris: Hachette, 1981.

Deleuze, Gilles and Félix Guattari. "Mai 68 n'a pas eu lieu." *Les Nouvelles,* 3–9 (May 1984): 75–76.

Delphy, Christine. "Les origines du MLF en France." *Nouvelles questions féministes,* 16–17–18 (1991).

Déon, Michel. *Les Gens de la nuit.* Paris: La Table Ronde, 1958.

———. *Lettre à un jeune Rastignac.* Paris: Fasquelle Editeurs, 1956.

Descotes, Maurice. *L'Epreuve.* Paris: Editions Julliard, 1951.

———. "Le Mal du siècle n'est pas seulement littérature." *La Nef* 77–78 (June–July 1951): 25–30.

Dine, Philip. *Images of the Algerian War: French Fiction and Film, 1954–1992.* New York: Oxford University Press, 1994.

Dormann, Geneviève. "Les Jeunes filles réduites à rien." *Arts,* 18–24 (January 1961): 3.

Douglas, Mary. *Purity and Danger.* New York and Washington: Praeger, 1966.

Dubois-Jallais, Denise. *La Tzarine. Hélène Lazareff et l'aventure d'«Elle».* Paris: Editions Robert Laffont, 1984.

Duchen, Claire. "Occupation housewife: The Domestic Ideal in 1950s France." *French Cultural Studies* 2 (1991): 1–11.

———. *Women's Rights and Women's Lives in France 1945–1968.* London and New York: Routledge, 1994.

En souvenir de René Julliard. Paris: Editions Julliard, 1963.

"Evolution of Adolescence in Europe, The." *Journal of Family History* 17, no. 4 (1992).

Faligot, Roger and Rémi Kauffer. *Porno Business.* Paris: Librairie Arthème Fayard, 1987.

Ferro, Marc. "Présentation." *Annales. Economies, sociétés, civilisations* 38, no. 4 (July–August 1983): 821–26.

Finas, Lucette. *Les Chaînes éclatées.* Paris: Mercure de France, 1955.

Fourastié, Jean. *Les Trente glorieuses ou la révolution invisible de 1946 à 1975.* Paris: Fayard, 1979.

Francis, Claude and Fernande Gontier, eds. *Les Ecrits de Simone de Beauvoir. La Vie — l'écriture.* Paris: Editions Gallimard, 1979.

———. *Simone de Beauvoir: A Life . . . A Love Story.* Translated by Lisa Nesselson. New York: St. Martin's Press, 1987.

Franck, Bernard. *Le Dernier des Mohicans.* Paris: Fasquelle, 1956.

———."Grognards et hussards." *Les Temps modernes,* 86 (December 1952): 1005–18.

Freud, Sigmund. "The Taboo of Virginity." *Standard Edition.* London: Hogarth, 1957, 11:193–208.

Friedan, Betty. *The Feminine Mystique.* New York: Norton, 1963.

Galland, Olivier. *Sociologie de la jeunesse. L'Entrée dans la vie.* Paris: Armand Colin, 1991.

Gallop, Jane. *The Daughter's Seduction: Feminism and Psychoanalysis.* Ithaca: Cornell University Press, 1982.

Gayraud, Amélie. *Les Jeunes filles d'aujourd'hui.* Paris: G. Oudin, 1914.

Giett, Sylvette. "Vingt années d'amour en couverture." *Actes de la recherche en sciences sociales* 60 (1985): 17–22.

Girardet, Raoul. "L'héritage de «L'Action française»." *Revue française de science politique* 7, no. 4 (October–December 1957): 765–92.

Giroud, Françoise. *La Nouvelle vague. Portraits de la jeunesse.* Paris: Editions Gallimard, 1958.

———. *Si je mens . . . Conversations avec Claude Glayman.* Paris: Editions Stock, 1972.

Godard, Jean-Luc. *Masculin/Féminin: A Film By Jean-Luc Godard.* New York: Grove Press, 1969.

Goodman, Paul. *Growing Up Absurd: The Problems of Youth in the Organized Society.* New York: Random House, 1956.

Grall, Xavier. *La Génération du djebel.* Paris: Editions du Cerf, 1962.

Gréco, Juliette. *Jujube.* Paris: Editions Stock, 1982.

Grosz, Elizabeth. *Jacques Lacan: A Feminist Introduction.* New York: Routledge, 1990.

Gurvitch, Georges. *La Vocation actuelle de la sociologie.* Paris: PUF, 1957.

Hacking, Ian. "Making Up People." In *Reconstructing Individualism: Autonomy, Individuality, and the Self in Western Thought,* edited by Thomas C. Heller et al. Stanford: Stanford University Press, 1986.

Hall, Stuart. "Cultural Studies: Two Paradigms." *Media, Culture and Society* 2 (1980): 57–72.

———. "Notes on Deconstructing the Popular." In *People's History and Socialist Theory,* edited by Raphael Samuel, 227–40. London: Routledge and Kegan Paul, 1981.

Hanoteau, Guillaume. *L'Age d'or de Saint-Germain-des-Prés.* Paris: Editions De-noël, 1965.

Hebdige, Dick. *Subculture: The Meaning of Style.* London: Routledge, 1979.

Hecquet, Stephen. *Les Garçons.* Paris: Fasquelle Editeurs, 1956.

———. *La Tête dans le plat.* Paris: La Table Ronde, 1989.

Heilbrun, Carolyn. *Writing a Woman's Life.* New York: W.W. Norton, 1988.

Heron, Liz. *Truth, Dare, or Promise: Girls Growing Up in the Fifties.* London: Virago, 1985.

Hewitt, Nicholas. *Literature and the Right in Postwar France: The Story of the "Hussards."* Oxford: Berg, 1996.

Higonnet, Margaret Randolph et al. *Behind the Lines: Gender and the Two World Wars.* New Haven: Yale University Press, 1987.

Houbre, Gabrielle. *La Discipline de l'amour. L'Education sentimentale des filles et des garçons à l'âge du romantisme.* Paris: Plon, 1997.

Houlding, Elizabeth. "Between the Lines: Women Writing the Occupation of France." Ph.D. diss., Columbia University, 1991.

Huerre, Patrice, Martine Pagan-Reymond, Jean-Michel Reymond. *L'Adolescence n'existe pas. Histoire des tribulations d'une artifice.* Paris: Editions Universi-taires, 1990.

Huguenin, Jean-Paul. *Une autre jeunesse.* Paris: Editions du Seuil, 1965.

Humbert, Geneviève, ed. *Jeunesse et état.* Presses Universitaires de Nancy, 1991.

Ibert, Jean-Claude. "La jeune littérature féminine en France." N.p., 30 septembre 1957.

Irigaray, Luce. *Ce sexe qui n'en est pas un.* Paris: Editions de Minuit, 1977.

———. *Speculum de l'autre femme.* Paris: Editions de Minuit, 1974.

Jameson, Fredric. "Periodizing the Sixties." *Social Text* 9–10 (1984): 178–209.

Jay, Karla and Joanne Glasgow, eds. *Lesbian Texts and Contexts: Radical Revisions.* New York: New York University Press, 1990.

Jeanneney, Jean-Noël and Monique Sauvage. *Télévision, nouvelle mémoire. Les Magazines de grand reportage 1959–1968.* Paris: Editions du Seuil and l'Institut National de l'Audiovisuel, 1982.

Jéglot, Cécile. *La Jeune Fille.* Paris: Editions Spes, 1948.

———. *La Jeune fille et le redressement national.* N.p. 1942.

"Jeunesses XXe siècle." *Le Mouvement social* 168 (July–September 1994).

Johnson, Lesley. *The Modern Girl: Girlhood and Growing Up.* Buckingham, UK: Open University Press, 1993.

Jouffa, François and Jacques Barsamian. *Vinyl fraise. Les Années 60.* Paris: Michel Lafon, 1993.

Jousselin, Jean. "Actualité d'une politique de la jeunesse." *La Nef* 12, no. 8 (March 1955): 148–62.

———. *Jeunesse. Fait social méconnu.* Paris: PUF, 1959.

Judt, Tony. *Past Imperfect: French Intellectuals, 1944–1956.* Berkeley: University of California Press, 1992.

Kanters, Robert and Gilbert Sigaux. *Vingt ans en 1951.* Paris: Editions Julliard, 1951.

Kessel, Joseph. *Le Procès des enfants perdus.* Paris: Editions Julliard, 1951.

Knibiehler, Yvonne, Marcel Bernon, Elisabeth Ravoux-Rallo, and Eliane Richard. *De la Pucelle à la minette. Les Jeunes filles de l'âge classique à nos jours.* Paris: Messidor, 1983.

Kuisel, Richard F. *Seducing The French: The Drama of Americanization.* Berkeley: University of California Press, 1993.

Labarthe, André. "Préparons des Français pour l'an 2000," *La Nef* 12, no. 8 (March 1955): 5–19.

Lamy, Jean-Claude. *René Julliard.* Paris: Editions Julliard, 1992.

——. *Sagan.* Paris. Mercure de France, 1988.

Laqueur, Thomas. "Orgasm, Generation, and the Politics of Reproductive Biology." In *The Making of the Modern Body,* edited by Thomas Laqueur and Cathleen Gallagher. Berkeley and Los Angeles: University of California Press, 1987.

Laroque, Pierre, ed. *La Politique familiale en France depuis 1945.* Paris: Documentation Française, 1985.

Laubier, Claire, ed. *The Condition of Women in France 1945 to the Present: A Documentary Anthology.* London and New York: Routledge, 1990.

Laurent, Jacques. "Plat du jour," *La Table ronde* 20–21 (August–September 1949): 159.

Leduc, Violette. *La Bâtarde.* Paris: Editions Gallimard, 1964.

——. *Ravages.* Paris: Editions Gallimard, 1955.

——. *Thérèse et Isabelle.* Paris: Editions Gallimard, 1966.

Lefebvre, Henri. "La Jeunesse aurait-elle découvert le bonheur?" *L'Express,* 19 December 1957: 10–12.

Lejeune, Philippe. *Le Moi des demoiselles. Enquête sur le journal de jeune fille.* Paris: Editions du Seuil, 1993.

Lenoir, Rémi. "L'effondrement des bases sociales du familialisme." *Actes de la recherche en sciences sociales* 57–58 (1985): 69–88.

——. "Transformations du familialisme et reconversions morales." *Actes de la recherche en sciences sociales* 59 (1985): 3–47.

Lessalier, Claudie. "Aspects de l'expérience lesbienne en France 1930–1968." Thesis for the DEA in sociology, Université de Paris 8, November 1987.

Lévi, Giovanni and Jean-Claude Schmitt, eds. *Histoire des jeunes en Occident.* Vol. 2, *L'Epoque contemporaine.* Paris: Editions du Seuil, 1996.

Lottman, Herbert R. *The Left Bank: Writers, Artists, and Politics from the Popular Front to the Cold War.* Boston: Houghton Mifflin, 1982.

Louvier, Nicole. *Qui Qu'en Grogne.* Paris: La Table Ronde, 1954.

Macaigne, Pierre. "Ils ont vingt ans." *Le Figaro* 21–22 mai 1960: 9.

Mallet-Joris, Françoise. *Le Rempart des béguines.* Paris: Editions Julliard, 1951. Translated by Herma Briffault as *The Illusionist* (New York: Farrar, Strauss and Young, 1952).

Manévy, Alain. *L'Algérie à vingt ans.* Paris: Editions Grasset, 1960.

Marks, Elaine. *Colette.* New Brunswick: Rutgers University Press, 1960.

Martin, Henri-Jean, Roger Chartier, Jean-Pierre Vivet, *Histoire de l'édition française.* Vol. 4. Paris: Promodis, 1986.

Martin, Marc. "La Radio dans les crises politiques contemporaines." In *Techniques et politiques de l'information. Actes du séminaire Histoire des politiques de la communication,* edited by Jérôme Bourdon and Cécile Méadal, 171–86. Paris: CNRS, 1987.

Matlock, Jann. *Scenes of Seduction: Prostitution, Hysteria, and Reading Difference in Nineteenth-Century France.* New York: Columbia University Press, 1994.

Mauriac, François. *Le Romancier et ses personnages.* Paris: Editions Corrêa, 1952.

Maurienne, *Le Déserteur.* 1960. Reprint, Levallois Perret: Editions Manya, 1991.

McRobbie, Angela and Mica Nava, eds. *Gender and Generation.* London: MacMillan, 1984.

Mendousse, Pierre. *L'Ame de l'adolescent.* Paris: Librairie Félix Alcan, 1909.

———. *L'Ame de l'adolescente.* Paris: Alcan, 1928.

Mendras, Henri. *La Seconde Révolution française 1965–1984.* 1988. Reprint, Paris: Editions Gallimard, 1994.

Michel, Andrée Michel and Geneviève Texier. *La Condition de la Française d'aujourd'hui.* Vol. 1, *Mythes et réalités.* Paris: Editions Gonthier, 1964.

De la Misère en milieu étudiant. Paris: Editions Champ libre, 1976.

Mitchell, Sally. *The New Girl: Girls' Culture in England, 1880–1915.* New York: Columbia University Press, 1995.

Modleski, Tania. *Loving With a Vengeance: Mass-Produced Fantasies for Women.* New York: Methuen, 1982.

Moi, Toril. "Appropriating Bourdieu: Feminist Theory and Pierre Bourdieu's Sociology of Culture." *New Literary History* 22, no. 4 (Autumn 1991): 1017–47.

———. "Simone de Beauvoir: The Making of an Intellectual Woman." *The Yale Journal of Criticism* 4, no. 1 (1990): 1–23.

Monchablon, Alain. *Histoire de l'UNEF.* Paris: PUF, 1983.

Morin, Edgar. *L'Esprit du temps.* Paris: Editions Grasset, 1962.

———. "Salut les copains I. Une Nouvelle classe d'âge." *Le Monde* 6 juillet 1963: 1.

———. "Salut les copains II. Le «yé-yé»." *Le Monde* 7–8 juillet 1963: 12.

———. *Les Stars.* Paris: 1957. Reprint, Paris: Editions Galilée, 1984.

Mossuz-Lavau, Janine. *Les Lois de l'amour. Les Politiques de la sexualité en France 1950–1990.* Paris: Editions Payot, 1991.

Le Mouvement social 168 (July–September 1994), "Jeunesses XXe siècle."

Muller, Martine, Danielle Tucat, Sylvie Van de Casteele-Schweitzer, Dominique Veillon, and Danièle Voldman. *Etre féministe en France. Contribution à l'étude des mouvements de femmes 1944–1967.* Paris: IHTP, 1985.

Murat, Pierre. "Les Unes l'autre. Les actrices et la naissance du mythe B.B." In *D'un cinéma l'autre. Notes sur le cinéma français des années cinquante,* edited by Jean Loup Passek. Paris: Editions du Centre Georges Pompidou, 1988.

Musset, Alfred de. *La Confession d'un enfant du siècle.* 1836. Reprint, Paris: Editions Gallimard, 1973.

Mypoint, Jean. *Une Jeune fille d'aujourd'hui.* Paris: Librairie de l'Arc, 1934.

Nabokov, Vladimir. *The Annotated Lolita.* Edited by Alfred Appel, Jr. New York: Vintage Books, 1991.

Nadeau, Maurice. "Une Génération perdue?" *Lettres nouvelles* 61 (June 1958): 948–54.

Nicholson, Linda. *Gender and History: The Limits of Social Theory in the Age of the Family.* New York: Columbia University Press, 1986.

Nimier, Roger. *Le Grand d'Espagne.* Paris: Editions Gallimard, 1950.

———. *Le Hussard bleu.* Paris: Editions Gallimard, 1950.

———. "Vingt ans en 1945." *La Table ronde* (August–September 1949): 1265–71.

Nora, Pierre. "Entrées et clés." *Le Débat* 50 (May–August 1988): 190–220.

———. "L'Evolution des best-sellers." *Lire* 181 (October 1990): 76–80.

Nourissier, François. *Les Chiens à fouetter.* Paris: Editions Julliard, 1956.

Ortner, Sherry. "The Virgin and the State." *Feminist Studies* 4 (1978): 19–37.

Parinaud, André. "La Génération des J-3 à la conquête de Paris." *Arts,* 657 (12–18 February 1958): 1.

Pauwels, Louis. "Lettre inutile à «Elle»." *Arts,* 17–23 July 1952: 1.

———. "Une génération." *Paris-Presse,* 17 January 1956: 1.

Perrein, Michèle. *La Sensitive, ou l'innocence coupable.* 1956. Reprint, Paris: Editions Grasset, 1986.

Perrot, Michèle. "Fait divers et histoire au XIXe siècle." *Annales. Economies, sociétés, civilisations* 38, no. 4 (1983): 911–19.

———, ed. *Une Histoire des femmes est-elle possible?* Paris: Rivages, 1984.

Perrot, Michèle, Jean-Claude Schmitt, and Arlette Farge. "Adolescences. Un Pluriel à l'etude des historiens." *Adolescences* 3, no. 1 (Spring 1985): 43–74.

Perruchot, Henri. *La France et sa jeunesse.* Paris: Hachette, 1958.

Peyre, Christiane. *Une société anonyme.* Paris: Editions Julliard, 1962.

Peyre, Henri. "Contemporary Feminine Literature in France." *Yale French Studies* 27 (1961): 47–65.

Planté, Christine. *La Petite soeur de Balzac. Essai sur la femme auteur.* Paris: Editions du Seuil, 1989.

Pollak, Michael. "Paul F. Lazarsfeld, fondateur d'une multinationale scientifique." *Actes de la recherche en sciences sociales* 25 (January 1979): 45–59.

———. "La Planification des sciences sociales." *Actes de la recherche en sciences sociales* 2–3 (June 1976): 105–21.

Prost, Antoine. "L'Evolution de la politique familiale en France de 1938 à 1981." *Le Mouvement social* 129 (October–December 1984): 7–28.

Radway, Jan. *Reading the Romance: Women, Patriarchy, and Popular Literature.* Chapel Hill: University of North Carolina Press, 1984.

Réage, Pauline. *Histoire d'O.* Paris: Editions Jean-Jacques Pauvert, 1954.

Rémond, René and Claude Neuschwander. "Télévision et comportement politique." *Revue française de sciences politiques* 13, no. 2 (June 1963): 325–47.

Remonté, Jean-François and Simone Depoux. *Les Années radio.* Paris: Editions Gallimard, 1989.

Rioux, Jean-Pierre. *La France de la IVe République.* Vol. 2, *L'Expansion et l'impuissance 1952–1958.* Paris: Editions du Seuil, 1983.

———, ed. *La Guerre d'Algérie et les Français.* Paris: Fayard, 1990.

Roberts, Mary Louise. *Civilization Without Sexes: Reconstructing Gender in Postwar France, 1917–1927.* Chicago: University of Chicago Press, 1994.

Rochefort, Christiane. *Les Petits enfants du siècle.* Paris: Editions Grasset, 1961.

———. *Le Repos du guerrier.* Paris: Editions Grasset, 1958. Translated by Lowell Bair as *Warriors Rest.* (New York: David McKay Company, 1959).

Ross, Kristin. *Fast Cars, Clean Bodies: Decolonization and the Reordering of French Culture.* Cambridge and London: MIT Press, 1994.

Rubellin-Devichi, Jacqueline. *L'Evolution du statut civil de la famille depuis 1945.* Paris: Editions du CNRS, 1983.

Ruddick, Sara. *Maternal Thinking: Toward a Politics of Peace.* Boston: Beacon Press, 1989.

Sade, Donatien Alphonse François, Marquis de. *Juliette.* Translated by Austryn Wainhouse. New York: Grove Weidenfeld, 1968.

Sagan, Françoise. *Bonjour tristesse.* Paris: Editions Julliard, 1954.

——— "Françoise Sagan vous parle." Interview by Madeleine Chapsal. *L'Express,* 13 September 1957: 15–16.

Saint Pierre, Michel de. *La Nouvelle race.* Paris: La Table Ronde, 1961.

Sand, George. *Lélia.* 1833. Reprint, Paris: Editions Garnier, 1960.

Santoni, Georges, ed. *Société et culture de la France contemporaine.* Albany: State University of New York Press, 1981.

Schneidermann, Daniel. *L'Etrange procès.* Paris: Fayard, 1998.

Schor, Naomi. "The Scandal of Realism." In *A New History of French Literature,* edited by Denis Hollier, 656–61. Cambridge: Harvard University Press, 1989.

Sérant, Paul. *Gardez-vous à gauche.* Paris: Fasquelle, 1956.

Simonin, Anne and Hélène Clastres. *Les Idées en France 1945–1988. Une chronologie.* Paris: Editions Gallimard, 1989.

Smith, Bonnie. *Changing Lives: Women in European History Since 1700.* Lexington, Mass.: D.C. Heath and Co., 1989.

Smith, Merrit Roe and Leo Marx, eds. *Does Technology Drive History?: The Dilemma of Technological Determinism.* Cambridge: MIT Press, 1994.

Stetson, Dorothy McBride. *Women's Rights in France.* New York: Greenwood Press, 1987.

Stone, Lawrence. *The Family, Sex and Marriage in England.* London: Weidenfeld and Nicolson, 1977.

Stora, Benjamin. *Appelés en guerre d'Algérie.* Paris: Découvertes Gallimard Histoire, 1997.

———. *La Gangrène et l'oubli. La Mémoire et la guerre d'Algérie.* Paris: La Découverte, 1991.

Sullerot, Evelyne. *La Presse féminine.* Paris: Librairie Armand Colin, 1966.

Sussman, Elizabeth, ed. *On the passage of a few people through a rather brief moment in time: The Situationist international, 1957–1972.* Cambridge: MIT Press, 1989.

Szacki, Jerzy. *History of Sociological Thought.* Westport, Conn.: Greenwood Press, 1979.

La Table Ronde 99 (March 1956): "Psychologie de la littérature féminine."

Talbott, John. "The Myth and Reality of the Paratrooper in the Algerian War." *Armed Forces and Society* 3 (Fall 1976): 69–70.

Thérame, Victoria. *Journal d'une dragueuse.* Paris: Editions Ramsay, 1990.

———. *Morbidezza.* Paris: Editions Julliard, 1960.

Tompkins, Jane. *Sensational Designs: The Cultural Work of American Fiction 1790–1860.* New York: Oxford University Press, 1985.

———. "Sentimental Power: Uncle Tom's Cabin and the Politics of Literary History." In *The New Feminist Criticism: Essays on Women, Literature, and Theory,* edited by Elaine Showalter New York: Pantheon Books, 1985.

Trévol, Elisabeth. *Mon amour.* Paris: Editions Julliard, 1954.

Vaisse, Maurice. *1961, Alger, le putsch.* Brussels: Editions Complexe, 1983.

Vance, Carole S. ed. *Pleasure and Danger: Exploring Female Sexuality.* Boston: Routledge and Kegan Paul, 1984.

Van Den Bosch, Paul. *Les Enfants de l'absurde.* Paris: La Table Ronde, 1956.

Vian, Boris. *Le Manuel de Saint-Germain-des-Prés.* Paris: Editions du Chêne, 1974.

Vidal, Guy and Alain Bignon. *Une Education algérienne.* Paris: Dargaud Editeur, 1982.

Vilaine, Anne-Marie de. *Des Raisons d'aimer.* Paris: Editions Julliard, 1959.

Vittori, Jean-Pierre. *Nous les appelés d'Algérie.* 1977. Reprint, Paris: Messidor, 1983.

Vincendeau, Ginette. "The Old and the New: Brigitte Bardot and 1950s France." *Paragraph* 15, no. 1 (March 1992): 73–96.

Vincent, Gérard. *Les Français 1945–1975. Chronologie et structures d'une société.* Paris: Masson, 1977.

Voldman, Danièle. "Mai 68 ou la féministe refusée." *Nouvelle revue socialiste* August-September 1985: 41–48.

Waller, Margaret. *The Male Malady: Fictions of Impotence in the French Romantic Novel.* New Brunswick, N.J.: Rutgers University Press, 1993.

Weiner, Susan. "La Consommatrice of the 1950s in Elsa Triolet's *Roses à crédit.*" *French Cultural Studies* 6 (June 1995): 123–44.

White, Barbara A. *Growing Up Female: Adolescent girlhood in American fiction.* Westport, Conn.: Greenwood Press, 1985.

Wilson, Elizabeth. *Only Halfway to Paradise: Women in Postwar Britain 1945–1968.* London and New York: Tavistock Publications, 1980.

Winock, Michel. *La République se meurt. Chronique, 1956–1958.* Paris: Editions du Seuil, 1978.

———. *Le Siècle des intellectuels.* Paris: Editions du Seuil, 1997.

Winship, Janice. *Inside Women's Magazines.* London and New York: Pandora Press, 1987.

"Women Writers." *Yale French Studies* 27 (1961): 11.

Yonnet, Paul. *Jeux, modes et masses. La Société française et le moderne.* Paris: Editions Editions Gallimard, 1985.

Index

Bettelheim, Charles, 177
Bibliothèque de sociologie contempo-
  raine, 126–27
birth control, 23, 24
Bissiglia, Paul, 133
Blier, Bernard, 133
Blier, Bertrand, 185–87
Blondin, Antoine, 82, 113, 119
Blondo, Lucky, 148
blousons noirs, 209–10n.32
Bonjour les amis, 150
book publishing. *See* fiction by female
  adolescents
Bourdieu, Pierre, 171
Bourgois, Christian, 73, 218n.19
Breton, André, 30, 35
Buran, Robert, 156

Camus, Albert, 114, 178
Carné, Marcel, 12, 124, 128, 140, 158,
  163–67, 168, 169, 229–30n.42
Carrère, Claude, 148
Carroll, Raymonde, 216n.87
Cau, Jean, 198, 226n.63, 229–30n.42
Cayatte, André, 131–38, 227n.80
Cazalis, Anne-Marie, 125, 226n.61
Cery, Yveline, 159
Chafe, William H., 215n.79
Chancel, Annie, 148
Chardonne, Jacques, 85, 101, 114
Charrier, Jacques, 165
chastity. *See* virginity
Chateaubriand, François-René de, 111,
  115–16, 223n.13
Chonez, Claudine, 88–89
Clark, Petula, 199
Cocteau, Jean, 13–14, 17, 97, 114, 133
Code de la Famille, 24
Coggio, Roger, 132
Colette, 43, 83, 101
Constant, Benjamin, 83, 111
contraception, 23, 24
Converse, Jean, 171
copains, 12, 13, 140, 146–50

copines, 146–53
Copjec, Joan, 5, 16, 208n.16
Cosima, Renée, 13
Coty, René, 215n.71
couture. *See* fashion
Croisille, Nicole, 147
Crouzet, Paul, 215n.80
Curtis, Jean-Louis, 73

Dalmas, Louis, 142–43
Dambre, Marc, 224nn.22, 27
D'Assailly, Gisèle, 72
Dean, James, 166
D'Eaubonne, Françoise, 73, 77, 88,
  217n.14, 219n.32
Debesse, Maurice, 175
Debord, Guy, 199–200
Debord, Michel, 190
Deharme, Lise, 101–2
Deleuze, Gilles, 202
Demy, Jacques, 163
Déon, Michel, 83, 113, 117, 120–22,
  123–24
Descotes, Maurice, 130
détournement, 200
Dieterlen, Germaine, 127
Disco Revue, 150
domesticity: Beauvoir's view of, 45–
  46; changing perception of, 25–28,
  52–54; in the postwar period, 32;
  young women's view of, 58–59, 64,
  66
Dormann, Geneviève, 7
Drouet, Minou, 76–77
Dubreuilh, Nadine, 7
Dumont, Louis, 127
Duport, Catherine-Isabelle, 188
Duras, Marguerite, 77, 116, 179–80

Elle magazine, 17–18, 21–22, 128, 204;
  Barthes's view of, 35–36; compared
  with *Mademoiselle,* 60–66; fashion
  in, 40–41; femininity as depicted in,
  36, 42–43, 54–60; housewives as de-

picted in, 52–54; influence of, 36–39; intellectual reaction to, 33–39; man's role in, 39–40; and the Minou Drouet affair, 76; and politics, 47–52; in postwar France, 22, 30–32; secretaries in, 41–42; sexuality in, 33–35; as voice of modernity, 30; women writers in, 43–47, 70

Ellul, Jacques, 19, 141

enfant terrible, 13–14; in fiction, 1, 18, 79; in film, 1, 204–5; forerunners of, 1–2. *See also* female adolescents

engagement, 70, 82, 116

Eternal Feminine, 38, 42, 43, 49

Eustache, Jean, 196, 204–5

existentialism, 11–12, 59; and *mal du siècle,* 116, 122–28

L'Express, 82–83, 219n.40

faits divers, 129

fashion, 40–41; ethnological examination of, 126–28

Faure, Edgar, 28

Fayet, Jacques, 133

Febvre, Lucien, 177

female adolescents: as authors, 67–71; as consumers, 150–53; French cultural conceptions of, 10; identity struggle of, 6–10, 16–19; and the mass media, 10, 17–18; sexuality of, 14–15, 67–68, 86–106, 112–13; surveys of, 174–75. *See also copines;* fiction by female adolescents; youth

female suffrage, 22–23, 47–50

female virtue, 2–4

femininity: definitions of, 17–18; as depicted in *Elle* magazine, 36, 42–43, 54–60

feminist movement, 203–4

femme fatale, 96–97

Fénelon, François de Salignac de la Mothe-, 2

Fête de la Nation, 198–99

fiction by female adolescents, 18,

67–71; antisentimental quality of, 85–106; marketing of, 68–77; and Françoise Sagan, 77–85; sexuality in, 67–68, 86–106, 113, 118

Le Figaro Littéraire, 73–74

Filipacchi, Henri, 72

films about youth, 184–96, 197–98, 204–5. *See also Adieu Philippine; Antoine et Colette; Avant le déluge; Les Tricheurs*

Finas, Lucette, 87

Flaubert, Gustave, 153

Fourastié, Jean, 10, 141

France: female suffrage in, 22–23, 47–50; social change in, 9–10, 22–25; working women in, 9–10

France Soir, 22

Frère, S., 177

Friedan, Betty, 222n.86

Fumaroli, Marc, 143

Galey, Mathieu, 87

Galland, Olivier, 16

Gallimard, Gaston, 77, 82, 217n.14

garçonne, 1, 3

Garric, Robert, 109–10

Gaulle, Charles de, 10–11, 23–24, 52, 123, 156, 168; use of television by, 157–58

Gayraud, Amélie, 174–75

Gérin, Paul, 53–54

Gide, André, 131

Girardet, Raoul, 114

Girardoux, Jean, 72

Giroud, Françoise, 30, 35, 40–41, 48, 51–53, 121, 181, 182, 212–13n.25, 219n.40, 229–30n.42

Godard, Jean-Luc, 19, 158, 168, 184–85, 187–96, 197–98

Gordon-Lazareff, Hélène, 30, 43

Goya, Chantal, 188

Grasset, Bernard, 71–72, 77

Gréco, Juliette, 1, 40, 123, 148

Guattari, Félix, 202

lescents, 68–77. *See also* films about youth; radio; television

Triolet, Elsa, 43
Truffaut, François, 144, 156–57

Vadim, Roger, 57, 103, 123, 182, 185
Van Den Bosch, Paul, 119, 120
Vartan, Sylvie, 1, 150, 198
Vian, Boris, 134
Vichy France, 10–11, 114
Vidal-Naquet, Pierre, 168
vieille fille, 3–4, 208n.12
Vilaine, Anne Marie de, 68, 97
virginity, 2–3, 208n.5
Vlady, Marina, 133
voting rights. *See* female suffrage

Waller, Margaret, 112, 223n.10
women: in *mal du siècle* fiction, 112;
political involvement of, 47–52;
wearing trousers, 31–32; in the work
force, 25–26, 211n.10; as writers,
43–47, 84–85, 219n.38. *See also*
domesticity; female adolescents;
motherhood

yé-yés, 146, 150, 152
youth: as consumers, 140, 141, 147,
149–53, 155, 199–202; disaffection
of, 110–22; and existentialism, 122–
28; films about, 184–96, 197–98;
images of, 11–12, 19–20; surveys of,
170–84; and the war with Algeria,
139–40, 141–42, 144, 153–56. *See
also* female adolescents